Municipal reform and the industrial city

Themes
in Urban
History

General editor: Derek Fraser

Municipal reform and the industrial city

edited by DEREK FRASER

Leicester University Press
St. Martin's Press, New York
1982

For Clio

First published in 1982 by Leicester University Press
First published in the United States of America by St Martin's Press Inc.
For information write: St. Martin's Press Inc., 175 Fifth Ave, New York, N.Y. 10010

Designed by Arthur Lockwood

Text set in 10/11 pt Linotron 202 Times, printed and bound in Great Britain at The Pitman Press, Bath

British Library Cataloguing in Publication Data
Municipal reform and the industrial city.–
(Themes in urban history)
1. Municipal government–England–
History–19th century
I. Fraser, Derek   II. Series
352'.00724'942   JS3078
ISBN 0–7185–1176–X

Library of Congress Cataloging in Publication Data
Main entry under title:
Municipal reform and the industrial city.
(Themes in urban history)
1. Municipal government–Great Britain–History.
2. Bradford (West Yorkshire)–Politics and government.
3. Leeds (West Yorkshire)–Politics and
government. 4. Manchester (Greater Manchester)–
Politics and government I. Fraser, Derek.
II. Series.
JS3065.M86   352'.00724'0941   81–21302
ISBN 0–312–55268–8   AACR2

FOREWORD

Urban history is an expanding field of study, sustained by a considerable volume of research. The purpose of this series, originally conceived by the late Jim Dyos, is to open a new channel for the dissemination of the findings of a careful selection of that research, providing a conspectus of new knowledge on specific themes.

For each volume in the series, each of the contributors is invited to present the core of his work: the essays, originating in theses but now specially written for this volume, are combined under the control of the editor, who writes an introduction setting out the significance of the material being presented in the light of developments in that or a cognate field.

It is hoped that in this way the fruits of recent work may be made widely available, both to assist further exploration and to contribute to the teaching of urban history.

The fourth volume in the series examines the impact of Victorian municipal reform upon three northern commercial and industrial cities. These studies not only illustrate the variations in municipal developments in Victorian England, they also exemplify the different perspectives historians may use in studying Victorian cities.

Derek Fraser
University of Bradford

CONTENTS

LIST OF ILLUSTRATIONS

LIST OF TABLES

Note Places of publication are given only for works published outside the United Kingdom. Commonly accepted abbreviations such as *J.* for *Journal, Rev.* for *Review* have been used.

NOTES ON THE CONTRIBUTORS

V. A. C. GATRELL obtained his Ph.D. from the University of Cambridge. He is a Fellow and Tutor of Gonville and Caius College, Cambridge, and University Lecturer in History. He has published on the nineteenth-century cotton industry, on Robert Owen, and on Victorian law and criminality, and co-edits the *Historical Journal*.

BRAIN BARBER obtained his Ph.D. at the University of Leeds. He is an assistant archivist in the West Yorkshire County Record Office. With M. W. Beresford he is joint author of *West Riding County Council 1889–1974: Historical Studies* (1979).

ADRIAN ELLIOTT obtained his Ph.D. at the University of Bradford. He is a deputy headmaster at a Blackpool comprehensive school. He has published in the journal *Northern History*.

Introduction:
Municipal reform
in historical perspective

DEREK FRASER

Introduction: Municipal reform in historical perspective

DEREK FRASER

1 The significance of 1835

It is sometimes loosely asserted that the system of English local government was reformed in 1835 by a municipal revolution, from which dates the establishment of democratic and effective urban self-government.[1] There are several misconceptions in such an argument. Prior to 1835 England was not blessed with a system of local government, for while the leading municipal historian of our day has written a book entitled *The Unreformed Local Government System* the main conclusion of that study is that what town government lacked above all was *system*.[2] What existed was a mosaic of manorial, parochial, township and borough institutions, many of which were effete and most of which were hopelessly ill-equipped to deal with the problems of a growing and changing urban society. We may adopt a simple classification of towns which divides them between corporate (those with a town corporation) and unincorporated (those without), though this is hardly an indication of how effectively a town was governed. It was not the *system* of English local government which was reformed in 1835, but the government of 178 named incorporated boroughs: in short a reform of the existing institutions of town government. Whether that alone constitutes a municipal revolution is open to doubt since in many places there followed not so much a change of system but a change of men.

We may also wish to reserve judgment on the 'democracy' of the 1835 municipal revolution. It is certainly true that corporations were opened up to the electoral process and it is equally true that the household municipal franchise adopted in 1835 was considerably more democratic than the £10 qualification incorporated by the 1832 Reform Act. Whig ministers intended that the municipal franchise should be more democratic than the parliamentary, as one of them recorded in his diary:

Decided . . . in favour of resident three year ratepayers instead of ten pounders. I think this is right . . . it is wholesome that the voters for Parliament should be

2

taught that they have not a monopoly of all rights – that others, incapable of voting on these occasions, yet enjoy privileges, and that it was not the intention of Parliament in extending the franchise to create any species of oligarchy in the country.[3]

Contemporary radicals applauded this aspect of municipal reform, and, for instance, Cobden drew attention to the democractic equality of the 1835 Act:

Every man's vote, however humble his circumstances may be, is of equal value with his wealthiest neighbour's. There is no clause borrowed from Sturges Bourne's Act giving six votes to the rich millowners and only one to the small shopkeepers. The banker or the merchant, though worth a million, and though he ride in his carriage to the polling booth, can only record the same number of votes as the poor artisan, who walks there perhaps slip-shod and aproned from his garret or cellar.[4]

Nevertheless while Cobden considered 'the corporation act the most democratic measure upon our statute book', Keith-Lucas has shown that in practice the residence and ratepaying qualification severely impaired the franchise and in many cases reduced the municipal electorate below that of the parliamentary.[5]

The role of the 1835 Act in bringing about effective municipal administration must also be questioned. Municipal reform, of itself, did not transform urban government since the reformers were primarily concerned with public participation and official propriety rather than with function. There was a profound transformation of town government during the nineteenth century which derived from rather than occurred in 1835. It was to be a long drawn out process taking many decades to accomplish, not something sudden resulting from a dramatic piece of radical legislation.

In very general terms we must agree that there was a major reform in 1835, which was something of a turning point, which did introduce a more representative system of town government and which did, in time, effect a change in urban administration. However, on each of these counts we need greater precision to sharpen our focus on what existed, what was changed and what resulted from those changes. It is through in-depth case studies of three industrial cities that this book hopes to illuminate the real significance and impact of municipal reform.

2   Municipal government and its reform

By the early nineteenth century, borough government in the incorporated towns had fallen into decay. Many ancient corporations had a distinguished history of protecting urban interests against encroachment from the landed élite. Indeed, historically the granting of a charter of incorporation had been a recognition of the separation of a town from its rural hinterland. Incorporation was something of a test of urban identity and when, for instance, anti-incorporation elements wished to inflict a humiliating blow upon Birmingham in the early Victorian years, they induced the county bench to levy the county rate upon the city. This was an assertion that Birmingham remained merely a township within the county. If the creation of a corporation demonstrated an autonomous urban existence, it did not guarantee effective town government. Corporations were not embryonic municipal authorities, despite being their historical antecedents, since their status was essentially private rather than public. When the mayor of Leicester claimed in 1822 that 'the Corporation were possessed of considerable estates in their own proper right and over those estates had by law as free and ample a dominion as any individual over his own property', he was stating the actual legal position. Similarly when new bye-laws were drawn up by Leeds Corporation in 1823 they were described as for 'the due ordering, good government and welfare of his corporation': for the welfare of the corporation, not for the welfare of the local community.[6] Corporations were private bodies whose primary responsibility was to their constituent members, and any public functions exercised 'for the good of the town' were merely incidental.

A few corporations had served their towns well. The Royal Commission, appointed by the Whigs in 1833 to report on the municipal corporations, concluded in the case of Liverpool that, 'in the main, the Corporation have evinced economy and good management in their affairs; that as magistrates they are attentive to their duties, and careful of the due regulation of the Borough; and that, as its governing body their conduct seems to have been materially influenced by a desire to promote its welfare'.[7] Liverpool was atypical and most corporations were corrupt, inefficient, and insensitive to real local needs. When the need was perceived to introduce new functions into local government, these duties were imposed not upon corporations but upon non-municipal institutions in which there was public confidence. As the Royal Commission explained,

> It has been customary not to rely on the municipal corporations for exercising the powers incidental to good government. The powers granted by Local Acts of Parliament for various purposes have been from time to time conferred, not upon the municipal officers, but upon trustees or commissioners distinct from them, so that often the corporations have hardly any duties to perform. They have the nominal government of the town, but the efficient duties and the responsibility have been transferred to other hands.[8]

Thus in corporate towns the improvement commissioners took on the character of a rival municipal authority, while in unincorporated towns they were a surrogate municipal authority.

The 1835 Royal Commission Report was a massive indictment of the municipal corporations and strengthened the prior ministerial resolve to reform them.[9] Much may be gleaned from the motives of the Whig government which were threefold – political, administrative and social. First the Whigs desired to complement the 1832 Reform Act. There was much more here than simply refurbishing the political system to bring it up to date. There was a very real political connection between 1832 and 1835. In general the corporations were Tory and grossly partisan during elections. If this electoral influence were to remain it would subvert the purposes of the Reform Act. The Whigs aimed to complete a process which had begun in 1832 and so Joseph Parkes, secretary of the Royal Commission, described the corporations act as 'our Postscript to the Reform Bills; in fact Municipal Reform is the steam engine for the Mill built by Parliamentary Reform.' Parkes, too, saw the party political advantage which the Whigs hoped to gain and he predicted that municipal reform 'will be poison to Toryism.'[10]

To this political aspiration was married a concern over urban administration of a limited sort. The Whigs had no vision of broad municipal functions but they were extremely worried about the problems of public order. It was noticed that the worst Reform Bill riots of 1831 occurred in Bristol and Nottingham, both corporate towns. Clearly the unreformed corporations were not dealing at all adequately with the policing of growing cities. So judicial functions and public order, the question of magistrates and police, were the limits of Whig administrative horizons and it is thus no accident that the only compulsory functions imposed on the new councils concerned the establishment of a police force.

Thirdly, Whig motives were related to the social aspirations of the bourgeois urban élite. Earl Grey, Prime Minister from 1830 to 1834, had been impressed by the new forms of wealth created by industrialization and urbanization and he had hoped in 1832 to draw enfranchised wealth into partnership with unenfranchised wealth. It was natural for economically successful businessmen to wish to translate their wealth into status in their own towns. The exclusive nature of the unreformed corporations prevented a painless absorption of the new men into the élite political structures of the old system. As a result these 'outsiders' became the political rivals of the 'insiders' and would supplant them upon municipal reform. The opening up of the corporations would allow the proscribed élite, often Whig in political sympathy, to participate in the exercise of local municipal power and to share in the spoils of office. There was thus some point to the criticism that reform was merely the robbery of one group to satisfy the social and political ambitions of another – that the outsiders wanted only 'power and influence and some share of the loaves and fishes of official rank.'[11] Such views were set to verse:

Indeed the Rads are working hard
Each in his own vocation
To get a finger in the pie
Of a *party* corporation.
The "Local" lies – it lied before
But oh! What an alteration
It now lies *for* what it lied *against*
A *party* corporation.[12]

This motivation, a mixture of political, administrative, and social objectives, explains the nature of the Municipal Corporations Reform Act. The Act sought to legitimize town government by opening it up to popular participation and by cleansing its public image. Representative and judicial propriety were the basis of the new system. Household suffrage was enacted, with the three year residence and ratepaying qualification, and both debates and accounts were to open to public scrutiny. Aldermen elected for six years and crown appointed magistrates tempered the radical transformation. Some safeguards had been imposed on the government by the House of Lords, but despite some shortcomings Parkes could conclude, 'the bill as a whole is more than we had any right to obtain this year . . . I am content'.[13] When the first municipal election results registered large Whig-Liberal successes, he described it as 'the greatest political revolution ever accomplished. I don't except the Reform Bills . . ., for though they were the keys to this change yet this Municipal Reform alone gives the vitality . . . It is the "breath of life".'[14]

It is important to appreciate that this municipal breath of life initially infused only the existing corporations. It had no immediate impact upon the unincorporated towns and this is why the description of 1835 as a reform of the local government *system* cannot be accepted. This is also why it is misleading to cite the many industrial cities without corporations as evidence of the need for municipal reform. If ministers viewed the absence of municipal government in cities such as Birmingham or Sheffield as a pressing evil, they sought to remedy the evil in a most roundabout way. The procedure for extending the principles of 1835 left the initiative entirely in local hands. It was 1838 before the first charters of incorporation were issued by the Queen in Council and, as is explained later, the legality of those charters was challenged. Radicals had indeed hoped that the 1835 reform would spread and Francis Place had predicted in 1836, 'the time shall come, as soon it must, and that too at no great distance, and the whole country shall be municipalized . . . I believe we shall have an incorporation of the whole country which will be the basis of a purely representative government'.[15]

Over several decades municipal government did extend itself to the unincorporated towns. When in 1879 a municipal antiquarian wished to demonstrate the growth of town government he was able to do so with an impressive array of figures:[16]

Table 1   Comparison of municipal government in 1835 and 1879

	1835	1879
number of municipal boroughs	178	240
population within municipal limits	238,226	8,152,444
voters on Burgess Roll	124,710	1,312,796
area of municipalities – in acres	470,992	760,942
annual corporate income – in £s	365,958	3,855,415

This extension of municipal government was accelerated by an act of 1877 which allowed the costs of incorporation to be met out of the rates, costs previously borne by the promoters. By the end of the century there were over 300 municipal boroughs and more had been created in the 20 years after 1880 than in the 45 years before. It is this self-sustaining process of municipal extension which is the most powerful evidence in support of the view that 1835 represented a 'municipal revolution'.

Yet it may be argued that the true municipal revolution of the nineteenth century involved the creation of powerful and effective urban authorities with broad social and economic, as well as judicial and political, functions. Hence the Victorian municipal revolution comprised not the extension of the principles of 1835, but their transformation. And for that transformation to occur three pre-requisites were necessary: the establishment of municipal authority; the creation and accumulation of powers; and the definition of a positive social role.[17]

To establish the status of urban authorities required the confirmation of their authority, legal, social and moral. The challenge to the legal status of the new councils mainly concerned the incorporation of industrial cities. The famous test case of *Rutter v. Chapman* disputed the legality of the Manchester charter, and on the outcome depended the charters for Birmingham and Bolton as well. It was not until the mid-1840s that this legal cloud was removed from these towns and their councils could emerge from a municipal limbo. The legal confirmation of authority did also involve those corporations where the outgoing political masters had distributed corporate property for fear of its transfer to their successors. Thus the legal actions for the recovery of town property, for instance in Leeds and Liverpool, were as important for the legal status of the reformed corporations, as *Rutter v. Chapman* was to the new incorporations.

Once confirmed legally, councils needed to establish their social status by the participation of leading urban citizens. In some cases the frustrated ambition for the mayor's chain or a seat on the bench was sufficient to secure immediate municipal participation of the industrial élite. In such towns there was no great difference in the social composition of unreformed corporations and elected town councils. Elsewhere it was more difficult. In Birmingham the élite had to be belatedly coaxed into municipal government by the famous 'civic gospel' and it was to the élite of Bristol that Canon Barnett addressed his message of civic conscious-ness in his celebrated pamphlet of 1893, *The Ideal City*.[18] In Sheffield the shunning of the municipal authority by the town's business leaders accounted for the council's low status: 'The main reason for the degradation of the Council has been that intellect and property of the town has stood aloof from it. The people have been taught that there was no one so ignorant or incompetent but he might become a town councillor . . . The Town Council has had no self respect'.[19]

Paradoxically, uniformly élitist municipal councils would emulate one of the worst defects of unreformed corporations – remoteness from their local commun-ity. To prevent a new form of oligarchy, municipal reform had to forge a strong link between the council and its community. The council had to become a focus of citizenship, as well as a fount of social authority. The moral authority of councils had to be secured by making the council the embodiment of *civitas* for all its citizens. The extensive municipal franchise established a common bond between the council and its community on the Benthamite principle of what was participated in by all would conduce to the benefit of all. As one municipal enthusiast argued, 'To afford a channel in which the political energies of townsmen may legitimately flow is a thing to be desired . . . the sense of local interest and self respect of the townsmen would find their legitimate gratification in the ability to elect and the possibility of being elected managers of their own local affairs'.[20]

If the authority of municipal councils could be established, the question would arise of what functions the councils should exercise. The nature of English law meant that local authorities had only those powers which Parliament had specifical-ly allocated, and in the case of 1835 they were precious few. The Benthamite J.A. Roebuck was one of a small group of radicals who advocated that the 1835 act should include a code of general powers.[21] In his series of radical pamphlets and, with Place, in a lively but short-lived newspaper, Roebuck argued for the allocation of extensive powers, foreseeing a sort of municipal collectivism.[22] As Roebuck anticipated, the Whigs did not grant many powers to the reformed councils, some of which had fewer functions than before because they lost control over charities. Powers had to be slowly acquired by municipal authorities, largely through local private acts.[23] The great turning point in most towns' civic history was not 1835 or the date of incorporation, but the date of the first major local act granting extensive powers to the council. Thus for Leeds this was the 1842 Improvement Act, for Manchester the 1844 Police Act and for Liverpool the 1846 Sanitary Act. These pioneering bills were but the first of many as each town accumulated powers through a code of private bill legislation. In so doing councils often faced resistance from rival competing authorities. Birmingham Town Council shared its authority with a much respected Street Commission and several minor boards of township surveyors. Any municipal progress in Sheffield was always resisted by the democratic anarchists led by Isaac Ironside who desired complete township autonomy. The gradual amalgamation of parochial, township and improvement institutions with councils and the consequent concentration of powers within the corporations enabled the 'Municipal Leviathan' to emerge.

The powers which authorities sought in private acts of parliament imposed in general legislation were determined by the conventional contemporary definition of the proper role of town councils. That definition changed and grew during the nineteenth century. It was wholly in keeping with the growth of the Victorian administrative state that the development of such a definition was pragmatic rather than ideological. Some individuals, notably municipal activists, struggled toward a definition of municipal collectivism which was to reach fruition as a philosophy of municipal welfare in the civic gospel of Dale and Dawson in Chamberlain's Birmingham. Perceptive and inspiring as that was, we have to note that it was the articulation in moral and religious terms of a concept which was already well rooted in municipal practice, elsewhere if not in Birmingham. Councils took practical steps to deal with practical problems and found as a consequence that they were drawn ever farther down an interventionist road. The pragmatic nature of municipal collectivism was never better illustrated than in Sidney Webb's celebrated individualist town councillor who extolled the virtues and achievements of self help in the context of massive municipal activity.[24] The commitment to municipal welfare invariably began in the field of environmental control. This may be understood as Helen Meller has argued, as a first stage of 'sanitation', to be followed by a second stage of 'civilization'.[25] Early Victorian councils built sewers and reservoirs, late Victorian councils built swimming pools and libraries. On the other hand, it may be more valuable to think in terms of a gradually widening definition of the social purposes of municipal reform. Concern for the urban environment was central and the desire to create a decent wholesome environment encompassed broader horizons as time went on. At first the wholesome environment was seen in physical sanitary terms; later it was perceived to encompass men's cultural and recreational needs as well. By the end of the century councils were supplying gas, water, electricity, education, housing and transport as the definition of the municipal role had enlarged to include responsibility for all that was conducive to the welfare of the urban community.[26] Hence the nineteenth-century municipal revolution was that process which took local authorities from the corporation reform of the 1830s to the 'municipal socialism' of the 1890s.

3 The historiographical context of the case studies

English town government has been an attractive field of study since municipal reform itself. The study of municipal history has thrown up a number of classic works of exhaustive proportions, each under joint authorship. The definitive history of the unreformed corporations appeared in 1835 and may be read as a corrective to the hostile Royal Commission Report.[27] The great socialist partnership of the Webbs produced a monumental nine-volume history of English local government of which at least three are of central concern to the municipal historian.[28] In the Edwardian years a Viennese lawyer and a London barrister published the best guide to the development of local government during the nineteenth century.[29] Alongside these works of reference may be placed two very thorough bibliographies.[30] In the twentieth century there have been a number of reliable general surveys to which the student may turn as an introduction to the subject.[31] The reform of local government stimulated much propaganda in the late Victorian period, from Liberals with strong municipal connections (such as Joseph Chamberlain and William Rathbone), in favour of the extension of democratic local government and the remodelling of local taxation.[32]

These and other specialist studies suggest that historians have examined the problem of town government from three types of perspective. These have not crystallized into three schools of interpretation; rather they have indicated that historians have asked questions in three main clusters. First, many scholars interested in local government have a political scientist's concern with central-local relations and this is very much the perspective of our own society. That this is so is an illustration of the tendency for historical writing to mirror movements in contemporary opinion. At a time when the autonomy of local government appears under threat from central government direction and control, there is much public interest in knowing how the relationship of central and local government has developed historically.[33] This perspective has focussed much attention on the issue of centralization versus local autonomy. England had traditionally been locally governed and there was a certain logic in its continuing to be so. As one of the philosophical radicals explained: 'it is only natural to conclude that those whose comfort and welfare are to be considered, who will be the first and principal sufferers by neglectful or bad government are much more likely to know what ought to be done than strangers, however well intentioned they may be, who have not the same knowledge and experience.'[34]

Yet when local authorities were a by-word for jobbery, corruption and inefficiency and the problems of urban growth beyond their competence there were many who wished the central authority to take a much more coercive line. This battle was personified in the argument between the antiquarian lawyer, Joshua Toulmin Smith and the Benthamite bureaucrat, Edwin Chadwick.[35] Fear of centralization has usually been cited as a negative factor restraining progress by enlightened governments, in such areas as public health. This is because so much history is written from the centre looking out, whence anti-centralization feeling appears backwoodsman reaction. Yet from a local standpoint anti-centralization was a stimulus to much local initiative, inspiring local councils to adopt new functions in order to forestall government intervention.[36] Municipal councils were often the pioneers of social reform rather than negative obscurantists resisting benevolent governments. This became even more important as central government created a machinery for dealing with urban authorities, first the General Board of Health, then the Local Government Act Office and finally the Local Government Board.[37] The transition from one to the other was symbolic of a greater reliance on compulsory rather than permissive legislation, as central government sought to impose duties on local authorities rather than relying on intermittent local initiative and enthusiasm. In the crucially important area of public health Sir John Simon moved slowly away from unfettered local autonomy.[38]

The second perspective concentrates attention much more directly upon urban society and the exercise of power within it. What part was played by municipal reform in reinforcing the authority of those who claimed a disproportionate share of urban wealth and property? How far did municipal reform merely serve the social and political aspirations of an emergent élite? Were municipal politics organized by class, by parties, by ideologies? These are the sorts of questions posed by such a perspective in which municipal government is viewed as a means of legitimizing social and political leadership in the city. On the one hand, town councils were politicized by being sucked into the contemporary political battle within the urban middle class, between old and new families, between Anglicans and Dissenters, between Tories and Liberals. On the other hand, municipal reform became part of a process whereby more popular forms of town government could be supplanted and by which social leaders could monopolize local office and patronage. Studies of the larger provincial cities provide ample evidence that real political battles were fought out in the municipal arena.[39] In Oldham and Salford pre-municipal town government provided opportunities for influence by working-class radicals, which were effectively removed by incorporation.[40] In such places municipal reform might appear less, rather than more democratic, since as one Manchester radical put it, incorporation represented 'the tyranny of the bloated rich'.[41]

The third perspective has concerned itself with the growth of urban administration, with those accumulating powers and broadening purposes discussed earlier. Of course the growth of administrative functions cannot be explored in isolation from the social and political context in which councils were operating. As Professor Hennock has shown in his work on Birmingham and Leeds, and Dr Meller on Bristol, the administrative role performed by a local authority bore a direct relationship to the social and political composition of its council.[42] With varying reference to this wider context, many historians have been primarily aiming to chart the growth of municipal activity in terms of services and functions. This was the main theme running through the great municipal history of Birmingham launched by J.T. Bunce in 1878 and the central purpose of the equally important civic history of Manchester, written to mark the centenary of its incorporation.[43] More recent research studies have also devoted considerable attention to the expansion of municipal administration, notably those on Liverpool, Bristol, Gateshead and Exeter.[44] Such a perspective has propelled historians also towards the controversial question of municipal trading, which so worried anti-socialist opinion in the Edwardian years.[45]

Each of these perspectives is illuminated by the three detailed case studies in this volume, which add considerably to our knowledge of municipal history. Dr Gatrell is exclusively concerned with the second theme, for he is attempting to identify the role of incorporation in establishing 'Liberal Hegemony'. Indeed incorporation marks the end and not the beginning of his study. Incorporation secured the victory in Manchester of the 'new' men over the 'old' and the Manchester study demonstrates the social and political framework within which the municipal question was understood by contemporaries. There is virtually nothing in Cobden's propaganda about the administrative service the new council could render to its community, nor about the potential for municipal welfare. Incorporation is seen as part of a battle against 'the Lords of Clumber, Belvoir and Woburn' and as a means of rescuing the town from the clutches of a 'booby squirearchy'.[46] It is also analysed as an expedient for securing the support of the 'shopocracy' and it is one of the author's main achievements to demonstrate how fragile Liberal control over Manchester was. Penetrating beyond the rhetoric of Manchester as a shock city dominated by class tension, Dr Gatrell argues that despite Peterloo and Chartism the Manchester bourgeoisie did not feel acutely threatened from below and that their outlook was 'self-referential'. The middle class was not united by fear of proletarian assault but divided internally by kinship, religion and politics and these factors are carefully delineated by reference to a wide range of sources. This acute definition of the protagonists makes clear how important it was for Liberal middle-class leaders to secure incorporation in order to reinforce that victory registered at the first parliamentary election in 1832. The political forces vanquished in the 1830s were to gain their revenge in the eclipse of the Manchester School in 1857.

Dr Barber is well aware that Leeds was as politically divided as Manchester and that its municipal history was more influenced by continued political dispute. In Manchester the boycott of municipal elections by disgruntled Conservatives led to an overtly non-political council, a development regretted by a distinguished later observer.[47] In Leeds, despite periodic waning in political partisanship, seats, offices and policies were normally subject to great political debate.[48] However, except insofar as politics affected administrative policy Dr Barber restricts his attention to municipal government itself, the third perspective. Here is an example based mainly on civic archives of a thorough review of the social, economic and administrative role of a Victorian town council. The local authority was faced with intractable environmental problems and as the author shows success was elusive. Dr Barber clearly undermines any notion of municipal government getting steadily and progessively better in the march of improvement. Leeds was pioneering in one decade, laggardly in another, and its municipal history neatly exemplifies the erratic nature of civic enthusiasm and enterprise. The author's views on the primacy of local or central innovation in public health reform forces a reconsideration of the part played by model clauses in the evolution of private local legislation. He also provokes a re-evaluation of the 1890 Housing of the Working Classes Act whose significance and impact he judges to have been under-estimated. He thus touches the theme of central-local relations. He also refers to the growth of a municipal bureaucracy, a much neglected topic of study.

It is to Dr Elliott that we may turn for an attempt to employ all three perspectives. His original thesis had been based on an attempt to place municipal government in a broad context. The incorporation of Bradford had much in common with the incorporation of Manchester a decade earlier. Some of Dr Gatrell's points find an echo in Dr Elliott's account – the same new *versus* old, Dissenter *versus* Anglican, Liberal *versus* Tory-Radical struggles. This sociopolitical perspective enables him to relate together the occupational and electoral composition of the council. Like Dr Barber, Dr Elliott surveys municipal government and administration, albeit necessarily in a briefer compass. The growth of public health activity brought Bradford Town Council into greater contact with central government and the author examines the relationship between the General Board of Health and the council. Here central-local relations emerge along the lines of accommodation and cooperation rather than of confrontation and conflict. As often the pragmatic and not the ideological carried the day.

The appearance together of these three case studies affords an opportunity for a comparative approach where this is not often attempted.[49] We may observe that each city has its own story to tell and that three industrial cities could display quite marked differences. We may also evaluate the implications of three historians approaching municipal reform in three quite different ways. Municipal history, like any other history, assumes different contours when viewed with different perspectives. Manchester, Leeds and Bradford were northern industrial cities: insufficient work has been done to decide whether the contrasts between categories of cities were greater than those within categories. How reliable was the prediction beforehand and the judgment afterwards that the extension of representative government to the counties had the effect of municipalizing the country? Were the county councils of the 1890s merely town councils in the countryside or did their social and political context breed a different species of local authority? More research is needed on both town and county before such questions can be fully answered. It is hoped that this volume by both precept and omission will encourage further studies of municipal authority and urban society.

NOTES

1 For a bold statement of the 'municipal revolution' argument, cf. Ivor Jennings, 'The passing of the first Municipal Corporations Act was described in 1835 as a revolution and may be so described a century later . . . It is substantially true . . . that the principles of 1835 dominate the whole field of English Local Government . . . the municipal revolution of 1835 was a great step in the history of England'. H.J. Laski *et al.*, *A Century of Municipal Progress* (1935), 55–65.
2 B. Keith-Lucas, *The Unreformed Local Government System* (1980).
3 A.D. Kriegel (ed.), *The Holland House Diaries 1831–40* (1977), 303.
4 *Incorporate Your Borough*, by a Radical Reformer (Manchester, 1837). The reference to Sturges Bourne is to the Parish Vestries Act of 1818 which gave votes on a sliding scale of one to six depending on rateable value. This was commonly referred to as 'bricks against brains'. This system of voting was used for Poor Law and Local Board elections.
5 *Manchester Guardian*, 10 Feb. 1838; B. Keith-Lucas, *The English Local Government Franchise* (1952).
6 R. Read, *Modern Leicester* (1881), 228; J. Wardell, *The Municipal History of the Borough of Leeds* (1846), cxxxix. Cf. D. Fraser, 'The Leeds Corporation c. 1820– c. 1850', *Publications of the Thoresby Soc.*, LIV (1979), 72–80.
7 *Report of the Royal Commission on Municipal Corporations*, PP (1835) XXIII, IV, 2706.
8 *Ibid.*, I, 17.
9 G.B.A.M. Finlayson, 'The Municipal Corporation Commission and report 1833–5', *Bull. of the Inst. of Historical Research*, XXXVI (1963), 36–52; *idem*, 'The politics of municipal reform 1835', *English Historical Rev.*, LXXI (1966), 673–92; B. Keith-Lucas, 'Municipal corporations' in *Aspects of Government in Nineteenth Century Britain*, ed. V. Cromwell *et al.* (1978), 70–89.
10 J. Parkes to Earl of Durham, Sep. 1835, quoted by J.K. Buckley, *Joseph Parkes of Birmingham* (1926), 122.
11 *Birmingham Advertiser*, 2 November 1837.
12 *Leicester Herald*, 19 December 1835.
13 Joseph Parkes to E.J. Stanley, 6 Sep. 1835, Parkes Papers (University College London).
14 Joseph Parkes to Earl of Durham, 5 Jan. 1836, quoted by W.E.S. Thomas, *The Philosophical Radicals* (1979), 289–90.

15 Francis Place to Joseph Parkes, 3rd January 1836, Place Papers (British Museum Add. MSS 35150, f.102).
16 Figures derived from J.R. Somers Vine, *English Municipal Institutions* (1879).
17 For a fuller exposition of this hypothesis and the case studies on which it is based see D. Fraser, *Power and Authority in the Victorian City* (1979).
18 E.P. Hennock, *Fit and Proper Persons* (1973); H.E. Meller (ed.), *The Ideal City* (1979).
19 *Sheffield and Rotherham Independent*, 7 July 1864.
20 J. Thompson, *An Essay in English Municipal History* (1867, repr,. 1971), 193–5.
21 For Roebuck see Thomas, *op. cit.*, 206–43; J.A. Cruikshank, 'John Arthur Roebuck' (M.A. thesis, University of Manchester, 1977); S. Wilks, 'An independent in politics: J.A. Roebuck 1802–79' (D.Phil thesis, University of Oxford, 1979).
22 J.A. Roebuck et al., *Pamphlets for the People* (1835–6); *The Municipal Corporations Reformer* (1835–6).
23 F. Clifford, *A History of Private Bill Legislation* (2 vols., 1885–7); F.H. Spencer, *Municipal Origins* (1911).
24 text quoted from S. Webb, *Socialism in England* (1889) by D.Fraser, *Power and Authority*, 171.
25 H.E. Meller, *Leisure and the Changing City* (1976).
26 Cf. S.A. Barnett in his pamphlet of 1893, quoting a Cobden Club essay, 'A true municipality should completely grasp the life of the community . . . The work of a town should be done with such completeness as to leave no sort of danger or evil unchecked, no material defect uncured, no intellectual want cared for.' Meller, *Ideal City*, 65.
27 H.A. Merewether and A.J. Stephens, *The History of the Boroughs and Municipal Corporations of the United Kingdom* (3 vols., 1835; new edn, ed. G. Martin), 1973.
28 S. and B. Webb, *English Local Government* (9 vols., 1906–29); see particularly vols. 2 and 3 *The Manor and the Borough* and vol. 4 *Statutory Authorities For Special Purposes*.
29 J. Redlich and F.W. Hirst, *Local Government in England* (2 vols., 1903).
30 C. Gross, *A Bibliography of British Municipal History* (1897; 2nd edn, ed. G. Martin, 1966); G.H. Martin and S. McIntyre, *A Bibliography of British and Irish Municipal History* (1972).
31 Laski, *op. cit.*; K.B. Smellie, *A History of Local Government* (1968); J.J. Clarke, *A History of Local Government in the United Kingdom* (1955); B. Keith-Lucas, *English Local Government in the Nineteenth and Twentieth Centuries* (1977).
32 J.W. Probyn (ed.), *Local Government and Taxation* (1875, revised edn 1882); W. Rathbone et al., *Local Government Taxation* (1885); J. Chamberlain et al., *The Radical Programme* (1885; new edn, ed. D.A. Hamer, 1971); E.A. Hart, *Local Government as it is and as it ought to be . . .* (1885).
33 The SSRC has launched a major research initiative in this field and during 1980–1 a special Social Science Research Council Study Group on Urban Politics and History explored central-local relations as one of its main programmes.
34 A. de Fonblanque, *How We Are Governed* (1872), 54; for Fonblanque see Thomas, *op. cit.*, 305–37.
35 Cf. J. Toulmin Smith, *Local Self Government and Centralisation* (1851) and E. Chadwick, *On the Evils of Disunity in Central and Local Administration* (1885).
36 Cf. W. Lubenow, *The Politics of Government Growth* (1971); R.M. Gutchen, 'Local improvement and centralisation in nineteenth century England', *Historical J.*, IV (1961), 85–96.
37 R.J. Lambert, 'Central-local relations in mid Victorian England', *Victorian Studies*, VI (1962), 121–56; M.E. Craig, 'Bureaucracy and negativism: the Local Government Board 1886–1909' (M.A. thesis, University of Edinburgh, 1975).
38 R.J. Lambert, *Sir John Simon and English Social Administration* (1964).
39 A. Briggs, *Victorian Cities* (1968); D. Fraser, *Urban Politics in Victorian England* (1976). Cf., for a twentieth-century example, G.W. Jones, *Borough Politics* (1969).

40 J. Foster, *Class Struggle and the Industrial Revolution* (1974); J. Garrard, *Leaders and Politics in Nineteenth Century Salford* (University of Salford, n.d.).

41 W.E. Axon, *Cobden as a Citizen* (1907), 88.

42 Hennock, *op. cit*; Meller, *Leisure*; cf. A. Briggs, *A History of Birmingham* (1952), vol. II.

43 J.T. Bunce, C.A. Vince *et al.*, *A History of the Corporation of Birmingham* (6 vols., 1878–1957); A. Redford and I. T. Russell, *The History of Local Government in Manchester* (3 vols., 1939–40).

44 B.D. White, *A History of the Corporation of Liverpool* (1951); G. Bush, *Bristol and Its Municipal Government 1820–51* (1974); F.W. Rogers, 'Local politics and administration in the borough of Gateshead c. 1835–c. 1856' (Ph.D. thesis, University of London, 1971); R. Newton *Victorian Exeter* (1969).

45 H. Finer, *Municipal Trading* (1941); J.R. Kellett, 'Municipal Socialism, enterprise and trading in the Victorian city', *Urban History Yearbook* (1978), 36–45; M.E. Falkus, 'The development of municipal trading in the nineteenth century', *Business History*, xix (1977), 134–161; N. Solden, 'Laissez-faire as dogma' in *Essays in Anti-Labour History*, ed. K.D. Brown (1974), 208–33.

46 *Incorporate Your Borough*, 2–4.

47 S.D. Simon, *A Century of City Government* (1938), 398.

48 D. Fraser (ed.), *A History of Modern Leeds* (1980).

49 For a rare example of a comparative approach see R.A.H. Smith, 'The passing of the Municipal Corporations Act . . . with reference to selected boroughs (Ipswich, Hull, Preston, Norwich)', (M.Phil. thesis, University of East Anglia, 1974).

Incorporation and
the pursuit of Liberal hegemony
in Manchester 1790–1839

V. A. C. GATRELL

Incorporation and the pursuit of Liberal hegemony in Manchester 1790–1839

V. A. C. GATRELL

1 Introduction

The thesis from which the following chapters have been extracted in somewhat abbreviated and revised form is only incidentally concerned with the politics of municipal incorporation in Manchester. Entitled 'The commercial middle class in Manchester, c. 1820–1857' (Ph.D. thesis, University of Cambridge, 1971), it addresses more widely the local social and political context out of which by the late 1830s a caucus of wealthy businessmen emerged to assert their interests in national affairs, and which in some degree accounts for the subsequent disintegration of their purposes in the decade following corn-law repeal in 1846. In effect, the thesis is about the social genesis of the Manchester School in its home base and about its subsequent eclipse.

In this town notorious for the intensity of class division, it is striking how 'self-referential' middle-class political concerns generally were – a theme briefly aired in the first of the chapters below. By way of preliminary, and to explain this more ambitiously, part I of the thesis (not represented here) addresses some of the key variables which weakened the effectiveness of working-class opposition in that unequal society: the diversity of its occupational structure, for example, the adverse market conditions in which labour was sold, and the inability even of Chartism to break the confidence which propertied men rightly had in their own security.

The second part of the thesis, of which the following chapters are a distillation, examines the emergence in these conditions of a distinct Liberal caucus opposed to Tory influence in local affairs, and the municipal and parliamentary constituencies from which Liberalism and Toryism alike drew their support. The élites engaged in the party conflicts of 1790–1838 and the sources of their backing are examined through political narrative, through the analysis of kinship and similar linkages, and through the analysis of the pollbooks of the 1830s. The borough's incorporation in 1838 is seen to have played as crucial a part in the consolidation of liberal support as did the borough's parliamentary enfranchisement in 1832. Nonetheless the fragility of Liberal hegemony in the 1830s receives due emphasis, for it is a theme of some subsequent relevance.

The third part of the thesis (again not represented here) is concerned first with the economic rationality of the free trade movement built on these constituency foundations, as it struck cotton men increasingly anxious about their industry's prosperity. It then focuses on the gradual isolation of the League machine in its home town after its apotheosis in 1846. This process is explained partly in terms of altered export patterns in the late 1840s and 1850s, which rendered cotton men more susceptible to the appeals of Palmerstonian foreign policy than they were to Cobdenite panaceas, and partly as a function of the fragile electoral base upon which the League depended, as already referred to. The thesis concludes with a study of the 1857 election in which the Manchester School was defeated.

2 The setting

Many historians who have written about Manchester politics in the first half of the nineteenth century have been perhaps excessively preoccupied with the seeming polarization of the town's social structure into the class of the rich and the class of the poor. Their interest in this theme is understandable. Many who visited the town in the 1830s and 1840s went there, it often seems, expressly to indulge their sense of alarm at the depth of its class division. Of this 'classic type of the modern industrial city'[1] class division was the emblem. Its population was 'an aggregate of masses, our conceptions of which clothe themselves in terms that express something portentous and fearful'. 'At Manchester industry has found no previous occupant . . . There is nothing but masters and operatives.'[2] Observations of this kind were numerous, and they have left their mark on the later diagnoses of historians who should have known better.[3] Manchester, of course, was never as starkly polarized as this: the gap between rich and poor was appalling, but the occupational structure was nonetheless very complex, as befitted a retail and servicing as well as manufacturing conurbation of this size. Even more to the point, the issue of class did not dominate the political thinking of one social group at least – and those the most powerful in the community with whom these chapters are concerned. The response of the native middle class to their own community was likely to be altogether more equable than that of outsiders: 'always a little commotion in Manchester, but nothing very material', as one manufacturer put it in 1833.[4] There were tense months and years when the propertied and the respectable had to defuse the clamour of the poor by charity or propaganda or quell their demands by force. But the mentality which generally prevailed among them was characteristic of many similar groups who hold secure economic, social and political status in analogously divided societies. The very depth of the chasm between rich and poor and the sanctions it acquired in law and ideology almost guaranteed in the rich an inward-turning or self-referential mentality. The political issues that counted for them were not centrally concerned with the demands of the poor. They were more to do with who among themselves should wield local power and the status attached to it. Indeed, viewed from the middle class perspective, Manchester's political life in the first half of the nineteenth century was dominated less by overt class conflict than by the competitive pursuit of power by groupings within the middle class community. Some of these were closely integrated enough (by denominational, marital, and commercial bonds) to be termed 'élites'.

We should pay attention to this view of the meaning of Manchester politics if for no other reason than that a new form of political Liberalism was generated out of the feudings between these groups. The political history of the Manchester middle class in this period was in effect the history of the defeat and replacement of Tory and High Church authority in the town by 'Liberal' and largely dissenting authority. The aftermath of this protracted battle had great significance for the nation's history. Forged in a long confrontation with local Toryism, the 'Liberalism' for which Manchester became famous was to be inevitably – almost by birth-right – 'radical' in its attitudes to all interests which claimed a greater moral or political authority than its own. By natural extension this included the authority of land and aristocracy in the nation at large. Resolutely commercial and urban in its predispositions, moreover, Manchester Liberalism by the 1840s was, in the Anti-Corn Law League, to acquire from its antecedent history a thrust and momentum of which even Westminster had to take account. To be sure, after 1846, it flew too high. The defeat of the Manchester School in its home town in the 1857 election did not entirely surprise those who recognized that the Liberal hegemony in Manchester had been built upon less stable electoral foundations than its protagonists liked to pretend: Conservatism remained a vital force in the town, even (or rather, particularly) among the commercial classes. Nonetheless, even in the third quarter of the century, some Manchester Liberals under Richard Cobden's leadership were still claiming to represent the interests not of a town but of a class, not of an industry but of all industry; and there were many who knew little of Manchester who took that claim seriously. So these chapters, contemplating the town's politics through the experience of the middle class, are concerned with the genesis of a real political force in the land. They are concerned above all with the process by which the Liberal caucus attained that fragile hegemony in Manchester politics upon which the League was to rest its authority. The central achievements in that process were twofold: the conversion of Manchester into an ostensibly Liberal borough through the electoral victory made possible by the town's enfranchisement in 1832, and the municipal incorporation of the borough in the Liberal interest in 1838. Both achievements were indispensable to Liberal authority in the town; however, surprisingly perhaps, it was the last that was the more conclusive for Manchester's 'Liberal' future.

Municipal politics have not, in the present century, been a subject to engage the minds of those interested in 'real' power. Local politics take what colour they possess today from the greater doings of the parliamentary parties. In the early nineteenth century, however, local politics could claim greater autonomy. For most of urban and provincial England, they were what politics was 'about'. In 1828 the Duke of Clarence told Croker that party labels 'are mere nonsense nowadays'. Croker agreed that such might be the case at Westminster, but he 'still thought there were two marked and distinct parties in the country, which might for brevity be fairly called Whig and Tory'.[5] Croker's implied distinction between the nebulousness of party alignments at the legislative centre and their significance in the country at large was a valid one, and it held true for a decade after 1832 as well as for the years preceding it. However great the confusion about the role and the identity of party in parliament, in many provincial towns like Manchester the labels Whig, Tory, Liberal, and radical *did* denote meaningful and specific positions acknowledged as such by all politically literate and articulate men. To that extent, 'party' in the country tended to antedate 'party' in Westminster. The formal machinery of party government which began to assert itself in the first years of Victoria's reign built upon, exploited, and expressed, the already existing structure of local allegiances defined in the pre-reform period: its greatest achievement was to imbue them with a generalized ideological significance which pertained to the national society as a whole.

But that lay in the future. In Manchester, until 1838, 'party' was a vehicle by which groups competing for local power defined and resolved their local antagonisms, and involved in their own struggle social groups who looked to them for leadership. The wider national implications of these locally defined values could become apparent only when the immediate contest about local power had been resolved. Only after 1838 was the League, for example, able to elevate the local conflict into a national one; for only in the wake of incorporation was it certain of its ability to stave off the still very real power of the middle-class Toryism it had just supplanted. Only then was the intense localism of 'party' in Manchester (as elsewhere) to be changed utterly. Indeed the national 'formation' of the popular Liberal party, so often located in the late 1850s and 1860s,[6] cannot really be understood without reference to the antecedent history of that process in the urban politics of the 1820s and 1830s.

The looming presence of the League in the 1840s can only be fore-shadowed in the following discussion. The crisis in textiles which gave its economic panaceas credibility cannot here be at all considered.[7] Municipal incorporation provides the focus of what follows; but, even then, less the act of incorporation itself than the context in which it must be understood, and its longer term significance. If we are to grasp the meaning of 'party' in Manchester, the way in which incorporation consolidated that meaning, and the sense in which incorporation at last gave the Liberal caucus a political credibility in the town, we must cast our net much wider than is customary in such exercises. We must look to the social identities of the protagonists in the protracted battle between the 'ins' and the 'outs' waged from the 1790s onwards; we must note the earliest challenges to the Tory stranglehold which prevailed until at least the 1820s; we must attend to the parties who fought for the parliamentary seats of 1832; and, in the 1830s, we must note the progressively important role which the enfranchised shopocracy and artisanate were to play in local affairs. It is extraordinary how little it has been recognized that these last provided the electoral footsoldiers without whom the big battalions of the Anti-Corn Law League would have been impotent. In many towns like Manchester, it was the issue of incorporation that thus consolidated their 'Liberalism' – long before Dr Vincent, for example, would have us believe.

Let us first, however, attend briefly to the political arena in which the middle classes conducted their feuds. For it was implied at the beginning that this was virtually an *apartheid* society, in which the well-heeled could play out their contest for authority with next to no reference to the poor on the other side of that vast chasm which divided Manchester society. We need to understand why this was so before we proceed further. It is not, of course, a matter for great puzzlement. There were powerful guarantees of the stability of the social order in which the middle class could rightly be confident. To the most important we can do no more than refer in passing here: the occupational and status differentiation of the workforce, far more complex than contemporary alarmists perceived; its subjection to a glutted labour market which worked emphatically to the employers' advantage; the presence of a military and later a police force which, though in chartist years sorely stretched, proved sufficient to cope with the threat from below; the institutional underpinning of middle-class control, through churches, schools and institutes. The condition of stability most germane to this argument, however, relates to the distribution in the town of political influence – and particularly to the demarcation in law itself of the political arenas which men of property could legitimately colonize with little interference from the working class presence.

After the 1832 Reform Act the demarcation was to become very explicit indeed. It is almost a sufficient explanation of the self-referential nature of the middle-class political consciousness. In Manchester as elsewhere the division between Commons and People was throughout these years more directly influential on the borough's political history, and more intimately relevant to the political calculations of those whose actions brought Manchester to national attention, than the very much less clear-cut division between labour and capital, propertied and non-propertied, which obsessed as many contemporary observers as it has subsequent historians. For the distinction between the electorate and the non-electorate was after all the institutionalized and legally sanctioned expression of every other form of social and economic inequality within the town. No other statute asserted so unequivocally the ancient association of property with power than the Reform Act; no other Act so categorically sorted men into two distinct groups, one privileged, the other not, or so clearly defined the areas of political action each could legitimately inhabit. In Manchester as elsewhere, economic inequality was thus endowed with a political correlative, and given its statutory *imprimatur*.

It would be foolish to deny that a sizeable minority of the working and the middling classes were represented in the Manchester electorate. A sample analysis of the 1832 and 1839 poll-books suggests that some 4 per cent of those voting then were skilled operatives; shopkeepers made up another 23 per cent; and craft and building trades another 12 to 15 per cent. The 'middle class' were by no means overwhelmingly dominant. Professionals wielded only 6 per cent of votes, textile magnates only 20 per cent in 1832 and 13 per cent in 1839, 'subsidiary' textile men 9 to 10 per cent, and those in commercial and administrative callings 10 to 13 per cent (see table 4 below). In 1832, moreover, 14 per cent of all adult males were registered voters, and by 1841, 17 per cent. All of this made the parliamentary electorate more 'popular' than the local government electorate, before 1838 at least.

Even so, this popular presence does not seriously qualify our sense that the electorate was well suited to middle-class influence, or that middle-class preoccupations were little distorted thereby. The reasons are several. First, when all is said and done the constituency was an exceptionally wealthy one. It is all but impossible to specify the wealth structure of early nineteenth-century electorates, but some indication of the peculiarities of the Manchester case can be inferred from the rating returns for Manchester and comparable towns laid before parliament in 1847. These suggest that in 1846, thanks to a high incidence of commercial property, Manchester was probably the wealthiest industrial urban constituency in England and Wales (matched only by Liverpool). For every 100 householders qualified for the vote by rate assessment at £10 to £15, there were about 36 assessed at £100 and over. In Leeds, by contrast, the ratios were 100 to 25, in Birmingham

100 to 12, in Oldham and Rochdale 100 to 10, in Blackburn 100 to 7.[8] Seven per cent of the Manchester householders whose rateable value was specified in the returns were not registered for the vote, it is true. But this does not significantly weaken the impression of an electorate in which wealthy householders were more than commonly numerous relative to the rest of the electorate, for it was as much the disqualification of poor householders as dual ratings at the upper levels which accounted for the discrepancy. Also working to enhance élite influence in the parliamentary electorate was its very size: again with the exception of Liverpool it was the largest non-metropolitan borough in England. This admittedly fostered a high degree of electoral independence in the town, for employers' coercion and pressure was weakened thereby;[9] but then, conversely, the power of the non-electorate wielded by exclusive dealing or by direct intimidation was similarly weakened.[10] Even more to the point, the depersonalization of political relationships in a large borough engendered a high degree of electoral indifference as well. Percentage polls are notoriously difficult to measure in this period although a rough idea of how extensive electoral apathy could be in Manchester can be gained by seeing how many of the 1,379 names beginning with B in the manuscript electoral register closed in October 1838, on which the 1839 by-election was fought, appear as active voters in the 1839 poll-book. Since 81 per cent of these names can be identified occupationally by cross-reference to the 1838–9 directories, the analysis can be conducted in occupational terms. The percentages of those qualified who did not vote is as follows:

Table 2   Qualified voters not exercising their right in the 1839 election in Manchester

occupation	%	
major textile employers (155)*	36	* For composition of
professionals (76)	29	occupational groups,
subsidiary textile employers (135)	42	see Appendix, p. 53
commercial, scholastic, etc. (170)	38	below.
skilled operatives (43)	37	
craft and artisan (86)	29	
building (66)	24	
drink (112)	33	
food retailers (80)	29	
clothes retailers (73)	27	
sundry retailers (88)	36	
miscellaneous (31)	32	
not known (264)	86	
total (1,379)	44	

These figures cannot of course pretend to accuracy, since they were distorted by the incidence of double assessments and non-residence, especially among the wealthier ratepayers, as well as by familiar deficiencies in the registration process. However, accepting the figures as approximate indications, it is striking that even among craftsmen and shopkeepers who were unlikely to be doubly assessed or non-resident, anything between one third and one quarter of those registered did not go to the polls; and since most double assessments and non-residents are in fact, in this table, included among the 'not knowns', some similar inferences can be drawn from the figures for the wealthier groups as well.

For the purposes of the present argument, the effect of all this was important. It reinforced greatly the need for electoral party organization. This need arose from the expensive 'necessity of employing hired canvassers, and other similar means, to overcome the indifference of the voters, and induce them to come to the poll'.[11] (Significantly, the Manchester election expenses in 1832 and 1841 were among the highest in Britain.)[12] In this sense Manchester was wholly characteristic of those large and wealthy constituencies in which political influence fell unavoidably not into the hands of one man, nor as in Oldham into the hands of a radical caucus with the non-electorate's backing, but into the hands of caucuses with the will, wealth, authority, and experience, which enabled them to control well-financed organizations. This was an electoral structure which conduced naturally to its manipulation by highly mobilized and experienced élites.[13]

Before 1832 Manchester was not enfranchised; however, the arenas in which the disputes for authority in *local* government were conducted were no less conducive to an uncontaminated middle-class influence. It is true that in principle the Manchester and Salford Police Act of 1792, which applied until 1828, offered opportunities for a wider participation in local government than the ancient Court Leet and manorial authorities. But in terms of the 1792 Act, commissioners had to occupy or own property with an annual rent or value of over £30 *per annum*. This effectively excluded the participation of all wage-earners and of many small shopkeepers. The new Police Act of 1829 set the minimum requirement for voters at £16, and for the 240 commissioners to be elected on that franchise at £28. But by 1835 even this Act had enfranchised a mere 8½ per cent of adult males in Manchester (i.e. 4,242 voters) and heavily biased the representation in favour of the richer districts of the Manchester township.[14] Again: the fuller democracy even of the municipal charter of 1838 was to be vitiated by massive electoral indifference: by 1860 the Tory election agent John Sudlow could point out that of about 33,000 householders assessed at under £10 in 1859, fewer than 200 had claimed to be put on the municipal register.[15]

We have stressed here the relative exclusiveness of the middle-class political arenas. But it was not merely the poor who were excluded from participation in them: it is worth noting that county influence was virtually excluded as well. The town was innocent, indeed, of all forms of inherited influence, relatively speaking. Although before 1838 Manchester was subject to the jurisdiction of the county magistracy and ultimately that of the Lord Lieutenant, it was largely spared the attentions of landed political patrons because it had been so long unrepresented in parliament. It lacked even a resident gentry. Gentle blood had begun to desert the town long before the 1820s as it grew larger, dirtier, and smellier. As early as 1728 all the chief houses illustrated and named in Whitworth's panorama of Manchester and Salford belonged to merchants. By 1795 the only family of antiquity in the neighbourhood were the Traffords at Trafford Hall. Merchants had moved in to Broughton and Smedley Halls, and also into the seats of the Mosleys at Ancoats and Hulme after the Mosleys retired to Staffordshire; Lord Ducie owned Strangeways Hall but lived in Gloucestershire.[16] Another 30 years and the mercantile appropriation of the old family seats was all but complete. Of the 37 seats within five miles of Manchester in 1825, seven were occupied by merchants, four by manufacturers and spinners, two by bankers, one by a barrister.[17] By 1842, those halls which were left were 'much degenerated': 'several . . . are divided into separate dwellings, and are tenanted by persons of the poorer classes of society'.[18] Only one magnate of consequence survived this exodus in the Manchester vicinity, Lord Francis Egerton at Worsley; but his preserve was the South Lancashire constituency, and in Manchester affairs he was impotent. Such as it was, Manchester's political relationship with the county was to derive from Mancunian incursions into county affairs, and not vice versa – before 1832 through urban representation in the county electorate, and in the 1840s through the League's registration efforts in the counties.

So much by way of context. But what now of the middle-class protagonists who worked within this structure, and with whose feuding we are now mainly concerned? For over half a century, in the local government as later in the parliamentary arenas, a small group of High Churchmen and Tories on the one hand did battle with a select handful of Unitarians, Quakers or Whig-Radical families on the other, together with their less elevated political henchmen and the *menu peuple* whom they attached to their respective causes. Relatively stable political and social nuclei in the expanding commercial society, they acted as focal points of authority to one or the other of which newly risen men tended to attach themselves to attain a vicarious status; each nucleus was represented in the possession of a second- or third-generation fortune; the identity of each was starkly clarified in the course of the denominational and political disputes of the revolutionary and post-revolutionary decades, and above all in the course of the battle for control of local government and parliamentary representation in the 1820s and 1830s.

With the incorporation of the borough in 1838 Manchester at last witnessed the temporary resolution of this competition. The Tory oligarchy which had long controlled the vestry, the police commission, the Court Leet, and the magistrates' bench, was defeated by a coalition of 'Liberals', many of whom were still drawn from the network of Unitarian families whose political interests had been first defined in the 1790s. From this victory, quite as much as from that of 1832, Manchester Liberalism was to derive its strength for another 20 years; the achievement of the dissenting group was the indispensable basis of the Anti-Corn Law League.

We should begin by examining some of the protagonists in this local saga. It is the Liberal-Radical groups, whose star was to rise, who are the most easily identified in the decades 1790–1832. In those years, Manchester Toryism drew much of its strength from the prevailing political climate in the nation at large. It was not nearly as integrated as its opponents were. By contrast, the as yet excluded but ascendant élite drew their strength from denominational cohesion. The reference is particularly to the Unitarian families worshipping at the Cross Street and Mosley Street chapels. 'Marginal men' in the nation as well as the locality, their self-appointed mission was to destroy the High Church and Tory hegemony in the town which denied them, it seemed, the proper status which their wealth and education merited. Their vigour was long sustained, and it was to be effective. It was from the Gregs, the Potters, the Philipses, and their like that the Anti-Corn Law League in its heyday was to draw some of its most stalwart supporters. It was for these people that the borough's enfranchisement in 1832 and incorporation in 1838 had a truly epic meaning. By the 1830s they had 'arrived'. In the course of the nineteenth century as a whole, the trustees of Cross Street Unitarian chapel alone were to provide Liberal Manchester with seven of its Mayors, and the nation at large with a dozen M.P.s.

3 The protagonists defined

The Unitarian community

By the end of the eighteenth century the ambiguous status of Manchester's Unitarians all but guaranteed the vigour with which they were to challenge the Tory and Church establishment. They were wealthy and well-educated; some were entrepreneurial giants. Their denomination was exclusive; their families were closely intermarried; they subscribed jealously to an intellectual tradition which was rationalist and in that sense potentially 'radical'. Self-perceived status notwithstanding, they were to bear the full brunt of the tory reaction which the French Revolution let loose in Manchester as elsewhere. The consequent need to reconcile a strong sense of their material, intellectual, and familial wealth with the equivocal status accorded them by the 'official' culture propelled these people, as it is likely to propel all such minorities, into an overt form of political radicalism.

The material solidity of eighteenth-century Unitarians, as of eighteenth-century Quakers, has been as often remarked upon as its sources have been misunderstood. To regard their wealth and business success as a *product* of their puritanism – of the ethic of thrift and diligence which Old Dissenting doctrine enjoined on those who subscribed to it – is to misconstrue the causal relationship between wealth and doctrine. A family's material comfort was as often a *pre*condition of its adoption of Unitarianism as its consequence: for only moderate and pre-existing wealth could purchase the education which made accessible the rational theology developing among early eighteenth-century Presbyterians and General Baptists, and out of which Unitarianism was conceived. When for example the Manchester chapel at Cross Street turned Unitarian under the ministry of the Rev. John Seddon (1739–69), 200 families worshipping there seceded in protest. On the whole, those who did not secede were the more prosperous of the congregation, as surviving wills indicate.[19] To be sure, as time passed, the sophistication, general affluence, and business connections of the Cross Street community attracted its share of new men. These were seldom fortune-hunters, however, but men of established business standing and again (significantly) of some education. By the beginning of the new century the chapel's trustees were deeply enmeshed in the leading business enterprises which were rapidly converting Manchester into the urban pace-maker of the industrial revolution. Thus the Heywoods and the Loyds were Manchester's most prominent bankers; the Gregs, the Potters, the Philips brothers, James M'Connel, A. and G. Murray, and James Kennedy were among Lancashire's greatest cotton men. The trend to business success manifested itself unequivocally in the new century. Of the 73 men who acted as trustees at Cross Street in the period 1713 to 1802, 22 per cent had been 'gentlemen' or professional men, 25 per cent had been traders or retailers, 53 per cent had been merchants or manufacturers. Of the 100 trustees listed for the period 1802–54, 24 per cent were gentlemen or professional men, only five per cent were in trade or retail, and the proportion of manufacturers and merchants had risen dramatically to 71 per cent.[20]

The material security of the community was further guaranteed by its exclusiveness. Unitarians were not a proselytizing denomination. Expansion was achieved by secession rather than by conversion, and the social dilution of the parent community was thus minimized. An Arian group had broken away from Cross Street to build the Mosley Street chapel in 1789; this in turn financed the erection of the Upper Brook Street and Strangeways chapels in 1827–9; a Unitarian chapel was built at Greengate, Salford, in 1824.[21] But this was a less than remarkable expansion. By 1851, in Lancashire as a whole, only nine Unitarian chapels had been added to the 26 occupied by the denomination at the beginning of the century, and this across a period when every other denomination except the Quakers had more than doubled the number of their chapels. In Manchester itself by 1851, unitarians comprised a bare 1.8 per cent of the total church-going population.[22] Cross Street remained dominant, with the Mosley Street chapel its social adjunct. Intermarriages between members of both chapels were frequent, as were familial migrations from one to the other. By 1820 the Mosley Street membership included the Gregs, the younger Philipses, G. W. Wood, and William Henry, for example, all prominent in dissenting politics and descended from or connected by marriage to Cross Street trustees of the eighteenth century. But between Cross Street and the other newer chapels founded in the early nineteenth century there were real social differences, partly expressed in organizational forms. The new chapels were run by elected committees whose membership changed frequently; Cross Street, by contrast, was governed by a well entrenched hierarchy of trustees through whom the control exercised by a group of eighteenth-century families was perpetuated into the new century. The social consequences of this distinction were fully evident by the 1830s. The new chapels attracted large numbers of dissentient Methodists which made them both more sectarian in attitude and more 'popular' in membership. The old chapel (as the Strangeways congregation complained), failed to attract anyone but 'respectable' people; its sermons were 'literary' in tone; and its pews were expensive.[23] More select in membership, the Cross Street chapel also remained more liberal in doctrine and more jealous of its intellectual distinction. It was right to be so: few who worshipped at Cross Street lacked an education at the Warrington Academy, or at Manchester College in York, or at Lant Carpenter's school in Bristol. Many could trace their ancestry back to the seventeenth century; others boasted an unbroken ancestral commitment to the Presbyterian and Unitarian ministry which was the central fact of their lives.[24]

The third condition of Unitarian status in Manchester resided in their extraordinary kinship linkages. This alone justifies our regarding them as an 'élite'. Their business success, their political opinions, their sense of their own identity, were all supported by, and in some part attributable to the close kinship ties by which they had linked themselves to each other over the preceding century. This web of family connection was the source of the Manchester Unitarians' greatest strength. It guaranteed a reserve of capital for the entrepreneur, an electoral fund for the politician; and in a society which barred or made difficult their advancement to positions of authority, it bolstered and sustained a degree of social resentment which stimulated them to political action. They were fortunate in this. Their Tory and High Church opponents lacked any support-system of this kind. Such eminent Tory families as there were, were centrifugal in their kinship linkages; the Unitarians were centripetal. While the comparable Tory dynasties, the Peels, the Birleys, the Flemings and the Wanklyns, loosened their kinship links by seeking their wives across the breadth of two or more counties, the leading Unitarian dynasties almost unfailingly sought their wives at Cross Street, Mosley Street, or at Dob Lane, Failsworth, or at Toxteth Park chapel, Liverpool. They had done so for a century. In the new century, too, they were to draw into their orbit, by marriage, many of the most dynamic newcomers in the community of Old Dissent. Not only were the roots of Manchester Unitarianism deeply planted: fresh roots were being put out all the time.

Let us take for example one sequence of familial linkages at Cross Street which may represent several such.[25] The Heywoods, Percivals, Naylors, Philipses, Hibberts, Bayleys, Henrys, Potters, and Gregs, provided late eighteenth- and early nineteenth-century Manchester with a good number of its leading commercial, professional, scientific and literary men, and the nation at large later, incidentally, with near on a dozen members of parliament. Several families within this network traced their ancestry back to ejected ministers of the seventeenth century. Most, in their history, testified eloquently to the judicious marriage system by which they had assisted themselves to financial and social dominance by the end of the Napoleonic Wars.

Of this process the Heywoods were wholly representative. Descended from two ministers ejected in 1662, the family initiated its fortune by marriage into the Graham family of Drogheda, and into the fortune of the Pembertons of Liverpool in the 1730s and 1740s. This connection put them at the top of Liverpool's merchant hierarchy. In 1757 they assisted Thomas Bentley and Thomas Wharton in the founding of the Warrington Academy. In 1774 the eldest of the brothers went into partnership with his sons as bankers; four years later the youngest brother and his sons Benjamin and Nathaniel followed suit by opening their bank in Manchester. Here they moved straight into the milieu of Cross Street. Nathaniel became a trustee and married the daughter of Thomas Percival, F.R.S., a founder of the Literary and Philosophical Society. Three of the five sons of this marriage were Cross Street trustees; James, the youngest, went to Cambridge, was called to the Bar, was returned as M.P. for North Lancashire in 1847 and 1852, and was elected to the Royal Society. The eldest, Benjamin, went to Glasgow University, succeeded in the bank's management in 1828, sat for Lancashire in 1831, was knighted in 1838, and joined his brother as Fellow of the Royal Society in 1843. His sons took over the bank until its business was transferred to the Manchester and Salford Bank in 1874.

This familial apotheosis was not unique at Cross Street. Given appropriate marriages and sufficient business wit, many of those who possessed even moderate fortunes in the first half of the eighteenth century were transformed in the latter half into men of substance: in an expanding society those who possessed or had access to capital early on had little competition to encounter until the huge expansion of enterprise in cotton in the 1820s and 1830s. The father of the Hibbert family, to take another example, was a linen draper who combined trusteeship at Cross Street with the position of Constable of Manchester in the 1740s. The local trade prospered: estates were bought in Jamaica. The second son became a West India merchant, followed his father as trustee and Constable, and begat a son who entered parliament and the Royal Society. The three daughters married directly into Manchester's most prominent mercantile families: the youngest was to be paternal grandmother of Benjamin Heywood's wife; another, having married Nathaniel Philips, was to be paternal grandmother of Mark Philips, M.P. for

Manchester 1832–47, and of R.N. Philips, M.P. for Bury 1857–9 and 1865–85; the eldest, having married into another Cross Street family, the Bayleys, eventually became paternal grandmother of the wife of Thomas Potter, first mayor of Manchester, and of the wife of Manchester's most distinguished medical man, William Henry, yet another Cross Street F.R.S. With the marriage of Henry's daughter to W.R. Greg and of Mark and Robert Philips' sister to R.H. Greg, this Byzantine network was significantly consummated: in the Philips, Potter, and Greg families it encompassed what were to become three indispensable bastions of the Liberal and free-trade movement in Manchester in the 1830s and 1840s.

In the case of each of these last three families the Cross Street community provided an entrée into Manchester's dissenting politics in the nineteenth century: they were loosely associated with the chapel but they were not, in the way that the Heywoods or Hibberts were, of it. The elder Philips brothers were educated at Manchester Grammar School and their son appears to have worshipped at the Presbyterian chapel rather than at Cross Street. The Gregs were all unitarians but since they were engaged in manufacture in Styal they were too remote for the Sunday journey to worship in Manchester. The Potters were Unitarians but newcomers. Thomas, William, and Richard were sons of a Tadcaster farmer and draper and began business in Manchester as late as 1802; Thomas alone became a Cross Street trustee, and that only in 1828. But as their marriage links testify, all three families gravitated naturally into the Cross Street milieu. Even the Philipses accommodated themselves to the Unitarian community, for Mark was sent to Manchester College, York, of which his father was a generous benefactor. In part this was the centripetal tendency of a family isolated in its wealth: the Manchester presbyterian community harboured few great manufacturing magnates, and the Philips brothers, who in the post-Napoleonic decade owned one of the five Manchester firms employing over 1,000 factory hands, may have drifted into the Cross Street milieu on that account. (Significantly the Scots engineer William Fairbairn followed their example in this.) The Greg marriages might equally have expressed an awareness of economic status, for by the 1820s they were among the largest country manufacturers in Lancashire. But in each instance additional factors drew these families within the Cross Street orbit – real confessional sympathy, and almost certainly a similarity of cultural interest and political opinion. Two principles united this complex family network: a more or less intense political radicalism which diversely expressed itself, for example, in Sir George Philips' advocacy of female suffrage in 1782 or, later, in the Potter brothers' cabal which, as we shall see, was to constitute the nucleus of Manchester Liberal politics in the 1820s; and a more or less explicit commitment to the dictates of political economy, manifested, for instance, in the writings of the Greg brothers or the public works of the Heywoods, and ultimately enforcing the Unitarian support of the Anti-Corn Law League.

These political alignments, it is true, were not invariable at Cross Street. Another major Cross Street connection, the Jones and Loyd families, deeply entrenched in Manchester banking, were to turn Tory in their second generation at Cross Street; Samuel Jones Loyd became Tory M.P. for Hythe from 1819 to 1826 and in 1832 stood as unsuccessful Tory candidate in Manchester itself. By then, too, the family had connected itself through marriage to William Entwistle, Tory candidate for Manchester in 1841 and Tory M.P. for South Lancashire from 1844. Locally, the family bank became the guardian of almost Tory wealth: an account there, in Tory eyes, was to be a measure of Tory respectability, along with occupancy of a pew at the Old Church. But the Loyds were exceptional among Manchester Unitarians in their apostacy from the prevailing Liberalism of Cross Street, and it is understandable that relations between the Loyds and the Cross Street politicians should have become strained. The truth is that the correlation between association with Cross Street and commitment to Liberal causes was almost invariable in the late eighteenth century and the first four decades of the nineteenth; it was a correlation that was jealously guarded.

The peculiarities of Unitarian doctrine all but ensured that this should be so. The Cross Street congregation shared a tradition common to all long-established Unitarian chapels. Characteristically it entailed a profound confidence in the worth of man and in the power of reason as a foundation of faith. But it also committed them to a quite distinctive ethic of toleration which had been sharpened in those congregations which had borne the full brunt of the semi-persecution of the previous century. It is true that in eighteenth-century Manchester such people by dint of their wealth and respectability had been able to hold local office. But their status was uneasy, and as the century progressed it became more so. Those in the 1790s who were to flirt with Jacobinism were to pay for it. For Burke, 'Unitarians were united for the express purpose of proselytism' and aimed 'to collect a multitude sufficient by force and violence to overturn the Church . . . concurrent with a design to subvert the State'. In law if not in practice, to be a Unitarian was a criminal offence until 1813.[26] Animosities in the nineteenth century were accentuated by the growth of Methodism and Evangelicalism: profession of Unitarianism remained a political, social, and doctrinal liability. At the 1839 Manchester election the Tory candidates felt it worthwhile to draw the attention of electors to the heterodoxy of the Liberal candidate W.R. Greg.[27] A year before, even as one of Manchester's most eminent Unitarians (J. Potter) became the borough's first mayor, a concerted attempt was made to exclude the denomination from office in the Athenaeum, which Cobden and James Heywood, himself a Cross Street trustee, had founded three years previously.[28] From 1825 until the final resolution of litigation in the Dissenters' Chapel Bill of 1844 the Cross Street congregation had to resist a sustained assault on their right to occupy and administer property in contravention of the terms by which it had been entrusted to their trinitarian ancestors in the seventeenth century.[29]

The effects of this adverse climate on the cohesion of the Cross Street congregation were profound. Clearly, kinship served a protective function. For most of them, too, their religion was no embellishment. Of the unitarians more than of many other denominations Taine's comment on English nonconformists is perhaps most strictly true: 'respectable, middle class people very correctly dressed, and with serious sensible faces. They are here [at chapel] to refurbish their principles . . . Apparently they consider morality not an object of curiosity, but of use – a tool in daily requisition, so that, on Sundays, it needs sharpening.'[30] However, in the late eighteenth century the most remarkable aspect of the Unitarians' accommodation to this climate – as well as the most expressive of their rationalism – was an institutional one. The Manchester Literary and Philosophical Society was one of the most vivid expressions of English provincial culture of those decades. That it derived its tone from its Unitarian membership is no real conundrum. Its brighter luminaries, Percival, Henry, Thomas Robinson, for example, had for the most part received their early education at the Warrington

Academy during the decade 1757–67 when it was run by a brilliant partnership of which Joseph Priestley was the most famous. There, trained in the principle of open debate, they sought in their maturity in Manchester to recapture the intellectual excitement of their earlier environment. 'Men, however great their learning', the preface to the first volume of the Society's *Memoirs* observed, 'often become indolent and unambitious to improve in knowledge, for want of associating with others of similar talents and acquirements. . . . But science, like fire, is put in motion by collision. Where a number of such men have frequent opportunities of meeting and conversing together, thought begets thought, and every hint is turned to advantage. A spirit of enquiry glows in every breast.'[31] The Society was established in 1781 by a group who had met regularly at Percival's house. Of its 43 members in 1785, 15 were trustees or ministers, or were closely related to trustees or ministers, of the Cross Street chapel, and the proportion increased somewhat in the ensuing decade. The office-holders Percival, Loyd, Barnes, Henry, Robinson, were chiefly from the same circle.[32] Within a very few years it was people of this kind, we shall see, who were to bear the brunt of the Tory reaction of the 1790s. That spirit of enquiry which they so valued drove them into positions which their local opponents could castigate, as Burke did in parliament, as subversive of the established order. In the 1790s the first salvoes were fired in that battle between middle class 'radicals' and Tories respectively which was to be concluded only with incorporation in 1838.

Manchester Tories
Manchester Conservatism in the late eighteenth and early nineteenth centuries lacked the institutional underpinning the Cross Street network gave its opponents. To be sure it had its fair share of second- or third-generation fortunes upon which much of its business status rested. J.B. Wanklyn for example, was typical in the range of his public commitments: constable of Salford in 1826 and boroughreeve in 1829; senior churchwarden of Manchester in 1835; member of the Billiard Club, the Broughton Archers, and the Chetham Society; Tory manager 1832–9 for the candidatures of William Garnett in Salford and of Hope and Murray in Manchester – Wanklyn's status turned on the prestige of his father's merchant house. Thomas Fleming serves as another example: as treasurer of the police commission he was the undisputed autocrat of the town's local government between 1810 and 1819, and he continued in public office until 1828: his fortune had been initiated by his grandfather who had developed a new dying process.[33] Men of this type, however, were never quite the dynasts the Heywoods, the Philipses, the Hibberts were. In Leeds, the dynastic cohesion of their Tory equivalents appears to have been much stronger. But Leeds' wealth was built upon a woollen industry which had been Britain's staple product long before cotton had acquired its dominance. If there were Lancashire equivalents to the great Leeds Tory dynasts, they were to be found among the West Indiamen of Liverpool.[34] In Manchester, although mercantile wealth in the late eighteenth century could plausibly pretend to be largely Tory wealth, the range of familial connection which might have supported it was relatively limited. Manchester churchmen, too, subscribed to no intellectual and hence political tradition as coherent as that prevailing at Cross Street; there is also less evidence that they were prepared or called upon to deploy a pool of wealth in support of a political cause.

Indeed, the Tory manufacturing families with the greatest influence in Manchester remained relatively remote from the town even in those years when they might have wielded most influence to their own political advantage. The Peels in the late eighteenth century and the Birleys in the early nineteenth century provide the classic cases in point. Let us dwell at some length on the Birleys, for example. By the mid-nineteenth century they were at last to fulfil their appropriate role in Manchester by giving leadership to local Toryism and ultimately by providing the borough (in 1868) with its first Conservative M.P. Before the 1840s, however, they stood in marked contrast to their Cross Street counterparts in two respects. First, while the Unitarian families nearly always married *into* Manchester society, they always married *outside* it; secondly and in part following from this, their business and social interests were such as to make them in some degree alien to the town. In important ways, too, their claim to act as leaders of an independent Conservatism was deeply compromised by the fact that willy-nilly, as leading manufacturers, they tended in some measure to share the economic beliefs of their Liberal rivals.

The Birleys' distance from Manchester was a literal one.[35] The family home was at Kirkham, whence the foundation of their fortune had been laid in the West India interests built up by John Birley (1710–67). Their ties with Kirkham were not relinquished, and it is this that partly accounts for that geographical diffusion of their kinship links. The closest relationship was with the Hornby family, also of Kirkham, with whom intermarriage was so frequent as almost to indicate a family policy deliberately sustained over three generations. Five further marriages – with the Cardwells, the Backhouses, the Yates and the Addisons – cemented the family's connection with the Tory and mercantile élite of Liverpool. The third generation (born in the first decades of the nineteenth century) consolidated this already tight network by marrying Birley cousins, so that by the 1820s Birley marriages straddled the county. Richard Birley alone (1812–74) married into a Manchester manufacturing family (that of James Kennedy): his daughter was to marry the engineer William Fairbairn in 1864. The family's business interests reflected this kinship pattern in respect of both partnership structure and location: only in 1827 did the Birleys become an exclusively Manchester-based manufacturing firm. An early partnership with the Cardwell family seems to have been supplanted round about 1779 when Richard Birley (1743–1812) moved from Kirkham with his brother-in-law John Hornby to establish the putting-out weaving business at Blackburn which remained the bed-rock of both families' fortunes until the dissolution of the partnership in 1827. (How the early Blackburn business prospered is witnessed by the increase of John Hornby's estate from £3,131 in 1786 to £26,242 ten years later). Richard's sons appear to have moved to Manchester only after their father's death in 1812, two of them, Joseph and Hugh Hornby Birley, to manage the Chorlton (spinning) branch of the partnership, which they expanded by the purchase of Charles Macintosh & Co, thus becoming Manchester's most substantial employers. The dissolution of the Hornby partnership did not entirely confine their interests to Manchester: with Hornby they retained shares in Thos Orrell, Sons & Co, of Stalybridge, and probably in several smaller concerns as well.

In the scale and diversity of their manufacturing interests the Birleys were not radically different from the Gregs, for example, in whose business records we witness a similar diversification of enterprise and a similar narrowing down of the partnership to the immediate family circle once the family fortune was independently established. The chief difference, obviously enough, lay in the fact that probably by inclination, to some extent by business interest, and certainly by marriage, the Birleys' social horizons were not limited to the immediate environment of Manchester. If the Gregs lived out of Manchester by necessity (their largest works were at Styal) the Birleys lived out of town by choice – John and Joseph in the then still remote villages of Rusholme and Didsbury, Hugh Hornby Birley still further away, at Eccles. If Samuel Greg's sons were educated in local unitarian academies, at least one of Joseph Birley's sons (Hugh, the future M.P.) was educated at Winchester. If the Gregs sought to assert their status in the Liberal/dissenting institutions and cabals in Manchester, the Birleys were assured of a ready-made status in county society: the brothers John, Hugh Hornby, and Joseph were each of them Deputy Lieutenants. No Birley appears in the membership lists of John Shaw's Club in the years 1800–60, an aloofness from the social milieu of Manchester Conservatism in marked contrast to the participation in the club of nearly every other local Conservative of note – Fleming, Crossley, Sudlow, Sowler, for example.[36] If the Gregs could claim kinship with Manchester's Liberal élite, the younger Birleys in the 1840s could claim first-cousinhood with the Peelite Edward Cardwell. The Birleys, in short, were of the county and potentially of the national establishment, and this seriously qualified their interest in the affairs of Manchester itself.

One individual alone broke the family habit. Hugh Hornby Birley quickly asserted himself as one of the bulwarks of the local governmental oligarchy before incorporation by associating himself with Fleming's rule in the post-war years: he became boroughreeve in 1814–15, a leading architect of the 1829 Police Act, and was active thereafter on the Gas Commission. But although with his brother Joseph he signed the petition for the transfer of the Penryn seat to Manchester, and also gave tardy approval of Manchester's enfranchisement,[37] H.H. Birley could in no plausible sense act as public, let alone popular figure-head of Manchester Conservatism, and this for two reasons. First, as one of Manchester's greatest manufacturers, he was obliged to associate himself with causes which Manchester Liberals even then were trying to make their own. In his capacity as first president of the Chamber of Commerce he adopted at the outset a strong aversion to factory regulation, communicating to Peel in 1825, for example, the Chamber's and his own opinion 'that the regulation of such matters by law, seems to be objectionable on general principles, to be difficult of enforcement, and to afford means for the gratification of revengeful feelings, to the serious injury of individuals'. If regulation was to prove necessary (and he believed a commission desirable to investigate the question), he and his fellow masters argued that it should 'extend to all mills where machinery is used, and not be confined, as at present, to persons of a certain age, and to one particular trade'.[38] By 1832 the family had, if anything, become less compromising in the face of Sadler's Bill.[39] Despite some relaxation of their opinion ten years later, when H.H. Birley could confess himself ready to accept the limitation of children's hours and their education under the church's guidance as one sure means of regulating their political passions,[40] it remained the case that the family stood thus far compromised in the eyes not only of the working population but also of the non-commercial Conservative community, the clerical part of which, at least, was shortly to demonstrate their commitment to the short-time movement. The second reason for the Birley's equivocal popular status in Manchester needs less elaboration though if anything it was more conclusive. The memory of Peterloo died hard: even Cobden invoked its memory to justify incorporation in 1837–8. On 16 August 1819, Hugh Hornby Birley, major of the Manchester Yeomanry, had led the fateful charge.

These vignettes may suffice to demonstrate the central point that Manchester Toryism lacked the cohesiveness of those who opposed it. Its leading families did not constitute, in the same sense, an integrated and operational élite. It was to find other sources of strength. As we shall see in the next section, even in defeat, it was to remain a more formidable force than Liberal mythology would have us believe.[41] But in these early years, as the rival groups first squared up to confront each other over the distribution of local authority, Manchester Tories and churchmen were to find strength mainly outside themselves. This came from the tide of national opinion flowing their way in the wake of the so-called counter-revolution unleashed by the French Revolution. It was in the 1790s that Manchester Unitarianism first declared and acted upon its radical predisposition. The successful Tory counter-attack was to seal the pattern of Manchester politics for the next two generations, and to define for Toryism the identity it might otherwise have lacked and the position it was successfully to hold for 20 years.

Tory dominance established
The history of this first skirmish must be briefly dealt with. Although the promise of religious freedom held out by the Rockingham interest had long aligned respectable dissenters with the Whigs, there were interesting exceptions in late eighteenth-century Manchester to the over-worked equation of Anglicanism with Toryism, dissent with radicalism. The local radical movement which was to provoke the political feuds of the 1790s and onwards was commercial in origin. It developed out of mercantile opposition to Pitt's fustian tax in 1784–5 and resulted in the establishment of the General Chamber of Manufactures. Its leader in Manchester had been the Anglican and Foxite merchant Thomas Walker: and it was he who led the local opposition to the Test Act in 1789 and proclaimed most loudly his approval of events in France in 1790.[42] It was Walker again who established the radical *Manchester Herald* in 1792, in association with the Anglican and Oxford-educated Thomas Cooper. And it was Cooper and James Watt, son of the engineer, who delivered the address of the Manchester Constitutional Association to the Jacobin Club in the same year, to provoke Burke's memorable denunciation in the Commons. Throughout these proceedings, and in the course of his subsequent trial, Walker apparently had good cause to deplore the indifference of those from whom he had expected full-blooded support: 'The Dissenters . . . have as a body constantly fallen short of their own principles – through fear or some other motive they have been so strongly the advocates of an Overstrained Moderation, that they have rather been the enemies than the friends of those who have ventured the most and effected the most for the rights of the people.'[43] Walker would have made exception for individuals, however and those largely Unitarians. If unitarians did not initiate the reform movement of the 1790s they provided the troops. And in their dominance of the Literary and Philosophical Society they provided its intellectual centre.

It was in this period with Percival as its president that the Society was at the height of its influence in Manchester. Percival's reflections on the conditions of public health and the Rev. Thomas Barnes's advocacy of a college of the arts and sciences in Manchester were merely the most conspicuous of the proposals emanating from it in the 1780s; a considerable number of the papers published in the first decade were appropriately concerned with the relation between technology and industry (a theme which came to provide the chief rationale for the Society's survival in the ensuing century).[44] Its influence spread beyond Manchester: honorary members in 1785 included Erasmus Darwin, Benjamin Franklin, Josiah Wedgwood, and Priestley. Consistently with this support, the Society quickly manifested an overt philosophical and political bias. Thomas Cooper was elected in 1785, James Watt junior in 1789, and Thomas Walker in 1790; two of those to be tried with Walker in 1794, Samuel Jackson and Joseph Collier, were elected in 1788 and 1792 respectively; a young and insecure Robert Owen became a member in 1793. It was a period of bright hope: the Society listened to Coleridge on the pantisocracy, and to Owen (not very effectually, for his papers were not published) on the effects of environment on character. Percival delivered himself in 1790 of *An Inquiry into the Principles and Limits of Taxation as a Branch of Moral and Political Philosophy* and Cooper of *Propositions Respecting the Foundations of Civil Government* in which, *inter alia,* he defended the political and social rights of women. In 1792 George Philips advocated female suffrage in his *Necessity of a Speedy Reform in Parliament.* A Manchester élite was training itself in the subversion of the established political society.[45]

It was thus predictable that in the loyalist reaction of the 1790s the Society's members should have been subjected to heavy pressures to conform to the prevailing patriotism; and some did so. As early as 1791 the Society saw fit to equivocate over Jackson's motion 'that the Society do write to Dr Priestley, being an honorary member, expressing their concern at the losses he has sustained by the late disgraceful riots at Birmingham'.[46] Other members refused to conceal their views. Early in 1793, with the formation by a group of local Tories of a Society to Put Down Levellers, the local persecution, which was to result in the trials of 1794, began in earnest. The trials have been adequately examined elsewhere.[47] What is relevant here is the identity of the 34 people whom the loyalist society subjected to secret examination and marked out for possible prosecution. Of these, 13 were or had been members of the Literary and Philosophical Society, and at least nine – W. Hibbert, Samuel Greg, Thomas Robinson, Rev. M. Hawkes, George Philips, Ottiwell Wood, John Grimshaw, William Rigby junior, and S. Hardman – were identifiably associated with the Unitarian congregation at Cross Street.

Walker and his associates were acquitted in 1794, but this Tory offensive against the Manchester radical movement effectively succeeded. Tory success was witnessed even in the fate of the Literary and Philosophical Society. The Society no longer speculated in political philosophy, but ceded primacy to scientific investigations represented at their best in the work of John Dalton. Where its interests were not scientific they were antiquarian. By 1805 a new type of member was being admitted, Tory, High Church, politically respectable: Hugh Hornby Birley, Robert Peel, Robert Peel junior. Henceforth the Society was neutralized, and for another half century admission was to be virtually guaranteed to local worthies and politicians, regardless of literary, philosophical, or scientific credentials.[48]

That, however, was the least of the effects of the new climate. Unitarian radicals and their associates capitulated to it cravenly, and their fate as status-bearers in Manchester was thereby sealed. By 1803 the erstwhile philosophers of political change were publicly demonstrating their loyalism by subscribing handsomely to the General Defence Fund, largely to support the Manchester and Salford Volunteers: Samuel Greg £100, the Philips family between them £400, Thomas

Percival £100, Thomas Barnes £21, M'Connel and Kennedy £52 10s. 0d. – sums which often matched the £100 subscribed by Sir Robert Peel himself (and which perhaps had to).[49] The old radical phalanx disintegrated. Thomas Cooper emigrated to America, Ottiwell Wood went to Liverpool, Walker died in 1817, and George Philips 'retreated into the ranks of the Whigs'. To be sure, as the years passed, good external reasons could be found for this state of affairs. Church and King riots had given way to food riots as early as 1796. The Exchange riot of 1812 developed out of a mass protest meeting against a Tory memorial to the Regent to congratulate him on the retention of his father's ministers after Percival's assassination. Propertied men were finding good cause to unite as popular clamour mounted, not least as it coincided with affronts to all commercial interests, regardless of politics: the new corn law and the rising poor rates which came with the end of the French Wars. As Prentice was to put it laconically, 'the commercial spirit' began to 'mitigate against the virulence of party spirit'.[50] All this, however, had important costs for an élite which found itself increasingly excluded from local authority.

Until the 1790s, local government had been relatively open to gentlemen of wealth and standing, regardless of political or denominational hue, and this had long been a matter for self-congratulation. 'Towns where manufactures are most flourishing are seldom bodies corporate', Thomas Walker observed, 'commerce requiring universal encouragement instead of exclusive privileges to the natives and freemen'.[51] Walker himself served as boroughreeve in 1790–1, and in the half century before that the trusteeship of the Cross Street chapel alone had provided Manchester with three boroughreeves and eight constables, and Lancashire with at least one Deputy Lieutenant and three High Sheriffs. Suspicion of Unitarians' heterodoxy certainly impeded their entry into the parliamentary arena in Westminster: but locally in Manchester as in Lancashire, the more prominent Unitarian families had been emphatically of the political establishment.[52]

The reaction against them in the 1790s therefore involved a challenge to their political and social status as well as to their opinions, and its effects were on that account the more keenly felt. The Cross Street trustee William Rigby found his nomination as High Sheriff of Cheshire in 1810 over-ruled on account of his Liberal politics, and he was not alone in this: between 1800 and 1838 only one trustee was to be elevated to local manorial or county office.[53] What happened was clear: exploiting the prevailing climate which had so triumphantly swung in their favour, and certain now of their ability to maintain political control, a small group of Tory merchants took the opportunity in 1792 of reforming the local government structure. The Manchester and Salford Police Act set up a new body of independent police commissioners, consisting of the boroughreeve and constables of the manorial Court Leet, the Warden and Fellows of the Collegiate Church, and every other person who owned or occupied a building valued or rented at £30 *per annum* and over.[54] This was a wider and more open body than that which had administered Manchester hitherto and it had greater statutory power. But in the current climate the expectations of the Act's initiators that its control would fall to them proved justified. By 1807, despite financial and organizational difficulties, the Police Commission was the most important governing body in the town. Under the treasureship of the Tory dye-manufacturer Thomas Fleming, from 1810 to 1819, it became the preserve of an allegedly corrupt but certainly Tory oligarchy which soon monopolized all significant posts in the town – churchwardens, constables, boroughreeves, and police commissioners alike.[55] As significant a change took place in the county authority structure to which Manchester was subject until the enfranchisement of 1832. Manufacturers and dissenters alike were almost invariably refused the commission of the peace, in part as an act of policy on the part of the Chancellor of the Duchy, in part as an expression of candid social prejudice.[56]

The 'Liberal' offensive

The discomfiture of Old Dissent in Manchester was not of long standing. In the second phase of the battle which opened in 1819, the Unitarian caucus adopted new tactics and drew into its orbit fresh supporters. These last were not exclusively Unitarian or even exclusively middle class. New alignments were being drawn, new weapons deployed. Manchester embarked now on the classic phase of the contest over local authority to which the events of the 1790s had been mere preliminaries. In the aftermath of Peterloo, events began to acquire a certain inevitability in their momentum, and not without reason. Peterloo polarized middle-class opinion for the first time in 20 years. It was not merely the enormity of the event which provoked the division. The Six Acts served middle-class politicians well by enabling them for the first time in years to initiate political debate without fear of the intervention of what even Prentice regarded as 'noisy demagogues'. If before Peterloo 'to have any sympathy . . . with the poverty-stricken multitude, except when they came with baited breath and pauper accents, was to forfeit all claim to the name of gentleman', from 1820, serious radical debate even among the respectable became a legitimate if not a popular pastime.[57]

The focal group of Liberal politics in Manchester had already been formed in a 'small but determined band' which began to meet in the Potters' warehouses in 1815. Although they were united in the first instance by opposition to the Corn Law, it was significant that the acknowledged leadership of the group came at first from the older veterans of the 1790s – Samuel Greg senior, Robert Philips, and Samuel Jackson. Under their aegis the Potter brothers themselves moved into prominence by attracting younger men to the circle, and those not exclusively Unitarian. John Edward Taylor, by 1840 a trustee of Cross Street and at this date making his name as political journalist on the *Manchester Gazette*, brought with him into the group the Quaker cotton-manufacturer John Shuttleworth, to whom Taylor had been apprenticed on his first arrival in Manchester. They were joined by the Independent Thomas Kershaw and by the cousins and business partners, Joseph Brotherton and William Harvey, both Bible Christians. The group was young: in 1815 the Potter brothers were 42 and 37, Brotherton and Harvey were 32 and 28, Shuttleworth and Taylor were 29 and 24 years old. Of those who were to join them subsequently, Archibald Prentice, Presbyterian, was 23, and the Independent George Hadfield was 28. It was in this spectrum of dissent, this range of occupations, and this age group that the source of Manchester commercial Liberalism first defined itself.[58]

It was appropriate that the challenge to Tory dominance should have been initiated on a denominational issue – the vestry's proposal to erect new Anglican churches out of parish funds. No proposal could have been better calculated to provide the middle-class radicals with a strong popular support. Dissenters had always been numerous in Manchester, but they probably expanded most rapidly in the 1790s and early 1800s. In 1784 there had been three Anglican churches to every dissenting chapel. By 1804 the balance had altered rapidly: three churches were now matched by four chapels, and notwithstanding the rate of building by the Established Church in subsequent decades this ratio was maintained in favour of dissent until mid-century.[59] If this growth was most marked among working men, and if its appeal was diverse and sometimes idiosyncratic, it nonetheless served in the post-Napoleonic period to generate a new assertiveness among middle-class nonconformists to which Richard Potter, Taylor and Hadfield first gave expression at the vestry meeting of January 1820. Under their leadership an unprecedented opposition of 367 votes was raised against the 415 in favour of the church-building proposal. And at a second meeting they succeeded in passing a motion against the imposition of church rates on dissenters for the equipping of the 'parliamentary churches' by a resounding 720 votes to 418.[60] In the prevailing climate the political implications of these incidents were not ignored. The denominational issue shortly merged naturally into the much wider confrontation between Church and Police Commission on the one hand, and the Liberal group on the other – the latter drawing now on the support of the dissenting élite and an increasingly articulate class of shopkeepers.

The first clear assertion of the Liberals' longer-term purpose was the establishment of the *Manchester Guardian* in May 1821. Edited by Taylor, financed among others by the Potter brothers, George and Robert Philips, Edward Baxter, and G.W. Wood, and declaring that its three-fold purpose was to 'enforce the principles of civil and religious liberty', to 'advocate the cause of reform', and to diffuse 'the just principles of political economy', the paper for half a dozen years institutionalized the opposition of men who were committed alike to the tenets of contemporary economic science, and to the assertion of their religious independence and eligibility for political office, against the hitherto barely-questioned ascendancy of the Tory oligarchy. But the hopes pinned on the paper were of short duration. In dim presentiment of the journal's more emphatic reversal of allegiance in the late 1840s, Taylor and his chief assistant Jeremiah Garnett had by 1826 so softened the aggressive radicalism of its earlier issues as to provoke an irremediable breach with the Potter group which widened considerably in the ensuing years.[61] It was by resort to an expedient other than journalism that the Potters were to sustain the Liberal cause in the 1820s, and one of far-reaching significance for Cobdenite Liberalism in the decades to come. This was by contracting an alliance with the shopocracy. If by mid-century in the nation at large the *menu peuple* were to find their characteristic role in the Liberal Party, in Manchester this alignment had been predicated in the 1820s in the association of the middle-class radicals with the shopocracy, over the issue of local government reform.

The genesis of the alliance was hardly auspicious of its subsequent significance.[62] Except in the case of a few individuals, shopkeeper radicalism was wholly unfocused. It turned largely on a self-interested hostility to the exactions of imposed authority in the localized context of Manchester itself. It was characteristic of these preoccupations that the shopkeepers were brought into an alliance with the Potter group over the question of gas profits. The Police Commission wished to deploy these for town improvement; publicans and shopkeepers, the chief consumers, wished gas prices to be reduced in proportion to profits. 'The question became one almost of politics', as Prentice put it, 'and it was discussed with even more than political rancour. The taxed shopkeeper was the radical, and the untaxed warehouseman was the conservative.' It was this issue that precipitated the first real defeat of the Tory oligarchy since its consolidation some 20 years earlier. Under the leadership of a corn dealer and two drapers, increasing numbers of those shopkeepers qualified as police commissioners at £30 *per annum* rental hastened to take the qualifying oath to 'gain the opportunity of putting a check to "oppression"': the stimulus to wider participation in public affairs which the Tories had feared and the Potters had sought was now discovered. In 1826 more than one thousand new commissioners were sworn; by 1828 about half of the 1,800 commissioners by then qualified habitually attended the commissioners' general meetings. Meetings grew tumultuous, the ballot was demanded, and business finally broke down at the meeting of 28 January 1828.

The Tory group felt their hand forced. Led by H. H. Birley,[63] supported by newly 'respectable' Whigs like G.W. Wood, and now applauded by the *Guardian*, they drew up a new Police Act designed to diminish the number of commissioners directly involved in the conduct of local affairs by about one quarter, and calculated to exclude chiefly small shopkeepers and others 'of those classes which have enough to do in their own affairs without any further interfering in police matters than to pay their rates'. The Potter group seized their opportunity. A committee was formed under Richard Potter and William Harvey; Potter, Baxter, Brotherton, Prentice and two shopkeepers travelled to London in May, there to confront a Tory deputation before a committee of Parliament. As a result of this the tories had to accept a compromise Act. The £25 qualification for voters which Birley and Wood had demanded was reduced to £16; the qualification for the 240 police commissioners to be elected on the franchise was likewise reduced from the original £35 to £28.

The triumph was qualified. By concession the Tories gained a new lease of life for a decade; the gas dispute was shelved, the electorate was curtailed, and many of the radicals were excluded from direct participation in general meetings.[64] The new Act was a victory nonetheless. It resulted in an enforced sense of the Tories' vulnerability which combined with a simmering resentment among the shopkeepers at their continuing dominance. An experience was gained of the effectiveness of organized opposition within legally sanctioned limits which was significantly to inform the movement, from 1829 onwards, for parliamentary reform. Above all, there survived the satisfaction of political self-assertion essential to the maintenance of the Liberal cause. 'A most splendid victory', Prentice had written to Potter of an earlier concession: the final victory seemed even better. The source of the satisfaction was expressed candidly enough. 'Our Opponents of the Broad Cloth will never again have it in their power to Domineer over the humbler fellow Townsmen', Daniel Holt wrote to Potter. Baxter concurred: 'One good at all events will be derived from it, and that is, the lesson our Tory neighbours have had of their littleness when they come here [Westminster] and I trust this produces less arrogance in their conduct and more moderation.'[65] The 'outs' had perceived their final destination.

4   The achievement of Liberal hegemony 1832–8

Elites and the electorate

For six years after the 1829 Police Act, Manchester politicians were distracted from the further pursuit of local government reform by the campaign for and the effects of the borough's parliamentary enfranchisement in 1832. It was a campaign whose outcome was greatly to allay many of the ancestral resentments which the 'outs' had nurtured since the 1790s. In the 1832 polls, the Liberal candidates Mark Philips and Charles Poulett Thomson defeated the Tory candidates S.J. Loyd and J.T. Hope, and the 'low' Union's candidate William Cobbett, by narrow but convincing margins. In parliamentary terms, Manchester was now a Liberal borough.

This achievement was in the long term to have profound implications for the meaning and purposes of the campaign for municipal incorporation when again, at last, the political action was to be refocused on local government reform in 1837–8. Local parliamentary and local government politics were in these years to be so closely intertwined in politicians' calculations that the meaning of incorporation must be understood in that context. The reference here is to the meaning which incorporation came to acquire for a Liberal caucus whose thoughts were ever more compulsively turning towards a campaign against the corn laws, but which still felt politically insecure. The commercial electorate remained in large part vociferously Tory, while the police commission was still in Tory and respectable Whig hands. Incorporation was necessary if Manchester was to present a plausibly 'Liberal' face to the nation at large; it was also necessary as a means of attaching critically important groups in the electorate to the Liberal interest, to offset the powerful Tory vote which could still quite possibly undo the electoral triumph of 1832. In 1832 these calculations were far from pressing ones: but a brief consideration of the electoral events of that year will show why they were to become so. We must note in this connection an interesting shift in the political preoccupations and membership of the Potter circle. Even in the process of selecting candidates their interests were becoming more overtly 'commercial' than they had been, and their commitments to the 'people' somewhat less than rhapsodic. In part this was a reaction to the hostility and power of the low Political Union, which had scared them greatly in the months leading up to reform.[66]

In part, it was the natural inclination of businessmen who at last had the whiff of power in their nostrils. It was inevitable that they should reject the low Union's candidate, Cobbett; it was interesting that they did so (publicly) because 'his qualifications to represent this great commercial district have yet to be learnt'.[67] Mark Philips was chosen as the Potters' candidate not only because of his political and denominational antecedents, but also because he was by now the dominant partner in one of the town's largest cotton firms. Some in the reform group suspected that Philips lacked 'experience in parliamentary and public business'. Hadfield, Dyer, Benjamin Heywood, and several new men only now becoming prominent in Manchester politics, J.B. Smith, George Wilson, W.R. Callender, and Kershaw, after some equivocation about the suitability of Loyd,[68] presented a second candidate in the person of C.P. Thomson, protegé of Bentham, M.P. for Dover, and Vice President of the Board of Trade since 1830. With their return, and Brotherton's in Salford, the Liberal and Radical hegemony of Manchester politics seemed to have been secured.[69]

In fact it was secured on terms which were to give popular radicals good cause to complain of middle-class betrayal. The election had been fought in large part on the candidates' attitudes to reform: Philips had advocated shorter parliaments and the abolition of sinecures and tithes and in this had been echoed by Brotherton; shortly after his return Thomson repudiated Stanley's assertion that the Reform Act was a finality. Had Richard Potter's influence not been removed by his election to Wigan, this spirit might conceivably have been kept alive. As it was, all three local M.P.s very shortly found themselves moved by a consideration best expressed as early as

December 1832, when Thomson 'boldly denounced the absurdity of frequent and unnecessary change in what is but the instrument of legislation; called on his friends to look to practical rather than theoretical grievances; and declared that he was prepared to resist the adoption of principles or measures, however good in themselves, if brought forward inopportunely, or so as to obstruct greater and more pressing objects.' What these pressing objects were Thomson made clear as follows: 'They are the most perfect freedom of exchange, a fair field for our industry, and no restrictions, beyond what for fiscal purposes are necessary, upon the exertions of our manufacturers: – in one word, to buy as cheap, to sell as dear as possible.' Lest this sound bleak to an audience long nourished on a diet of political rights, Thomson hastened to elevate this programme into a crusade of international significance:

> By extending and developing our industry at home, by giving it its fullest extension as regards foreign countries (and we can only give it that extension by consenting to receive from foreign countries that by which they are able to pay us), we extend the benefits of a common bond of union . . . founded upon a feeling of common interest. Make foreign nations dependent upon you for some of their comforts and conveniences, encourage them in the prosecution of their industry by becoming their customers, give to them the products of your own, on an exchange advantageous to both parties, and you raise up mutual feelings of affection and sympathy, which will go further than anything else to prevent that which in my mind has been, and is, the greatest curse that has ever afflicted mankind – war.

Thus early, and by a member of the government, the new creed of Manchester Liberalism was publicly announced, the germ of the Anti-Corn Law League planted.[70]

How secure, though, was the electoral basis from which any such creed was to be propagated? On the face of it, all boded well. Thomson and Philips were comfortable victors over the weak Tory candidate Benjamin Braidley in the 1835 elections, and they retained their lead in 1837 when they beat Gladstone with similar ease. Thomson was justifiably contemptuous of his Tory opponent in 1835 ('Never read such trash as Braidley's addresses. Has he nobody to translate what he wishes to say into English?'), and properly confident of the efficiency of his election committee ('I appear in the Legislature as the Representative of one of the most important constituencies in the Empire, without having solicited a vote, without having expended a shilling, ignorant of every detail of Election proceeding.').[71] In parliamentary elections, the Tories appeared to have been suffering a paralysis of will. Notwithstanding continuing influence on the police commission, few obstacles were outwardly apparent in the way of Manchester's continuing, credibly, to speak on commercial affairs with one voice – and that a Liberal voice.

There were, however, good reasons for caution in this matter, and they were directly connected with the social locations of the Liberal and the Tory votes respectively. Light can be thrown on this through a sampling analysis of the two surviving Manchester poll-books, relating to the 1832 and 1839 elections. To refer to the 1839 by-election admittedly takes us beyond the terminal point of this analysis, the incorporation of 1838: but the reference is justified on the grounds that these results expose the enduring nature of the party allegiances and occupational biases with which the Liberal caucus had to deal in the 1830s, and throw some retrospective light on the reasons for approaching the issue of incorporation in the way they did. Above all, both the 1832 and the 1839 polls will explain the importance the Liberal caucus were to attach to the support of the urban *menu peuple*, the artisans and shopkeepers whose numerical role in sustaining the Liberal interest was greater, if anything, than that of the 'middle class' proper. It was the support of these people that the incorporation movement was designed to consolidate, and with good reason.

Let us note first of all in this connection that the electoral support which would most have guaranteed free-trade M.P.s their credibility was in fact less than overwhelming (table 3). In 1832, only 24 per cent of the votes of major textile

Table 3   Percentage of votes cast for each candidate by different occupational groups in samples of the Manchester electorate, 1832 and 1839*

| occupation | 1832 | | | | | 1839 | |
	Philips (L)	Thomson (L)	Loyd (C)	Hope (C)	Cobbett (R)	Greg (L)	Murray (C)
major textile	24	20	30	23	3	53	47
professionals	23	15	28	30	4	33	64
subsidiary textile	32	27	17	16	8	64	36
commercial etc.	28	22	23	22	5	48	52
skilled operatives	27	15	5	20	33	51	48
craft and artisan	37	22	13	12	16	60	40
building	30	19	17	17	17	39	61
drink	34	13	12	13	28	45	55
food retailers	34	28	9	9	20	62	38
clothes retailers	34	31	7	9	19	59	41
sundry retailers	32	16	14	16	22	48	52
miscellaneous	27	27	5	16	25	41	59
not known	30	23	16	16	15	51	49
total in sample	608	440	375	364	270	770	731
	(30%)	(21%)	(18%)	(18%)	(13%)	(51%)	(49%)
distribution of	2923	2068	1832	1560	1305	3234	3058
all votes	(30%)	(21%)	(19%)	(16%)	(14%)	(51%)	(49%)

* For explanation of sampling process and details of occupations, see appendix to this chapter.

merchants and manufacturers were cast for Philips, and 20 per cent for Thomson. The Tory Loyd by contrast received 30 per cent of their votes, while even the non-Mancunian Tory Hope beat Thomson by winning 23 per cent of their votes. Nearly one quarter of the votes cast by this group for Loyd were plumped votes, as were over a fifth of those cast for Hope: those voting Liberal seldom plumped but tended to divide their votes between Philips and Thomson, or – less frequently – between Philips and Hope. As table 3 further shows, the professional classes were even more committedly Tory. Among the middle to middling classes only the lesser textile employers (and to a much lesser extent clerical and administrative employees) exhibited a pronounced Liberal bias.

Surprisingly these biases were to be only slightly altered by the time of the 1839 by-election. Analysis of that election, indeed, demonstrates with painful clarity the effectiveness of League propaganda in hiding from contemporaries – and for that matter from later and even recent historians – how dubious was the over-worked association of the Manchester middle class with 'Liberalism'. To be sure, the continuing strength of Manchester Conservatism in 1839 must have owed something to the flagging credibility of the Whig government. But this does not greatly diminish the extraordinariness of the voting patterns that year in a borough which had by then been incorporated in the Liberal interest, in a community which was feeling the pinch of deepening depression in the cotton industry, and among men to whom the diagnoses of the Anti-Corn Law League were being explicitly directed. Moreover, the Tory candidate Sir George Murray was another non-Mancunian, and not a strong contender ('when he comes to act, he fails'),[72] whose ambivalence on the matter of the corn laws disconcerted even his nominators. The League candidate, R.H. Greg, by contrast was certainly handicapped by his Unitarianism, but he was a local worthy of great eminence, partner in one of the largest of Lancashire's cotton firms, and an effective public speaker and man of affairs. The fact that under these circumstances Greg was returned by the narrowest of majorities (51 per cent of the vote) was itself unexpected, but less so than the weakness of his support among his status equals. He won two-thirds of the vote of lesser ('subsidiary') textile employers, to be sure – which suggests that the League's diagnoses at this stage had greatest impact on men operating on narrow credit margins and on a small scale. His majority among the major textile producers, however, was astonishingly narrow: as many as 47 per cent voted for the protectionist Murray. Two-thirds of the borough's professional classes voted Tory; less predictable was the newly-pronounced Toryism of the clerical and administrative strata (table 3).

These patterns provide one explanation of the Liberal caucus's attention to the artisanate and the shopocracy in the 1830s. The electoral strength of these latter groups provides another. As is shown in table 4, the so-called 'middle class' (including white collar) in 1832 and 1839 alike comprised no more than 46 and 41 per cent of the voting electorate respectively. Operatives and artisans made up a surprising 16 to 18 per cent, and shopkeepers 22 to 23 per cent. More important, these groups evinced a healthy predisposition to vote Liberal. In 1832 Cobbett, to be sure, had predictably found most of his support among these people; their votes for Philips and Thomson, however, had almost invariably exceeded their votes for Cobbett, while their Tory vote (except among building workers and the group here categorized as sundry retailers) was correspondingly weak. Altogether, in 1832, operatives, artisans, the drink trade, and shop-keepers, provided Philips and Thomson with 46 per cent of their total vote, to be compared with the 17 per cent provide by major textile men, the 12 per cent provided by subsidiary textile men, and the 43 per cent provided by the whole 'middle class'. By 1839 the contribution of the *menu peuple* to the total Liberal vote had, significantly, increased to 49 per cent, as against the 'middle class' 42 per cent. The drink interest and the building trades were going Tory; by 1839, however, the rump of operatives, craftsmen, and food and clothes retailers were more visibly Liberal in their biases than they had been in the multiple-choice election of 1832 (table 5).

Table 4 Occupational composition of samples of Manchester electorate voting in 1832 and 1839*

occupation	1832		1839	
	no.	% of total	no.	% of total
major textile	228	20	194	13
professionals	68	6	90	6
subsidiary textile	115	10	141	9
commercial etc.	118	10	196	13
skilled operatives	42	4	45	3
craft and artisan	78	7	118	8
building	53	5	99	7
drink	63	6	141	9
food retailers	80	7	103	7
clothes retailers	68	6	100	7
sundry retailers	98	9	128	9
miscellaneous	26	2	34	2
not known	90	8	112	7
totals in samples	1127	100%	1501	100%
totals voting	5267		6292	
samples as % of full totals	21.4%		23.9%	

* For explanation of sampling process and details of occupations, see appendix.

Clearly in a borough in which the Liberal leadership was ever more candidly flying the flag of commercial Liberalism, it was something of an achievement thus to maintain a hold on the artisanal and shopocratic vote – and a necessary achievement at that. For among all electoral strata, Toryism still remained a threatening force in the town, as these tables show. Admittedly, these were years when some Liberal complacency was justified: the Tory threat was as yet potential rather than real. Thus, for all their control of local government until 1838, Tory notables seem little to have exploited the immense powers of patronage this control gave similar agencies in other boroughs. If, too, Manchester churchmen found public causes enough to reassert the political content of their faith (church rates and church education in particular), few of these issues were relevant to the town's more pressing social and economic problems; and in any case many of the leading clergy were woefully lacking as yet in popular credibility. The collegiate church was in need of reform; the Rev. W.R. Hay never overcame popular resentment at the part he had played at Peterloo; Canon Wray, no less damagingly, saw no reason to conceal his loyalty to the repressive principles of Pitt and Eldon.[73] The most damning weakness of the Tory camp in the 1830s lay in their resolute failure to select electoral candidates appropriate to the largest manufacturing constituency in the kingdom. J.T. Hope was an aristocratic Scot; Benjamin Braidley, a local commission agent, is revealed in his diary as a political innocent whose main interest in life lay in his Sunday School work;[74] Gladstone was to be damned for his

Table 5   Occupational distribution of sampled votes for each candidate, 1832 and 1839*

| | 1832 | | | 1839 | |
occupation	Philips and Thomson (L) %	Loyd and Hope (C) %	Cobbett (Rad) %	Greg (Lib) %	Murray (Con) %
major textile	17	29	4	14	12
professionals	4	10	2	4	8
subsidiary textile	12	10	6	12	7
commercial etc.	10	13	4	12	14
skilled operatives	3	3	9	3	3
craft and artisan	8	5	8	9	6
building	5	4	6	5	8
drink	5	4	12	8	11
food retailers	9	4	11	8	5
clothes retailers	8	3	10	8	6
sundry retailers	8	7	15	8	9
miscellaneous	2	1	4	2	3
not known	9	7	9	7	8
total	100	100	100	100	100

* For explanation of sampling process and details of occupations, see appendix.

West India interests; Sir George Murray was a soldier first and a politician second.

When so much has been said, however, the Tory interest was not entirely moribund. Its main vehicle was the Church. Nearly 35 per cent of the churchgoing population in the town were to attend Church of England services in 1851 – a congregation of the well-heeled and predominantly enfranchised which was far more uniform in its political interests than the divided ranks of nonconformity. Nor was the influence of the Church, for all its parlous state in the 1830s, confined to the middle classes. Denominational interest must have accounted for a good part of the popular Tory vote evident in our tables – and not without reason. The Church controlled one quarter of Manchester Sunday School pupils in the 1830s, and seems also to have taught them more effectively than its dissenting rivals if the ratio of pupils to teachers is anything to go by.[75] Denominational interest could be reinforced at these levels by collective occupational interest in some cases (*vide* the pronounced Toryism of the drink and building trades in 1839) and doubtless by coercive patronage in others.[76]

Most important in accounting for the party's power in the 1830s, however, was the vitality of Church and Tory commitment among the town's 'respectables'. Manchester Toryism might have lacked the leadership of closely integrated dynasties comparable to those centred on Cross Street, although this was not entirely disadvantageous. Leading Tories could at least not be accused of aloofness from the town's life. Most were born of modest backgrounds; most were as involved in industrial and commercial pursuits as their Liberal rivals. Most, too, were educated at the Grammar School, an almost exclusively Tory enclave which was, however, in no sense the forcing-ground of an upper crust: in the years 1834 to 1837, 46 per cent of the boys there were sons of gentlemen, clergy, and professionals, but 11 per cent were the sons of textile men, 11 per cent of craftsmen, 30 per cent of tradesmen and respectable shopkeepers.[77] The invariable conservatism of the School's products testified to the formidable influences of the High Master, the Rev. Jeremiah Smith, himself the son of a small tradesman and a living exemplar of the upward mobility of many of his pupils who went on to become prominent Tories – Holland Hoole,[78] for example, or the Sowlers, whose editorship of the *Manchester Courier* made the newspaper, after the *Manchester Guardian*, the second most influential paper in the town.

As developments in the 1840s were to show, there was more than enough potential in this communal structure for toryism to revitalize itself and validate anew the often reiterated claim that 'all the wealth, talent, character, and influence of Manchester are Conservative'. After the shock of incorporation, Toryism was indeed to assert itself as a popular force – in churchmen's support of the short-time movement, for example, in more vocal opposition to the New Poor Law, in a campaign for more Tory magistrates, in the formation in 1846 of an Association for the Reform of the Ecclesiastical Provision for the Parish of Manchester, and in the re-emergence of the Birleys into the forefront of the party leadership in the run-up to the 1841 election. It was then as a matter of fact that the 'new toryism' which Professor Hanham identified in Manchester in the 1850s and 60s first became apparent.[79]

In this light – and in the light of our pollbook analysis – we may understand the Liberal caucus' interest in cultivating the support that so vitally mattered, of shopkeepers, artisans, clerks and the like. Their tactics took two forms, and we may briefly consider the first – the cultivation of nonconformist support in the 1830s – before we turn finally to the issue that brings this study to its close: the issue of incorporation itself.

Incorporation of the borough

By 1829 the dissenting population of the Manchester townships amounted to some 19,800,[80] and it was fast expanding – a cross-class interest group which no Liberal manager could ignore, even if 8,000 were Methodists and so in all likelihood Tory, if politically active at all. It was inevitable that popular nonconformist animosities, first expressed at the vestry meetings of 1820, should again in the 1830s become one of the staples of political debate in Manchester, and that it should be the Liberal élite which was best placed to give them focus.

Their calculations, needless to say, were in this connection wholly uncynical. The dominant stimulus behind their actions was as ever the sense that their political and economic status ill accorded with their civil status, and this sense could only be exacerbated by their recent enfranchisement and by their electoral dominance. Despite their political power, Hadfield felt in 1833, dissenters were 'left out of the social compact, and degraded'. And when the Manchester United Dissenters' Committee petitioned against Peel's Marriage Bill in 1835, it was on the grounds that its discriminatory clauses were calculated 'to wound their feelings, to inflict injury on their families, and to fix on the dissenting body at large the badge of perpetual inferiority and disgrace'.[81]

In the 1820s the Potter group had been hard put to it to rouse wide non-conformist participation in denominational protest. But in the wake of the Reform Act all things seemed possible, and protest was impressive for its numerical support. In 1834 a petition in favour of disestablishment was signed by as many as 34,000 dissenters in Manchester and the surrounding districts. And as Hadfield revived the hitherto dormant issue of the church rates at the successive vestry meetings of 1833, 1834, and 1835, he was gratified at the cumulative response he received. A poll of 3,506 was raised against the rates in 1833, to achieve a majority of one. In 1834, 'Mills were stopped that the men might vote, bands of music preceded long lines of voters and waggons, and carts full of voters poured in from the out-townships amidst loud cheers from the people': Hadfield's amendment against the rates on this occasion received 7,119 votes against 5,897, although subsequent scrutiny cast the validity of many of the votes into doubt. In 1835, Hadfield's motion was carried 'unanimously', and church rates in Manchester were finally abolished.[82]

The Liberal leaders could only benefit from this ground-swell of non-conformist discontent and its ultimate triumph. How centrally they stood with regard to the several movements of nonconformist opinion of the 1830s is evidenced in the genesis of the agitation for secular education. The Manchester Society for Promoting National Education, committed to further the education of the whole population 'upon liberal principles, untinged by sectarian prejudices', was established in October 1837 on the initiative of Mark Philips, Richard Potter, Brotherton and Cobden: its first committee included Cobden, S.D. Darbishire, Edward Herford, and Absolem Watkin, and its first life members Sir Benjamin Heywood, Thomas Potter, R.H. Greg, Alexander Henry. This close correlation between the names prominent in the pre-reform decades and those prominent in the diverse movements which acted as satellite and subsidiary causes to the League in the late 1830s, was sustained into the 1840s and 1850s: the consistency of the Liberal leaders' public action in the immediate local context on behalf of dissenting interests enabled them to build up a popular base which by mid-century was to be subsumed within the national party.[83]

By comparison with their attitudes to dissenters' rights, the Liberal caucus' approach to local government reform was calculative in the extreme. At issue here was the prospect of mobilizing Liberal opinion through incorporation, in order to consolidate the parliamentary Liberal vote. The architects of the Muncipal Corporations Act of 1835 had been explicit on this. 'It must', Parkes had written, 'break to pieces the Tory clique of the old Corporators, and in the article of patronage alone make a great dent in their influence over the *Parliamentary* elections'.[84] Why incorporation should be assumed thus to work in the Liberals' interest was equally clear: it would mobilize the latent Liberalism of the shopocracy. Of the 1860s, John Vincent has said that 'to vote liberal was closely tied to the growing ability of whole new classes to stand on their own feet and lead independent lives', particularly through 'a feeling of participation in a wider national life'.[85] In fact, the bases of shopkeeper Liberalism in many towns like Manchester had been laid some 30 years before the 1860s, and this with little reference, as yet, to the political life of the nation as a whole. The Liberal inclinations of what Croker had called 'a vulgar, privileged pedlary' had been explicitly anticipated in the parliamentary reform debates of 1831–2.[86] The characteristic political concerns of such people, however, were related closely to their need to assert their own status and interests in the local agencies which most affected them – as, in the Manchester case, the dispute over the use of gas profits had already shown. Their 'Liberalism' was in this sense, at this stage, a 'reactive Liberalism', activated by the fact that those agencies which discriminated against their interests were largely under Tory control. The man who in Manchester first perceived that the way to cement their loyalties was to enable them to assert their status in civic politics, had taken this point in 1837, when he had stood as Liberal candidate in Stockport: 'the butchers and the greengrocers in the market-place', Cobden noted, 'cry out from their stalls, Cobden beef, Cobden potatoes'.[87] As early as that he was wondering of Stockport whether 'a corporation, by periodically bringing the housekeepers of all classes together for the purposes of canvassing, selecting councillors, etc., [would] tend to give consolidation to the Liberal party'.[88] These were the kinds of calculation which, in the critical year of 1838, were to inform the campaign for Manchester's incorporation – and the Tories' opposition to incorporation as well.

The history of the incorporation battle is by now a well-rehearsed one, and it is not necessary to narrate it in detail here.[89] Our purpose rather, is to stress the role of the shopocracy in consolidating, through incorporation, the Liberals' narrow hegemony over Manchester politics. For what was achieved in Manchester in 1838 was the final apotheosis of the Liberal élite which in the League and its successor machinery, was to rule Manchester until 1857, and assert itself at last as the voice of commercial interest in the affairs of the nation itself. To this achievement the support of the *menu peuple* was indispensable.

The time was ripe for Cobden's initiative, for there was a real danger that the shopocracy would lapse into political passivity. Since the disputes preceding the Police Act of 1828 they appear, as a group, to have abstained from local politics, giving way in 1831–2, for example, before the assertiveness of the more committed popular radicals, and until 1838 lacking the will, or the organization, or the sense of corporate identity, which would have enabled them to take initiative on their own behalf. In any case, many of their grievances over the conduct of local government were softened, if not eradicated, by the indisputable fact that after 1828 the police commissioners were operating with unprecedented efficiency. With the passing of an Act in 1830 authorizing the extension of the gas works and detailed changes in almost every branch of their administration, they probably reached the height of their powers, accumulating an improvements fund out of gas profits, reconstituting the Board of Health, and reorganizing the watch. By 1835, furthermore, the Whiggish reformers G.W. Wood and J.E. Taylor and even Thomas Potter had been admitted to the Gas Board, and gas prices were lowered. By 1836 it was quite clear that the functions of the Court Leet were being energetically and effectively supplanted by the larger body, and it could be and was plausibly argued by several leading police commissioners, Whig and Radical as well as Tory, that incorporation in terms of the 1835 Act was made unnecessary by virtue of the fact that Manchester had never been better governed.[90]

Nonetheless, the popular resentments against Tory dominance still simmered. Potter and Hadfield found it possible to raise 22,800 names on a petition in favour of incorporation in 1835, although it was dismissed in parliament on the grounds that many of the signatories were unqualified to express an opinion on the subject, and that 'the property and prosperity of this borough are Conservatives'. A new Improvement Act of 1836 was vocally opposed by the 'low' radicals Wroe,

Nightingale, Abel Heywood and others, who advocated a wider franchise for the police commission comparable with that provided for in the Municipal Corporations Act. And from the point of view of the commercial classes the inadequacy of the dual administrative system of Court Leet and police commission was demonstrated both by its inability to run an efficient police force and by the increasing difficulty of finding candidates willing to serve on the manorial body. When William Neild was fined for refusing to accept the office of boroughreeve in October 1837, Cobden took the opportunity of denouncing the absurdity of running Manchester by resort to a 'booby squirearchy'; a declaration in favour of immediate reform was signed by the whole manorial jury: the local revolution in government was thus initiated.[91]

If Cobden was the chief architect of incorporation, it was because he alone appeared capable of regarding the task of achieving it with fresh eyes and from a quite original perspective: not exclusively as a way of settling old scores or of removing antiquated privileges, but more constructively as a way of broadening the Liberal base upon which the realization of his longer-term ambitions depended. An appropriate legatee of the Potter-led radicalism of the 1820s, at this stage he was loudly proclaiming the possibility of a popular coalition of middle class and people. His Sabden factory displayed slogans to remind his hands that education was the birthright of man; at their New Year supper in 1838 he pledged himself to help them win the franchise and the ballot: 'he would not separate himself from the people; and if they were determined to have both, he would go with them to the attainment of their object'.[92] Few, if any, of the older Liberal élite had said as much since 1832. It was understandable then that Cobden came to regard the Municipal Corporations Act as one of the several means now opening to the people to assert their political identity, and there can be no doubt that he shared the conviction of Joseph Parkes, for example, that the act was a triumph for democracy, and of Place that it was a piece of legislation more 'perfect' and 'extensive' (in its suffrage qualifications) than the Reform Act.[93]

In late 1837 or early 1838 Cobden published his anonymous pamphlet *Incorporate Your Borough*,[94] to awaken the 'people' to their dawning opportunity, to bring it home to them that the Corporations Act was indeed 'a charter of popular self-government', compiled by 'thorough Radicals'. The pamphlet's appeal was unequivocal:

The fundamental principles of the new municipal corporations act are – *the household qualification, and an equality of suffrage.* . . . The banker or the merchant, though worth a million, and though he ride in his carriage to the polling booth, can only record the same number of votes as the poor artisan, who walks there perhaps slip-shod and aproned from his garret or cellar.

[Corporations] are, in fact, so many little democracies, calculated to afford useful lessons of equality; to destroy the barriers behind which the proud and wealthy are too prone to thrust the poor and dependent; to teach the haughty few to respect the abject many; and, which is of greater value still, they tend to impart to the multitude the elevated feelings of self-respect.

The new corporations are trade unions, in opposition to the corn-law tyrants . . . .; they are the normal schools of agitation, for the education of orators and patriots.[95]

These populist appeals not only branded Cobden himself as an 'agitator',[96] they also failed where Cobden had hoped they would achieve most. The response of the artisan radicals was candidly hostile. Rightly arguing that at least one of the main purposes of incorporation was the establishment of an efficient police force to deal with riots and strikes, fearful that incorporation would involve an increase in the rates, and deeply sceptical of the good will of a party responsible for the new poor law, R.J. Richardson, Elijah Dixon, and James Wroe joined the Tory opposition to the incorporators, denouncing Cobden as 'a mere spouter to gain applause'. 'The object of Mr Cobden, and of those with whom he stood,' Wroe announced, 'was to ride rough-shod over his [Wroe's] party, and, in doing so, over the people. . . . The principle of the bill was said to be democratic; but he termed it to be the contrary, and compared the mayor, aldermen, and council, to king, lords, and commons . . . The people would have no power to prevent themselves being robbed.' The alleged tyranny of the manorial Court Leet, and of Sir Oswald Mosley, Dixon declared, was 'all fudge'. 'Bad as we are', Wroe said, 'there is no town in the kingdom where the affairs are managed in a better manner.'[97]

Cobden's appeal to the 'people' could not have been rejected with more contempt. But within his pamphlet, and within his speeches, there was an explicit appeal to a wholly different social stratum, and it is this that requires most emphasis in the present argument. In one notable passage he struck precisely the chord calculated to win the support of the shopkeepers, whose ambiguous social position allowed them no real consort with either the poor or the rich. What they were seeking was a social identity as well as a role, and Cobden showed them how to find both. Most effectively, he set about awakening the shopkeepers to the indignities of their present status in passages worth quoting at length:

> It has always been a maxim, at the election of municipal officers, that no retailer was eligible to fill the office of boroughreeve or constable! And so anxious have the Tory manufacturers and wholesale dealers been to apportion amongst their own order, dignities, however humble, that even the menial offices of Sir Oswald Mosley's feudal court have been distributed in the same spirit . . . The tone which has so long prevailed in the government of the town has naturally enough pervaded all our public institutions, and even entered into the private arrangements of social life. It is well understood, for example, that if the shopkeeper's family be not formally interdicted from entering our public assemblies, they will not be consulting their own interest or enjoyment by attending them, and the retailer would find it, probably, almost as difficult to gain admission to our clubs and our concerts, as he might to obtain the privilege of 'entre' to the Queen's court.

A pointed distinction follows:

> The *wholesale* dealer in fustians or fents, whose *bundles* occupy a garret or cellar, from which they only issue in the gross, may, however vulgar in mind or ill-bred in manners, gain admission without difficulty to places of privileged resort, from which the retail mercer or jeweller, with perhaps ten times the wealth, and whose vocation demands some refinement of manners and cultivation of mind, would find himself excluded. What wonder, with these facts in view, if we sometimes meet with Tory-radicals or operative Conservatives!

What wonder if the sincere democrat, finding a counterfeit aristocracy everywhere current, should grow bewildered at the sight of the spurious imitations, and, to escape deception, prefer such as bear the genuine stamp of nobility!

The consummation of the passage was delicate in wording, but its upshot was clear:

How different from the state of things just described, is the condition of social life in the city of London, where all distinctions of rank between the wholesale and retail dealer is unknown . . . But in the city of London, where you will find no manor court-leet diffusing its town of feudal insolence or slavish servility, there is a corporation renowned for its liberal character; and more than a moiety of its common councilmen, and several of its aldermen, are shopkeepers.

The results of this appeal were to be obscured for some months by the quite exceptionally hard fought and bitter contest which followed the preliminary meetings of January and February 1838. The opposition of the Tories was well financed. The out-townships remained sceptical about the advantages of joining the municipality until the very last. From March until May petition and counter-petition was sent to parliament, while bribery and forgery was practised by both sides.[98] The Whig ministry was unhelpful, and Cobden regretted that even Thomson shared their indifference to the question of local self-government. In May this indifference seemed to characterize the population of Manchester itself, and Cobden and his chief allies Thomas Potter, George Wilson and Neild, came near to despair. 'I am ashamed and disgusted at the utter destitution of every interest in the question', Cobden wrote to Wilson: '5,000 copies of the letter [*Incorporate Your Borough*] were distributed gratuitously, and yet not one reply! Shall we give up? So little public spirit in a plan that ought to be at the lead makes me almost inclined to turn hermit and let my beard grow'. In the event the Parliamentary Commissioners' scrutiny of the rival petitions in May allowed 64 per cent of the pro-charter signatures to be valid against 22 per cent of the opposition's. This gave the incorporators an unimpeachable majority: the charter was granted in October.[99]

Despite his disappointments, Cobden had no doubt that in their attendance at public meetings and in their support of the incorporation petition it was 'the shopocracy' who had 'carried the day', a conclusion confirmed perhaps by the radicals' clear affirmation in February that 'The Whigs are not our Friends, their reform tends to establish a shopocracy to rush over and grind down the poor'.[100] Few if any shopkeepers, however, appear publicly to have declared their motives in supporting incorporation, and it was only the subsequent course of municipal history which clarified the nature of their victory or the fact that in large numbers they must have been moved by precisely those considerations adumbrated by Cobden in the winter of 1837–8. For the establishment of the new muncipality entailed the establishment of no 'little democracy', no 'normal school of agitation', such as Cobden had anticipated: contrary to all expectation the municipal franchise proved more limited than the parliamentary. What was established, however, was a new power and status hierarchy in which shopkeepers – Liberal shopkeepers – came to play an increasingly dominant part.

Aftermath of incorporation

The failure of Cobden's more optimistic democratic fantasies is not entirely surprising. Russell had claimed, and Parkes, Place, and Cobden had hoped, that the municipal electorate would be a truly popular one, but they had all underestimated the restrictive effects of the $2\frac{1}{2}$-year residential qualification, of the frequent exclusion of the compound householder through landlords' failure to pay rates, and above all of the requirement that each man qualified should see to his own electoral registration. These impediments so diminished the number of poor householders enrolled that Manchester's municipal electorate in 1838 proved to be a meagre 9,118 as compared with the 11,185 on the parliamentary roll. The situation was not to change over the following years.[101]

The ease with which Cobden, Potter, and others allowed such a situation to pass is curious, at least in view of the principles they professed and the pledges they uttered in 1838. Throughout the 1840s no radical, real or alleged, whether in Manchester or in the nation at large, appears to have concerned himself about the fact that the expectations of the years 1835–8 remained unrealized. And when the Small Tenements Rating Act of 1850 allowed boroughs to extend the municipal vote to compound householders of £6 and under, no voice was raised in its favour in Manchester, where 10,000 would have been added to the burgess list: to the contrary the Council expressed its fear of 'the serious results which are likely to arise in all corporate towns from such a class of voters'.[102] Throughout these decades, then, the working man in Manchester remained as effectively excluded from his local as he was from his national citizenship, and the demarcation between the two political arenas which we have examined in a previous chapter was carried into the municipal sphere, with broadly comparable results in the structure of political participation.

There were of course good reasons in Manchester for the Liberals' acquiescence in this situation. The fact of the matter was that incorporation achieved everything which Cobden and his associates had hoped for in 1838 short of a full democracy, and this last, it became apparent, was for practical purposes a dispensable goal. The new corporation was, first of all, conceived as a base from which to launch an assault on the Corn Laws. It was desirable not simply because the effacement of a manorial structure of local government was an appropriate if largely symbolic overture to a full scale battle with hereditary privilege, but also because a national campaign would lose credibility if its advocates could not demonstrate a plausible facade of unity in their own town. How deliberately Cobden conceived the incorporation struggle in these terms was apparent in his pamphlet of 1837–8:

> The lords of Clumber and Belvoir and Woburn, although they can no longer storm your town, and ransack your stores and shops, at the head of their mailed vassals, are as effectively plundering your manufacturers and their artisans; for by the aid of their parchment votes and tenant-at-will serfs, they are still enabled to levy their infamous bread tax upon your industry . . . Amalgamate all ranks in your town, by securing to all classes a share in its government and protection; give unity, force, and efficiency to the intelligent and wealthy community of Manchester, and qualify it by organization, as it already is entitled by numbers, to be the leader in the battle against monopoly and privilege. In a word, *incorporate your borough.*

It was no coincidence that behind Cobden were ranged George Wilson, starch manufacturer, secretary to the incorporation committee, soon chairman of the League; Thomas Potter, James Kershaw, C.J.S. Walker, W.R. Callender sen., Paul Willert, Elkanah Armitage, and Henry Marsland, all merchants; and William Neild, like Cobden a calico printer. Not all of these could claim, as Potter, Kershaw or Walker might, a truly radical commitment to incorporation, and it was perhaps inevitable that in due course most were to find the League more amenable to their purposes once the Liberal base had been consolidated.[103] If Potter became Manchester's first mayor, Wilson, Callender, Marsland, all members of the first town council, refused to stand for re-election to the second, and the last council meeting Cobden attended as alderman was in April 1841.[104] The result was rather comparable to what later happened in Birmingham, where the old political élite tended to regard the magistrates' bench as the key position in the town's status hierarchy, shunned municipal elections, and left the town council to men 'of a vastly inferior sort'.[105] Although Potter, Neild, Shuttleworth, Armitage, and Willert remained in municipal office, and although the magistrates' bench remained under their control and was in no sense in competition with their authority, it was the case that the League attracted away the Council's wealthier and more active members, so that the social standing of councillors fell markedly, and its talent as well.

For a time this did not matter: from the point of view of many of its supporters, the new council had served its purpose merely by the fact of being established. Although they contested the validity of the charter until the final resolution of litigation in 1842, the Tories had at last been deflated and the local revolution in government begun in 1832 consummated: Liberal dominance of the council was assured (and remained so until 1890). No Tories were nominated at the first election, and the only contest was at New Cross ward, where the one radical candidate was heavily defeated by C.J.S. Walker. By 1842 after many disputes the Police Commission was in effect converted to an executive agency of the Corporation,[106] and Shaw's control of the police force reverted to the Council: the Liberal hegemony was further entrenched in control of the magistrates' bench.[107] It was important above all, however, that the League activists felt justified in leaving the exercise of this hegemony in the municipal context to their newly-risen allies, the shopocracy, who could be trusted to defend the base because it was entirely in their own interest to do so. How far in this respect Cobden's hopes had been fulfilled is witnessed in the fact that shopkeepers and tradesmen comprised just under one-third of the first council, and that they maintained and even improved this position over the ensuing couple of decades, at the expense of men in commerce and industry.[108] As Cobden had promised, grocers, publicans, and hatters had at last come into their own as functioning and influential members of the urban society, and they paid their debt in undeviating loyalty to the Liberal cause.

This they were prepared to do, because very shortly they were winning hands down in defence of their own interests. The worse for the quality of local government in Manchester, these interests had not changed very much since 1828. By 1846 the shopkeepers had solidified into a distinct pressure group backed by a Ratepayers' Association, opposed diversely to salary increases, to the erection of a new market, to the increase of the police force, and still resentful at the expenditure of gas profits on improvements which benefited the rich rather than the poor. These preoccupations dominated municipal politics throughout the 1840s, and with increasing force:

> The municipal elections [of 1848] . . . engaged the feelings and attention of the ratepayers to a greater extent than on any previous occasion . . . The great motto of all the candidates was 'economy and retrenchment', and politics as heretofore had nothing to do with the election. Every ratepayer had become sick of heavy taxation and the great aim of the voters has been to select parties who, in their opinion, are the best fitted to insist on carrying out the most rigid economy in municipal government.

Even by this date, however, the drive to economy was being carried to excess (there was a strong movement of ratepayers against the Public Health Act, for example):[109] by the 1850s the deterioration in the quality of council debates was being widely noticed. There were, to be sure, a few voices raised in favour of a more positive role for municipal government. The surgeon John Roberton in 1853 recommended that councils provide what can only be called a comprehensive welfare service to cultivate in the people those standards of hygiene and personal providence which alone would avert the peculiar evil of manufacturing communities – that 'culpable inequality' whose effects cause 'the multitude, a few of them highly talented, . . . [to] mar their own fortunes, and tumble down, the useless debris which lies thickly strewn around encumbering the base of the pyramid'. Pleas of this kind were fruitless, however. The malaise derived in part from the fulfilment of Liberal purposes in the senses referred to above, and in part also from the concurrent absence of real party conflict in municipal affairs: Tory bitterness over the ways in which incorporation had been achieved resulted in effect in a boycott of municipal elections.[110] As one correspondent of the *Guardian* put it in 1851, the lack of a real division of opinion on the council, 'the entire want of wholesome rivalry', whether on policy or on party lines, 'has tended more than anything to generate among the remaining portion of the constituency an apathetic disregard of the obligations resting on them in this matter, which has at length grown to such a pitch that hardly any of them care a rush who is to fill a vacancy which occurs in his ward.' When at last in 1861 mercantile and manufacturing interest in the council revived in the form of a Citizens Municipal Association, it was, in the words of one member, directed against 'a set of pot-house politicians, who regarded nothing but little matters brought before their little minds.'[111]

By 1861, of course the insult cost little: the Liberal machine in Newall's Buildings had collapsed four years before; the one which replaced it sought to draw sustenance from quite different sources. But unpalatable truth though it might have been to those whose conceptions of their own role in achieving the Liberal hegemony approached the grandiose, the fact of the matter was that over the preceding 20 years the pot-house politicians had served the Liberal cause better than they had served Manchester. Largely preoccupied with those issues which directly affected their pockets, inclined by interest (to the extent that they thought other than parochially) to subscribe to the economic formulae of the Liberal commercial community – with whom further they shared a strong and growing respect for the rights of private property and self-gained wealth – the prospering shopocracy as a group had little cause to defect to Toryism and still less to Chartism. No resident or extra-urban Tory gentry existed to sway them by its custom and in a community as large as Manchester the influence of the non-electorate on the municipal electorate was as faint as it was on the parliamentary. The independent Liberalism of the shopkeeper stratum was finally enforced by what may have been a subliminal but nonetheless real loyalty to the caucus which had thus brought them a status and a function in the local society which in the Tory years had been emphatically denied to them. It was now indeed the case, to recall Daniel Holt's words in 1828, that the Liberals' and Radicals' one-time 'opponents of the Broad Cloth will never again have it in their power to Domineer over the humbler fellow Townsmen'. In Manchester, Vincent's aphorism finds ample vindication: 'the victory of the people over their betters was the necessary cause of Victorian Liberalism'.[112]

APPENDIX

The Poll-Books for the Manchester Elections, 1832 and 1839

1 Tables 2 to 4 are based on a sample analysis of the poll-books for the Manchester election of 1832 and by-election of 1839 (Manchester Central Reference Library). Neither poll-book specifies the occupations of voters: hence the necessity of abstracting a sample of voters in each case and cross-referring to town directories. In the 1832 sample the occupations of 92 per cent of voters could be thus identified, and in the 1839 sample, 93 per cent.

2 In each poll-book all names beginning in A, B, and C provided the sample. In 1832 these amounted to 1,127 names out of 5,262 voting (21 per cent), and in 1839 to 1,501 out of 6,292 voting (24 per cent). (The 1839 total represents the average of all voters voting on the two days of polling (6,065 first day, 6,520 second day). Voters on one day and not on the other, and voters on both days, have in each instance been counted as individual voters.)

3. The occupational groups comprise the following:

> *Major textile*: cotton, calico, and silk spinners and manufacturers; cotton, silk, linen, twist merchants; 'merchants'.
> *Professionals*: medical, legal, banking, church and chapel, 'Mr'
> *Subsidiary textile etc.*: warehousemen, cotton dealers, finishing trades, design trades, components manufacturers, machine makers, ironfounders etc.
> *Commercial etc.*: commission, commercial, and local government agents; bookkeepers, clerks; scholastic and artistic; corn, coal merchants etc.
> *Skilled operatives*: managers, overlookers, millwrights, mechanics, a few operatives.
> *Artisan and craft*: printers, workshop manufacture (e.g. furniture), smiths, saddlers and curriers, clockmakers, plumbers etc.
> *Building*: builders, joiners, decorating; timber, stone, and glass merchants.
> *Drink*: licensed victuallers, beer-sellers, brewers, distillers.
> *Food retail*: butchers, grocers, provisions-dealers, bakers, flour-dealers.
> *Clothes retailers*: tailors, drapers, hatters, clothesdealers, boot- and shoemakers and sellers.
> *Sundry retailers*: chemists, booksellers, wine and spirit merchants, hairdressers, hardware, furniture brokers, pawnbrokers, 'shopkeepers'.
> *Miscellaneous*: coach proprietors, coachmen, porters, watchmen, gardeners, labourers, farmers etc.

SELECT BIBLIOGRAPHY

I Manuscript and local printed sources

Manchester Central Reference Library

General Defence Fund Accounts and Papers, 1803
Manchester Representation Committee Minutes, 1827–30
Manchester Statistical Society Minutes & Papers, 1834–8
John Shuttleworth Papers, 1809–39
J.B. Smith Papers, 1837–74
George Hadfield, *Personal Narrative* (1860)

Biographical and Obituary Collection
Electoral Registers
Manchester Poll Book, 1839
Manchester Directories, 1772–1850

Chetham's Library, Manchester

Manchester Poll Book, 1832

British Library

Chronicle of the City Council of Manchester, 1838–79 (n.d.)

London School of Economics

Richard Potter Correspondence and Diaries
Webb Local Government Collection, vols. 149–58

II Main contemporary and secondary sources

W.E.A. Axon, *The Annals of Manchester* (1886)
W.E.A. Axon, *Cobden as Citizen* (1907)
T. Baker, *Memorials of a Dissenting Chapel* (1884)
J. Birley, *Sadler's Bill: Cotton Branch* (1832)
A. Braidley, *Memoir of Benjamin Braidley* (1845)
M.L. Faucher, *Manchester in 1844* (1844)
J.F. Finch, *The Admission Register of the Manchester School* (3 vols., Chetham Soc. 1874)
G.B.A.M. Finlayson, 'The politics of municipal reform, 1835', *English Historical Rev.*, cccxxi (1966), 673–92
H.R. Fox Bourne, *English Merchants* (2 vols., 1866)
D. Fraser, *Urban Politics in Victorian England* (1976)
L. Grindon, *Manchester Banks and Bankers* (1877)
G. Hadfield, *The Manchester Socinian Controversy* (1825)
T. Heywood, *A Memoir of Sir Benjamin Heywood* (1888)
R.V. Holt, *The Unitarian Contribution to Social Progress in England* (2nd edn, 1952)
B. Keith-Lucas, *The English Local Government Franchise: a Short History* (1952)
F. Knight, *The Strange Case of Thomas Walker* (1957)
Manchester Literary and Philosophical Society, *Memoirs*
G. Meinertzhagen, *From Ploughshare to Parliament: the Potters of Tadcaster* (1908)
A. Prentice, *Historical Sketches and Personal Recollections of Manchester* (1851)
A. Redford, *The History of Local Government in Manchester* (3 vols., 1939–40)
G. Poulett Scrope, *Memoir of the Life of Charles, Lord Sydenham* (1843)

C. Seymour, *Electoral Reform in England and Wales: the Development and Operation of the Parliamentary Franchise, 1832–85* (New Haven, 1915)

R. Angus Smith, *A Centenary of Science in Manchester: for the Hundredth Year of the Literary and Philosophical Society of Manchester, 1881* (1883)

F.S. Stancliffe, *John Shaw's, 1738–1938* (1938)

F. Vigier, *Change and Apathy: Liverpool and Manchester during the Industrial Revolution* (Cambridge, Mass., 1970)

J.R. Vincent, *The Formation of the Liberal Party, 1857–68* (1966)

A. Watkin, *Extracts from his Journal, 1814–1756* (1920) (ed. A.E. Watkin)

E.W. Watkin, *Alderman Cobden of Manchester* (1891)

NOTES

1 Friedrich Engels, *The Condition of the Working Class in England* (1958 edn), 50.

2 W. Cooke Taylor, *Notes of a Tour in the Manufacturing Districts of Lancashire* (1841), 4–5; Leon Faucher, *Manchester in 1844* (1844), 21.

3 Cf. D. Read, 'Chartism in Manchester', in *Chartist Studies*, ed. A. Briggs (1962), 30.

4 *Select Committee on Manufactures, Commerce and Shipping* (Parl. Papers, 1833, vi), Q. 5166.

5 H.J. Hanham, *The Nineteenth Century Constitution* (1969), 203.

6 J. Vincent, *The Formation of the Liberal Party, 1857–1868* (1966).

7 See V.A.C. Gatrell, 'The commercial middle class in Manchester, c.1820–1857' (Ph.D. thesis, University of Cambridge, 1971), hereafter cited as Gatrell, 'Middle class', part III.

8 *Number of Registered Voters and Numbers of £10 Householders* (Parl. Papers, 1847, XLVI), 335ff.

9 This was not an invariable effect of constituency size (see C. Seymour, *Electoral Reform in England and Wales* (1970 edn), 181–5; what is striking about the Manchester case, however, is the virtual absence of any contemporary reference to corrupt voting.

10 Again the evidence for this is inferred from the lack of contemporary reference. Only in 1841 is there evidence of attempted intimidation of the shopkeeper vote on the League's behalf by the Irish in districts 1 and 2 of the central township. But although the tories attributed their defeat to this, it had no influence on voters in other wards, who made up the majority of the electorate: *Manchester Courier*, 3 and 7 July 1841.

11 *Select Committee on the Franchise* (Parl. Papers, 1860, xii), p.15.

12 N. Gash, *Politics in the Age of Peel* (1953), 16.

13 These organizations were as yet informal, in comparison with developments to come: see D. Fraser, *Urban Politics in Victorian England* (1976), 191–2.

14 F. Vigier, *Change and Apathy: Liverpool and Manchester during the Industrial Revolution* (Cambridge, Mass., 1970), 110–22, 148–9; A. Redford, *The History of Local Government in Manchester*, I (1938), 199–202, 230, 240–4, 245–6, 304–9.

15 *Select Committee on the Franchise* (Parl. Papers, 1860, xii), Q. 1836.

16 J. Aitken, *A Description of the Country from Thirty to Forty Miles Round Manchester* (1795), 207–11; W. Axon, *Annals of Manchester* (1886), 232; *Burke Peerage* (1857 edn), *passim*.

17 Seven of the rest were occupied by gentlewomen, three by clerics, one by the Earl of Wilton, who, like the Mosleys and Lord Ducie, played no part in local society. Ten further seats were occupied by men whose occupations or status cannot be traced in the directories: some were doubtless minor gentry, some were probably retired merchants

etc. E. Baines, *History, Director, and Gazeteer of the County Palatine of Lancaster,* II (1825), v–xiii.

18 B. Love, *The Handbook of Manchester* (1842), 12.

19 T. Baker, *Memorials of a Dissenting Chapel* (1884), 36; Ralph Harrison Papers (Manchester Central Reference Library, hereafter MCRL) wills: M/132/1.

20 Baker, *op. cit.,* biographies of trustees, *passim.*

21 *Ibid.,* 13–15, 94; Faucher, *op. cit.,* 22–3.

22 *Religious Census* (Parl. Papers, 1852–3, LXXXIX).

23 R.V. Holt, *The Unitarian Contribution to Social Progress* (London, 2nd edn, 1952), 338–9.

24 Biographies from Baker, *op. cit.;* cf. also the terms of the Rev. William Turner's letter reprinted in *Parliamentary Debates on the Dissenters' Chapel Bill* (1844), 426.

25 This discussion is based on the following biographical sources: Baker, *op. cit.;* L. Grindon, *Manchester Banks and Bankers* (1877), 321–32 and chs. 8 and 16; T. Heywood, *A Memoir of Sir Benjamin Heywood* (1888); W.E.A. Axon, *The Annals of Manchester* (1886); J.F. Finch, *The Admission Register of the Manchester School* (3 vols., Chatham Soc., 1874); G. Meinertzhagen, *From Ploughshare to Parliament: A Short Memoir of the Potters of Tadcaster* (1908); Potter Correspondence and Papers (MSS, London School of Economics), vol. XIV; H.R. Fox Bourne, *English Merchants* (2 vols., London, 1866). For fuller discussion, and family pedigree tables, see Gatrell, 'Middle class', 160–71.

26 Holt, *op. cit.,* 326–7. In 1813 those clauses of the Toleration Act were repealed which had excluded anti-trinitarians from the terms of the Act.

27 R. Cobden to G. Wilson, 22 March 1857: Wilson Papers (MCRL).

28 E. Watkin, *Alderman Cobden of Manchester* (1891), 122.

29 For the history of the 'open trust' dispute, *see* H. McLachlan, *Trans. Unitarian Historical Soc.,* II (1919–22) no. 2, 1–8; *Parliamentary Debates on the Dissenters' Chapels Bill*; G. Hadfield, *The Manchester Socinian Controversy* (1825). Hadfield, himself a Congregationalist, led the local attack on the Cross Street trust. The controversy was finally resolved in parliament on the initiative of two Manchester Unitarians, G.W. Wood (M.P. for Kendall) and Mark Philips (M.P. for Manchester), for whose role see introduction to second volume cited in this note. For the parliamentary petition of the Cross Street chapel in their support, see Appendix to 25th Report of the Committee on Public Petitions, p. 262.

30 Hippolyte Taine, *Notes on England* (1957 edn), 10.

31 *Memoirs of the Manchester Literary and Philosophical Society,* I, (1785), vi–vii.

32 *Ibid.* for members and officials; R.A. Smith, *A Centenary of Science in Manchester* (1883).

33 J.F. Finch, *The Admission Register of the Manchester School* (1874), III, 59, 102; II: 254; Redford, *op. cit.* I, ch.

34 R.G. Wilson, *Gentlemen Merchants: the Merchant Community in Leeds, 1700–1830,* (1971), 212 and *passim.*

35 On the Birleys: Finch, *op. cit.,* III, ii: 247; Axon, *Annals,* 396; Family pedigrees, kindly lent by N.P. Birley, Esq., of Marlborough; Birley Stockbooks and Partnership Records (John Rylands Library, Manchester: Eng. MSS 1199); R.C. Shaw, *Kirkham in Amounderness: the Story of a Lancashire Community* (1949), 696–9; G.C. Miller, *Blackburn, the Evolution of a Cotton Town* (1951), 371–3. For simplified family tree, see Gatrell, 'Middle class', 276.

36 F.S. Stancliffe, *John Shaw's, 1738–1938* (1938): membership lists.

37 A. Prentice, *Historical Sketches and Personal Recollections of Manchester* (1851). 375.

38 H.H. Birley to Peel, 2 April, 21 May, 1825: Peel Papers, (British Library, Add. MSS 40375).

39 J. Birley, *Sadler's Bill: Cotton Branch* (1832).

40 H.H. Birley to Lord Francis Egerton, 24 March 1843: Birley correspondence kindly lent
    by N.P. Birley, Esq.
41 See below, pp. 42–4.
42 T. Walker, *A Review of Some of the Late Political Events in Manchester* (1794), *passim*;
    F. Knight, *The Strange Case of Thomas Walker* (1957), *passim* for the General
    Chamber, the Constitutional Society, and the subsequent trials; D. Clare, 'The local
    newspaper press and local politics in Manchester and Liverpool, 1780–1800', *Trans.
    Lancs. and Cheshire Antiq. Soc.*, LXXIII–IV (1963–4) 101–23; F. Espinasse, *Lancashire
    Worthies*, II (1877), 306–13.
43 Knight, *op. cit.*, 172–3; Prentice, *Sketches*, 20–1; G.S. Veitch, *The Genesis of
    Parliamentary Reform* (1913), 189–90.
44 A.E. Musson and E. Robinson, 'Science and industry in the late eighteenth century' in
    their *Science and Technology in the Industrial Revolution* (1969).
45 *Memoirs of the Manchester Literary and Philosophical Society*, II (1785), 16–29; Smith,
    op. cit., ch. V and membership lists; *Memoirs*, vols. I and II; Smith, *op. cit.*, 189–91;
    Axon, *op. cit.* 428, 241. On Owen, see *Life* (1920 edn), 49–53, and V.A.C. Gatrell (ed.),
    Robert Owen: New View of Society and Report to the County of Lanark (1970), 23–4.
46 Smith, *op. cit.*, 173.
47 A. Mitchell, 'The Association Movement of 1792–3', *Historical J.*, IV (1961), 37–77;
    Smith, *op. cit.*, 173; Prentice, *Sketches*, 419–32.
48 *Memoirs of the Literary and Philosophical Society*, 2nd series, I (1805), for membership
    lists and papers read.
49 General Defence Fund Accounts and Papers, 1803 (MCRL BR. 356.M12).
50 Prentice, *Sketches*, 50–2.
51 Walker, *op. cit.*, 23.
52 Baker, *op. cit.*, biographies *passim*; J. Brooke, *The House of Commons, 1754–1790*
    (1964), 169–70, 173–4.
53 Baker, *op. cit.*, 97; for Thomas Heywood's elevation, see above, p. 26.
54 The unification of Manchester and Salford projected in the Act was not in the event
    implemented: Vigier, *op. cit.*, 117. For the inefficiencies of parochial government which
    it was meant to correct, *ibid.*, 110–49; for the expectations that the Act would provide
    means for the control of public disorder, *ibid.*, pp. 115–16.
55 Redford, *op. cit.*, I. 199–202, 230, 240–6; Vigier, *op cit.*, 118–22.
56 Prentice, *Sketches*, 153. See below, n. 107.
57 D. Read, *Peterloo: The Massacre and its Background* (1958), 7; Prentice, *Sketches* 130,
    179. Sixty-five manufacturers and 68 merchants and dealers signed the petition in support
    of the magistrates' actions; 71 manufacturers and 31 merchants and dealers signed a
    petition in criticism. These last are named by Prentice, *Sketches*, 165: they included all
    the Potter/Greg group.
58 Prentice, *Sketches,* 118–19; for the Potter group, *ibid.*, 74. Potter biographies: see
    above, p. 27, n.25; Taylor (1791–1844): Dictionary of National Biography (hereafter
    cited as DNB); Axon, *Annals*, 224–5; Shuttleworth (1786–1864): Axon, *Annals*, 292
    and Shuttleworth Papers (MCRL); Kershaw (1795–1864) and Harvey (1787–1870):
    Axon, *Annals*, 292–3, 325; Brotherton (1783–1857) and Prentice (1792–1857): DNB;
    Hadfield (1787–1879): DNB, *Personal Narrative* (MS: MCRL). All of these were to be
    prominent members of the League.
59 A.P. Wadsworth, 'The first Manchester Sunday schools', *Bull. J. Rylands Library*, XXXIII
    (1950–1) 319. By 1851 the distribution was as follows: Established Church: 32 churches,
    38,000 sittings, 36,000 worshippers; Dissent: 78 chapels, 40,000 sittings, 44,000
    worshippers (Religious Census: Appendix III).
60 *Manchester Gazette*, 29 Jan. 1820; Hadfield, *Personal Narrative* (1860, MCRL), 66.
    Thus began the campain against church rates which was to be won only in 1835: see
    below, p. 45. On the role of the vestry as a vehicle for radical assertiveness in this
    period, see Fraser, *op. cit.*, 25–8, 37–9.

61 Prentice, *Sketches*, 201–4, 212, 241, 245; Meinertzhagen, *op. cit.*, 227–33. For Garnett (1793–1870), D.N.B.: Axon, *Annals*, 324; O. Ashmore, 'Low Moor, Clitheroe: a nineteenth century factory community', *Trans. Lancs. and Cheshire Antiq. Soc.*, LXXIII–IV (1963–4), 124ff.

62 For the following narrative: Redford, *op. cit.*, I, 294–309; Prentice, *Sketches*, 312–21.

63 The Tory group included J.B. Wanklyn, William Garnett, Thomas Sowler, Benjamin Braidley. Thomis Entwistle: on Birley, see above, p. 31; on Sowler and Braidley, see below, 42–4.

64 On the franchise, see above, p.22.

65 Prentice to R. Potter, 7 May 1828; D. Holt to same, 10 May, 1828; E. Baxter to same, 4 July 1828: Potter Correspondence (MSS, London School of Economics), vol. XII.

66 For a narrative of the agitation for parliamentary reform 1828–32, see Gatrell, 'Middle class', 215–23.

67 1832 Broadside (J.B. Smith Election Papers: MCRL).

68 Although a Tory, Loyd was a moderate (and a Unitarian: see above, pp. 27–8), who pledged himself to the reform of the Church and of education, to retrenchment, and against slavery. Hadfield would have found him acceptable as a liberal candidate on grounds of his commercial standing in Manchester, 'if he had been hearty in our cause', but he was quickly adopted as the Tory candidate. (*Manchester Guardian*, 27 Oct., 13 Dec. 1832; Hadfield, *op. cit.*, 115–22; J.B. Smith to J. Shuttleworth, 24 Nov. 1832 [Shuttleworth Papers, Scrapbook, p. 96: MCRL]).

69 A. Prentice, *History of the Anti-Corn Law League* (2 vols., London, 1853), I, 8–9; Hadfield, *op. cit.*, 115–122; J.B. Smith to J. Shuttleworth, 26 May 1832: 'I like Mr P. Thomson's views of commercial affairs, and it will be important that they be sanctioned by his election for a place like this': Shuttleworth Scrapbook, 96; C.P. Scrope, *Memoir of Charles, Lord Sydenham* (1843), 52–62.

70 Prentice, *League*, I, 8–9; Scrope, *op. cit.*, 57, 59, 61–2.

71 C.P. Thomson to Shuttleworth, 11, 26 Dec., 1834 (Shuttleworth Papers); the same to J.B. Smith, 30 Apr., 1835 (J.B. Smith Papers.)

72 Charles Arbuthnot to Sir James Graham, 9 Sept. 1938: Graham Papers (microfilm, Cambridge University Library).

73 F.R. Raines, *The Vicars of Rochdale* (Chetham's Soc., Manchester, 1883), 297–306; *The Fellows of the Manchester Collegiate Church* (Chetham's Soc., Manchester, 1891), 336.

74 *Anon., Memoir of Benjamin Braidley* (1845), 54, 61.

75 *On the State of Education in Manchester in 1834* (Manchester Statistical Soc., 1835); E. Baines jun., *Social Educational, and Religious State of the Manufacturing Districts* (1843).

76 As noted on p 21 above, evidence of this is difficult to come by. The foundation of an Operative Conservative Association in Manchester in 1835, and the fact that even in the bitter year of 1841 as many as 800 operatives could be mustered to sign a testimonial in appreciation of Garnett's labours on behalf of the conservative party, suggest that patronage relations at that level, at least, were alive and well. (Operative Conservative Association *Minutes*, MCRL); *Manchester Courier*, 17 June 1841.

77 Based on full biographies in Finch, *op. cit.*

78 1796–1844: son of a shoe-maker, partner in Philips and Lee, cotton spinners, 1831–42; tory manager of the 1837 Salford election; later, however, free-trader and President of the Chamber of Commerce, 1843.

79 H.J. Hanham, *Elections and Party Management* (1959), 314–16. See Gatrell, 'Middle class', ch. 7 for further discussion.

80 'Return of the Places of Worship not of the Church of England in . . . the Diocese of Chester', 19 June 1829 (Lancs. Record Office, QDV/9/248–97).

81 N. Gash, *Reaction and Reconstruction in English Politics, 1832–1852* (1965), 67n.; Petition to Peel, Peel Papers (British Library, Add. MSS 40417, c.322).

82 Hadfield, *op. cit.*, 125–6; *Manchester Guardian*, 25 May, 1 June, 10 Aug. 1833; 6 Sept., 29 Nov. 1834; 11 July 1835; cf. the fuller account in Fraser, *op. cit.* 37–42.

83 S.E. Maltby, *Manchester and the Movement for National Elementary Education* (1918), 50ff. Dissenters' support for the Liberal cause in Manchester did not of course (especially in 1834–5) extend to the Whig government. See Thomson-Shuttleworth correspondence, March 1834 (Shuttleworth Papers), for Thomson's sense that Manchester dissenting opinion was 'anything but satisfactory': 'were an election to take place now, I should not be returned'. Thomson was, however, confident of most of the dissenters' 'warm feelings of attachment to myself personally'. For the role of the Dissenters' Marriage Bill and the church rates issue in precipitating this hostility, see Shuttleworth to Thomson, 2 March 1834, and more generally, Gash, *op. cit.*, 70–5.

84 G.B.A.M. Finlayson, 'The politics of municipal reform, 1835', *Eng. Hist. Rev.*, cccxxi (1966), 688.

85 J. Vincent, *op. cit.*, xiv, 80.

86 Seymour, *op. cit.*, 37–9.

87 J. Morley, *Life of Cobden* (1881), I, 116–17.

88 W.E.A. Axon, *Cobden as a Citizen* (Manchester, 1907), 66.

89 A.N. Redford, *op. cit.*, I, 321–56; S. Simon, *A Century of City Government* (1938). ch. II; Axon, *Cobden*; E.W. Watkin, *Alderman Cobden of Manchester* (1891).

90 Redford, *op. cit.*, I, 321–42, 349–56; II, 9.

91 Axon, *Cobden*, 1–28; Redford, *op. cit.*, II, 10–14; Simon, *op. cit.*, ch. II.

92 *Manchester Times* 6 Jan. 1838.

93 Simon, *op. cit.*, 425ff.

94 Reprinted in full in Axon, *Cobden*, 137–54.

95 Cf. Cobden's address at the public meeting of February 1838 (seconded by C.J.S. Walker): 'I pledge my word of honour that, by this Act, every individual, however low his assessment, shall have one vote'. *Manchester Guardian*, 10 Feb. 1838.

96 Cf. *Manchester Courier's* leader, 25 Aug. 1838.

97 *Manchester Guardian*, 10 Feb. 1838. This reaction seems to have surprised Cobden. 'Will you credit it – the low blackguard leaders of the Radicals joined with the Tories and opposed us': Cobden to W. Tait, 3 July 1838: Morley, *op. cit.*, I, 124.

98 Redford, *op. cit.*, II, 19–24; Simon, *op. cit.*, 83–95; Axon, *Cobden*, 101–20; Watkin, *op. cit.*, 25–44; Cobden to Wilson, 4 May, 5 May, 1838: Wilson Papers (MCRL).

99 R. Cobden to his brother, 4 May, 5 Oct. 1838: Morley, *op. cit.*, 124–5; Joseph Parkes to Wilson, 27 July 1838; Cobden to Wilson, 11 May 1838: Wilson Papers; Simon, *op. cit.*, 87.

100 Cobden to William Tate, 3 July 1838: Morley, *op. cit.*, 124; Simon, *op. cit.*, 81.

101 Not all boroughs showed the same imbalance: in a sample of 39 municipal boroughs in the first years of the Municipal Corporations Act the omission in the municipal franchise of the £10 qualification meant that some 12,578 out of 45,958 voters had the municipal vote who were excluded from the parliamentary franchise. For a critical account of the municipal franchise in England and Wales see B. Keith-Lucas, *English Local Government Franchise* (1952), 55–63. On the Manchester franchise: Simon, *op. cit.*, 429. See also p. 22 above.

102 Keith-Lucas, *op. cit.*, 69–71; Simon, *op. cit.*, 433–4.

103 Expectations that the Council might itself lead the anti-corn law agitation were soon dashed: the Council was quite incapable of coming to unanimity on the subject. As late as 1843 one Leaguer on the Council described his colleagues' equivocation about a proposal to send a free trade requisition to parliament:
'We had no *division*, but the requisition was withdrawn! ! ! Some strong reasons were given by Kay why it should be withdrawn – it appears we have some local act or acts to pass this Session, and on which the Standing orders of the H. of Commons have not been complied with. Lord G. Somerset can further those acts and it is understood he will do so, but if some strong resolutions were passed by the Council against the

Premier, and on a subject which did not legitimately belong to it, Kay feared we should have the opposition of the Ministry. Milne's compensation clause also must come before the Lords of the Treasury, and Mr Neild dreaded the effect of our onslaught on Peel.' Thomas Woolley to Wilson, March, 1843: Wilson Papers.

104 *Chronicle of the Council of Manchester: anon.*, n.d.

105 E.P. Hennock, 'The role of religious dissent in the reform of municipal government in Birmingham, 1856–76' (Ph.D. thesis, University of Cambridge, 1956).

106 For fuller discussion of relations between police commission and Council see Fraser, *op. cit.*, 98–100.

107 According to the analysis the Manchester Conservative Association sent to Peel in 1842, the bias of the county and the borough bench could be demonstrated as follows. Of the magistrates created from April 1819 to April 1832 and still living, four were Conservative and one was a Whig; of the four Conservatives, Foster (chairman of quarter sessions) and J. Heald 'never acted', W. Garnett was rarely resident in Manchester, and Mr Greaves was afflicted with palsy. Of the magistrates created between 1832 and 1841, only one was a Conservative, seven were Whigs, and twelve were radicals (a term which was flexible enough to include men like the Gregs). The borough magistrates appointed in the course of incorporation were similarly biased: five were Whigs, seven were Whig-radicals, six were radicals: there were no Conservatives (see Peel Papers, British Library Add. MS 40507, f. 106, for full listing of Manchester J.P.s in 1841 with occupations and political bias annotated). According to the Conservative Association two problems arose from this state of affairs. These were the men, firstly, upon whom would devolve the task of appointing commissioners to assess the new income tax: they would be enabled to exercise inquisitorial powers over 'the most respectable [i.e. conservative] part of this wealthy community'. Secondly, 'their being invested with such authority will be very harassing to the conservative party here'. In April 1842 the Manchester Conservative Association waited on Peel, Graham and Goulburn at the Treasury to press their case further. No longer, they pointed out, had the Conservative party 'the influence in the management of local affairs to which it was entitled by virtue of its property and respectability', because the overwhelming power and patronage given to their opponents by the late government was confirmed by the present through their acceptance of the incorporation charter. This state of affairs 'may probably extinguish the Conservative Party in Manchester'. (George Clark to Sir George Murray, 26 April 1842; the same to Sir Robert Peel, 25, 30 April 1842; Peel Papers, British Library, Add. MS 40507).

108 In 1839–9, 20 councillors were tradesmen, 13 were professional or commercial men, 21 were manufacturers, four were 'gentlemen', the occupations of seven were unknown. By 1856–7, these figures, respectively, had changed to 25, 11, 14, six, and eight. Occupational listings in *Chronicle of the City Council of Manchester, 1838–79* (1880).

109 F.H. Spencer, 'Review of the history of Manchester City Council' (n.d.), (MS. Report, Webb Local Government Collection [London School of Economics], vol. CLVIII), 21–3, 24; *Manchester Courier,* 4 Nov. 1848; Manchester Surveyors' Minute-books, 21 April 1847: Webb Local Government Collection, V, 156.

110 J. Roberton, 'Suggestions for the improvement of municipal government in populous manufacturing towns', *Trans. Manchester Statistical Soc.*, 1853–4, 81. Fraser, *op. cit.*, 143–4, 151 note, 152, for further discussion.

111 *Manchester Guardian*, 15 Oct. 1851; Spencer, *op. cit.*, 30–1.

112 J. Vincent, *Poll Books: How Victorians Voted* (1967), 21–2.

Municipal government in Leeds, 1835–1914

BRIAN BARBER

Municipal government in Leeds, 1835–1914

BRIAN BARBER

1 Introduction

The essay which follows is based upon a doctoral thesis entitled 'Leeds Corporation, 1835–1905: a history of its environmental, social and administrative services' accepted by the University of Leeds in 1975. The research was undertaken during the two years for which I held an SSRC postgraduate award, and continued intermittently over the subsequent five years while I was in full-time employment. Supervision was provided by Professor M.W. Beresford, for whose many academic and personal kindnesses I am more than grateful. The imminent departure of my supervisor to a visiting post at an American university finally precipitated the presentation of the thesis in the summer of 1975, when it was examined by Professor M.W. Flinn of the University of Edinburgh.

The thesis is composed of nine chapters. After an introduction outlining the structure of local government in the 1830s, chapter one examines the government of Leeds by the council, highway surveyors and improvement commission up to 1842, the date at which the municipality became responsible for the administration of the new Improvement Act. The next chapter considers the activities of the council over the following 20 years in public health, public utilities, amenities, and buildings, and the regulation of private enterprise and chapter three assesses the uneven and in many ways disappointing achievement of those years and suggests reasons for this.

In the post-1865 period the arrangement of chapters is thematic. Chapter four is concerned with public health over the 40 years up to 1905, and chapter five with the pronounced expansion of public ownership which occurred over the same period. Chapter six deals with a subject which was of no significance before the mid-1860s, and was, indeed, the subject of little activity before the 1890s, namely the 'housing problem' and slum clearance. Chapter seven contains a survey of labour relations and municipal unemployment programmes in the later decades of the period, and chapter eight examines some aspects of finance and administration over the whole 70 years. The last chapter reviews some of the issues raised in earlier pages.

The aim of the thesis was thus to provide as thorough a survey as possible of virtually the whole range of the activities of a major nineteenth-century municipal council, and the chapter in this book is an attempt to condense as much of the original work as possible with the aim of retaining its range. For reason of space, consideration of two topics, municipal labour relations and the administrative structure of the council have been excluded here. Education was not included as a subject in the initial research as until 1903 it did not come within the ambit of the council's functions. Although for the purpose of this chapter further research has been undertaken to extend the terminal date from 1905 to 1914, I have not incorporated any information about the council's activities in education after it had taken over from the school board.

This chapter, like the thesis, concentrates almost exclusively on performance and leaves politics very much out of account. Not to have done so would have involved duplicating work then being undertaken, from very different perspectives, by Professor D. Fraser and Professor E.P. Hennock. In many areas Professor Hennock and myself have covered common ground, and in doing so have produced some different conclusions. I need mention only two important ones here. The delays over the implementation of plans for a main sewerage network in the 1840s which in *Fit and Proper Persons* is accounted for by radical demands for maximum economy I believe to have been caused by other factors, which are explained in detail in section 3 below. Secondly, the Liberal opposition in the 1890s to Conservative plans to appropriate some of the trading profits of the utilities for the borough fund Professor Hennock sees as mere opportunism. It appears in fact to have been a genuine difference in policy dating back to the late 1870s, and demonstrates a fundamental difference in approach to municipal finance between Leeds and many other large municipalities.

The mention of this issue leads to one of the conclusions which are of general relevance. References to municipal enterprise often lead to the evocation of 'municipal socialism' a phrase as nebulous as it is pervasive. The extent to which this description can be applied to public utilities in Leeds is considered in section 5. Another general point to emerge in the course of research was the inaccuracy of the claims made by Professor Keith-Lucas for the pioneering importance of local legislation in promoting public health reform in the 1840s: evidence from Leeds and Liverpool suggests that the correct conclusions to be drawn from the evidence he presents may actually be diametrically opposed to those which he has drawn. More important, perhaps, is the significance which the Housing of the Working Classes Act, 1890 had on the inception of slum clearance projects in Leeds. The Act is usually dismissed as merely a consolidating measure, yet it is clear that the amendments which it made to the law of compulsory purchase as defined in the Lands Clauses Consolidation Acts was of major importance in inducing the council to embark on major clearance schemes. Perhaps its influence elsewhere would, in this light, repay examination.

2   From municipal reform to urban improvement 1835–42

The reform of municipal corporations carried out in 1835 was conceived as a political measure, a counterpart to the parliamentary reform undertaken three years earlier. As *The Times* stated in a leading article: 'the fact is that the parliamentary reform if it were not to include corporation reform likewise, would have been literally a dead letter, except in so far as the county representation was concerned.'[1]

In this context it is easy to understand why the provisions of the Act of 1835 concentrated upon electoral and administrative matters to the exclusion of those aspects of the role of local government which, in retrospect, might appear to have been of greater importance. The 143 clauses of the Act are concerned mainly with the provision of police and prisons, the administration of justice, local elections, questions of representation, council procedure, financial accountability, and the regulation of trusts in corporate administration. Indeed, it is probable that one aim of the Act was to reduce local government expenditure rather than to increase it. Over the subsequent 80 years, however, up to 1914 the character of municipal government underwent a remarkable change and the progressive transformation of one of the major municipal corporations of Victorian Britain is the subject of this chapter. Much of this book has been concerned with the politics of municipal government and although here we are concerned exclusively with functions it is important to remember that however circumscribed the role which the Act of 1835 envisaged for its progeny, this legislation, by altering the basis of political authority, laid the foundation for the developments which followed. The crippling disability which had restricted most unreformed corporations was highlighted by the assistant secretary to the royal commission which had investigated them. As he observed: 'the predominance of the political character in the municipal authorities, and their alienation from large bodies of the inhabitants, although they retained the administration of justice, lost them to a great extent the public confidence as trustees for numerous measures of local improvement, to the execution of which no other body could otherwise have laid claim.'[2] This state of affairs was exemplified in the politics of Leeds by the polarization of allegiance between the two main governing bodies before 1835, for prior to municipal reform 'in cases where the election is popular, as in the choice of commissioners under the local Acts, the persons selected are all of one political party, professing the opposite opinions to those entertained by the majority of the corporation; which is accounted for by the necessity of balancing the influence of the corporation.'[3] It was symptomatic of the change which the Act brought about that seven years later the commissioners' powers were merged with those of the reformed council. The simplest way to survey the variety of municipal functions as they had accumulated by the early twentieth century is to look at the statistics of capital expenditure as they were at the end of the financial year on 31 March 1914.[4] As can be seen from table 6, of the 18 million pounds which had been spent nearly half, £8.67m, had been spent on the four utilities: the waterworks, gasworks, tramways, and electricity supply. Nearly three million pounds had been spent on street improvements, highways, bridges and toll redemption, and almost two million on sewerage and drainage. Next in order of magnitude came education, with part of its capital expenditure inherited from the schoolboard in 1904, which had been superseded as a result of the Education Act, 1902. After that came 'unhealthy areas' – slum clearance – parks and recreation grounds, markets, hospitals and corporate buildings. All other services together represented less than 6 per cent of total capital expenditure.

This method of approach underestimates the importance of expenditure on the police force, which whilst of little significance in the capital account was of greater importance in current expenditure, particularly in the earlier decades. Before 1835

Table 6   Expenditure on capital account at 31 March 1914

waterworks	£3,989,551
street improvements, highways, bridges and redemption of tolls	2,942,194
drainage and sewage works	1,970,977
gasworks	1,948,067
education	1,644,844
tramways	1,571,196
electric lighting	1,162,643
unhealthy areas	813,772
parks, recreation grounds and allotments	570,990
markets	487,821
hospitals	452,949
corporate buildings	302,303
police stations and fire brigade buildings	125,757
baths	115,201
cemeteries	103,249
libraries	56,399
street lighting	53,765
other items	82,773
total	£18,394,451

the corporation had employed a 'day police' which consisted of only nine men, and a 'nightly watch' of 83 watchmen in the winter months, and 58 during the summer. The new corporations' first major decision, in April 1836, taken on the advice of the newly-constituted watch committee, was to adopt the metropolitan police model, based on the concept of a preventive force in the hope that 'both crime and expense' – a significant conjunction – might be reduced. This involved maintaining the strength of the existing night watch and augmenting the day police to 20 officers and men. Efficiency might have been increased, but expense was not reduced: in the last seven years of the unreformed corporation, around £3,000 a year was spent on the force, compared to an average of £6,000 in the period 1838 to 1844. Shortly after the reorganization of the police came the first moves to establish a borough prison, partly because of pressure from the home office and partly because of the cost of the borough's contribution towards the county prison. Fluctuating political pressures, however, delayed the final decision to build until 1842.

Two other issues of the late 1830s were harbingers of the changing role of the council. The first was the investigations undertaken by the council's statistical committee under the leadership of Dr Robert Baker, a councillor and inspector of factories, in the years 1837 and 1838.[5] Baker had already pioneered the topographical study of disease during the cholera epidemic earlier in the decade, and the statistical survey subjected the urban environment of Leeds to harsh and detailed scrutiny. The impressive array of information it produced may have increased public awareness of the need for wider legislative powers to combat the problems of public health – the sensational, if perhaps short-lived impact on the council itself is incontestable – but as will be seen, the stimulus to local action came from a less idealistic source. The second issue in these years was the reconstitution of the waterworks authority in 1837. Up to this time, the works had been under the ownership of the improvement commissioners, but in the middle of the decade a crisis developed, brought about by the commissioners' inability to agree over future sources of supply in the face of constantly growing demand. As a result, they lost control to a company which was owned by shareholders in the usual way but possessed a governing body one half of which was nominated by the shareholders and the other half by the borough council. The Act gave the council the option of purchasing the works from the shareholders after 1849, a significant indicator to future developments.

The first stage in the re-orientation of the role of the council came about with the local Improvement Act of 1842. This, the largest bill of the parliamentary session was, according to the historian of private bill legislation 'one of the most complete which had then been obtained by local authorities'.[6] It permitted the council to take over the authority of the improvement commissioners, greatly enlarging the existing powers which the improvement commission exercised in relation to markets, street lighting and street improvements, and in addition it contained wholly new powers for the council to adopt, such as the authority to create a sewerage system, to introduce building regulations, organize public cleansing and regulate smoke pollution. This Act was the first and most voluminous in a series of nearly two dozen local Acts, which took Leeds 'early and extensively out of the general law', although in this respect Leeds differed little from other major towns which in the course of the nineteenth century equipped themselves with local legislative codes.

Whilst the importance of local Acts in moulding the history of local government in this period is undeniable, it is important not to over estimate their significance. An extreme position in this respect has been taken up by Professor Keith-Lucas who has gone so far as to argue that, for example, in the 1840s much of the initiative in public health reform came from provincial towns which were obtaining 'new and remarkable powers' in their local Acts, and that, indeed, the Public Health Act of 1848 was 'composed essentially of a collection of clauses from local acts of the previous years'.[7] The more likely pattern of events, as the history of the promotion of the Leeds Act of 1842 demonstrates, was not so straightforward, and does not lead to the conclusions deduced by Keith-Lucas. Briefly, the event which galvanized the Leeds improvement commission into drafting the measure which eventually emerged as the 1842 Act was the introduction in the Commons by the home secretary, Lord Normanby, of three bills on borough improvements, building regulations and town drainage in 1841. To avoid inclusion in the government's bills, the improvement commission decided that the only alternative was for Leeds to promote legislation of its own. It is clear, however, that in preparing the bill, its authors transferred bodily from the Normanby bills many clauses which would be of use in their own. The legislators of Leeds, then, were parasites rather than paragons, and further research would probably reveal that these bills provided the stimulus and the substance for much local legislation of these years obtained by local authorities anxious to avoid the threat of 'centralization'.[8]

3   Public health

Public health reform was the most important single item on the agenda of any local authority in the nineteenth century, and by the early 1840s there was in Leeds not only ample evidence that certain major reforms were necessary – the introduction of sewerage and public cleansing, building regulations, and the control of smoke pollution, for example – but also local legislation available to enable them to be carried into effect. But in its public health administration, the council failed to sustain the expectations raised by the Improvement Act of 1842. By the end of the following decade the sanitary condition of Leeds, as revealed in its mortality statistics, was beginning to cause considerable disquiet both locally and nationally. The attention of the Medical Department of the Privy Council was focused uncomfortably on the town on at least five occasions. In 1858, 1865, 1870 (twice) and in 1874 medical officers from the Department visited Leeds and produced reports on conditions there which led the Medical Officer to the Privy Council, John Simon, to the barely qualified opinion that the sanitary condition of Leeds was 'in proportion to the importance of the town . . . perhaps . . . the worst that has ever come to the knowledge of this department'.[9] The principal reason for such strictures was the council's failure to provide an effective sewerage system.

The construction of a comprehensive sewerage system for the three urbanized townships of Leeds, Hunslet and Holbeck was recognized as one of the priorities of urban reform by the authors of the 1842 Act, and as soon as it became law, the council began to make plans for its realization. Unfortunately a series of problems, inevitable perhaps in the pioneering of so important a project, held back the beginning of work for eight years. The first difficulty arose over the design of the scheme. The council first selected Captain James Vetch of the Royal Engineers to provide a design. He visited Leeds in October 1842 and three months later submitted his report. The principles of his design were simple and commendable: they were to divert sewage then flowing into the river Aire and its tributaries in Leeds into sewers running parallel to each other on either bank of the river to carry their contents downstream from the town. They were not, however, to discharge into the river but into sewage works which would enable the effluent to be used to irrigate agricultural land. In this way Vetch intended to reduce the pollution of the river – since as he rightly observed, 'it is in vain to suppose that the condition of the town . . . can ever be materially improved until the rivers and becks are saved from their present pollution',[10] and, by utilizing the effluent to make the system virtually self-financing. He informed the Commissioners for Large Towns that after a decade he believed that the income from this source would be in excess of £10,000 a year. This prediction was printed in the first report of the Commissioners; their second report contained a fierce denunciation of the council for refusing to implement Vetch's plans,[11] giving the impression that the council was already reneging on the programme of reform contained in the Improvement Act. The truth was not so straightforward. Detailed investigations by the streets and sewerage committee had led it to the conclusion that there were serious defects in the Vetch designs: they involved the purchase of land which the council had no authority to take except by agreement with the owners, which would not be forthcoming; the diversion of Sheepscar beck, a stream which provided a source of water for the factories which lined its banks, where again the owners would refuse to negotiate; and finally there were suspicions that there were technical errors in the siting of the sewers. Furthermore, the very aspect of the plan which Vetch probably expected to impress a cost-conscious council most, the sewage utilization plan, met with some of the severest criticism. The acidity of the dyers' waste products were generally regarded as making the effluent positively harmful to agriculture, and his ignorance of this simple fact did nothing to support the reputation for practicality his plan aimed to cultivate. In March 1844, therefore, the council referred the whole question back to the streets committee, which chose J.W. Leather, a prominent local engineer, to reconsider the problem and present a report 'at his earliest convenience'. Unfortunately Leather proved dilatory, but his successful use of evasive tactics saved him from dismissal. He did not complete his survey until 1846, but he had, however, managed to solve the engineering obstacles which had negated the Vetch plan, and in June the council agreed to carry his proposals into effect.

In the course of the June debate three matters were raised which were to cause more delay. One was the need to come to an agreement with the Aire & Calder Navigation Company, whose statutory rights over the river and its tributaries would be affected by the works proposed. Another was the limitation to the council's borrowing powers, fixed at £100,000 by the 1842 Act, of which one half had been spent already. The third was the necessity to reach agreement with the owner of the Temple Newsam estate, on a peripheral part of which Leather proposed to site his main sewer outfall. Two years were spent in sorting out these problems, all finally settled in the Improvement Act of 1848. By this time, however, the local climate was not favourable to the prospect of major expenditure. The downturn in the trade cycle brought about a failure of political nerve as meetings of electors in several wards expressed their hostility to the levying of a sewerage rate 'until commercial prosperity and confidence are again restored'.[12] Motions to begin on the sewerage system were lost in January and again in February 1849, but when the issue was raised again in October the reappearance of cholera seems to have brought about a change of opinion and the streets committee was authorized to let the contracts. The first of these was let in 1850, and Leather's scheme was completed in 1855. Altogether it cost nearly £137,000, of which £109,000 was spent on the works and the remainder on legal costs, interest on loans, wayleaves and the like. Over the next decade, the council spent around £10,000 a year on extending the system.

Unfortunately, for several decades the network was severely under-utilized. In December 1854 the streets committee noted that the contractor was receiving very few applications for house drains to be installed, and three years later the inspection sub-committee reported that after a two-day tour through the drainage district, it 'regretted to observe the very large number of streets either wholly or inefficiently drained, not withstanding the excellent outlet which has in almost every instance been brought close to them by your main sewers; the owners of property having but in a few instances been at pains to drain their side streets into the new sewers'.[13] In the face of passive resistance by owners, the council took no action to compel the use of its sewerage system, indeed in May 1857 the streets committee advertised its decision not to sewer any street unless at least two-thirds of the property owners affected agreed to install house drains. Two years later, it attempted to rescind this resolution but the council directed that the decision be re-adopted. One member of the committee complained that since the cost of house connections was almost as great as constructing the main sewers, the effect of the motion would be to reduce the new sewer mileage from five to $2\frac{1}{2}$ a year; to which

68

another councillor reasonably retorted that there was little use in building sewers which went unused.

The most obvious index to the advance of modern sanitation is the number of water closets, and before the 1880s there were comparatively few in Leeds. In 1856 the council believed there to be only 1,000 in the town, just over 3,000 ten years later. By 1870 there were around 6,000. This meant that the great majority of the population relied upon the use of privies: in 1870 it was estimated that there were over 30,000 of them in the borough. Under these circumstances, public scavenging was obviously a vital sanitary service, but a service whose history is one of serious mismanagement by the council for more than 30 years. Before 1859, the emptying of privies was done by arrangement between the householder and private contractors, but in that year the council decided to adopt privy and ashpit-cleaning as a municipal service inside the drainage district of Leeds, Hunslet and Holbeck only. Initially this was done by direct labour but in 1863 it was decided to lease the work to the Leeds Economic Sanitary Company, established by a local doctor to make use of his patent deodorizing and disinfecting powder. Over-optimism on the part of this medical entrepreneur brought bankruptcy on his company and chaos to its operations. This crisis unhappily coincided with the arrival of Dr Hunter from the Medical Department of the Privy Council, who was sent down to investigate the 'pollution of the Aire and Wharfe rivers and other nuisances'. In an Olympian judgment, he placed two decades of public health administration in Leeds in cruel perspective: 'to the eye of an inspector who had just left Newcastle and Sunderland, and who in the same week visited Sheffield, Leeds in August 1865 presented a surprising sight, bringing to rememberance the condition of many English towns of twenty years ago, but finding hardly a standard with which to be compared in the present state of any great town'.[14] No immediate improvement in the privy-cleansing system followed Hunter's report. The council contented itself with a petition to the Privy Council, which amongst other things, claimed bombastically that 'we are not ashamed of our town, nor afraid to live in it'; the tenor of the whole petition was accurately caught by the *Leeds Mercury* which observed that 'hardly alleging a single fact in contradiction to his i.e. Hunter's statements, and merely charging him with prejudice and exaggeration',[15] was hardly likely to make a favourable impression in Whitehall. In the following 25 years the administration of the service was characterized by alternations between contractors and direct labour forming a saga of sordid inefficiency in which cheapness was the only criterion which the council applied. It was not until 1890 that the council finally accepted, after engaging a succession of neglectful, defaulting and bankrupt contractors, that the contract system was not an appropriate way of providing a vital sanitary service and that the only solution was to create a permanent municipal cleansing department. By this time, the growing adoption of water closets meant that the scavenging system was, fortunately, of declining importance. In the 1870s, the sanitary committee began a systematic campaign against the 'abominable midden-stead and cesspool', or at least the most offensive examples, and this, combined with the rising standard of housing had led by the end of the 1880s to a remarkable rise in the number of water closets in the borough. In 1870, just over 6,000 were known to have been installed; by 1889 there were almost 28,000.

A third reason for this development was the gradual extension of the sewerage system. Up to the mid-1860s it was confined to the three central townships of Leeds, Hunslet and Holbeck, which formed the central drainage district. The planning of the first major extensions in the late 1860s, which involved the creation of a drainage network for Armley, Wortley, Headingley, Chapel Allerton and Potternewton led initially to serious opposition from riparian landowners downstream from Leeds, who were apprehensive of the increase in the pollution of the river Aire which would be caused if the drainage area was extended. By December 1869 a Chancery injunction had been obtained to prevent the council from discharging more untreated sewage into the river. On several occasions in the 1850s the streets and sewage committee had considered, in a desultory manner, the prospect of 'turning the fertilising matters contained in sewage water to profitable account', but the search for some solution, profitable or not, was now made imperative by the injunction. One scheme which had been proposed in the year before the injunction was devised by the borough surveyor. He proposed that land should be acquired at Thorne Waste and that sewage should be conveyed there by a 37-mile conduit. The cost of the conduit, the purchase of the land and the laying out of the 2,000 acres to receive the effluent he estimated at £258,000. Not surprisingly, when the streets committee was obliged to consider some plan to meet the terms of the injunction, this was not the one which they selected. Instead an agreement was reached with the owner of the Temple Newsam estate, on whose land the main sewer outfall had been built 20 years before, for the sale of more land to build sewage works. Despite the urgency of the matter, eight years were wasted in commercially-oriented experiment, during which time a succession of ingenious and unsuccessful entrepreneurs came forward in the hope of realizing the council's hope that the plant might be a source of profit. Finally, in 1877 the streets committee opted for a lime precipitation process as the cheapest and most effective method.

Once this problem had been solved the extension of the sewerage system could begin, and between 1877 and 1900 nearly £600,000 was spent on sewerage and drainage. During the 1880s and 1890s approximately 120 miles of sewers were being built in each decade, and this, combined with the increasing number of water closets being installed, greatly increased the problems of sewage disposal. In 1900 the council decided to implement a plan very similar to that advanced by its borough surveyor 30 years previously: it approved the purchase of nearly 2,000 acres of the Gateforth estate, near Selby for £85,000 and decided to promote a local Act to authorize the use of the land for sewage disposal. The bill, however, was defeated in the Lords and nothing more was done until 1907 when the council was again provoked into action, this time by the West Riding Rivers Board. As the result of the providential death of the owner of the Temple Newsam estate, who had strenuously resisted proposals to sell land to extend the sewage works the council was able to acquire 600 acres from the new owner for this purpose, and in 1908 it obtained a local Act to allow the expenditure of £1,277,000 on land and purification plant.

Sixty-five sections of the 1842 Act were concerned with the lay-out of new streets and the regulation of the internal and external structure of houses. Owners could be obliged to pave and drain their streets, or in default have the work done by the council at their own expense. Once a street was made up, the council could formally declare it a highway, so making its repair the responsibility of the highway surveyors. Building sites were to be provided with covered drains, so that each house could eventually be connected with an artery of the sewerage system. The external features of buildings had long been partially controlled by the town's

Improvement Acts, for projecting porches, windows, steps and signs could be a public hazard; the powers in the 1842 Act to allow the council to control such features were thus no innovation. The new Act, however, also regulated the internal structure of houses for the first time to ensure minimum standards of space, light and ventilation. These provisions reflect some of the preoccupations of contemporary sanitary reformers, and it is not surprising to discover that, *pace* Professor Keith-Lucas, most of these sections were taken from Lord Normanby's building regulations bill of 1841. For the next 20 years, however, aspiration was not equalled by achievement.

The authority to supervise the building regulations was delegated to the streets committee, but it gave the matter very little attention. Before the creation of a building clauses committee in 1862, the occasional inspection of designs was usually assigned to an *ad hoc* group of streets committee members, but even this expedient was taken only infrequently. It would seem that builders and property owners only approached the committee if they hoped to gain exemption from the provisions of the Improvement Act, although such exemptions were never in fact approved. It would certainly be wrong to suppose that all other builders were conscientiously following the statutory code, and in 1866 one informed observer claimed that, 'if the cottage speculator chooses to disregard such regulations, he may do so with impunity. No summons has been issued for many years for any breach of the building regulations. The authorities are great friends of "moral suasion" pure and simple'.[16] The first occasion upon which the sanctions of the 1842 act were invoked against a builder was in February 1843, when significantly Dr Baker was the chairman of the streets committee. It was the last recorded instance until October 1863, shortly after the creation of the building clauses committee. One reason for the council's unwillingness to apply the sanction contained in the 1842 Act was probably its severity, for if the borough surveyor objected to the design of a building, 'the only resources he had was the rather cumberous one of pulling down the house'.[17] This difficulty could have been removed by having the building clauses amended, but no alterations were made until the improvement act of 1866. In the intervening years, more than 12,000 houses were erected in Leeds, an increase of over one third. There is of course no reason to suppose that the motives of speculative builders and the consequences of their activities were any different in these decades than those of an earlier generation castigated in the sanitary enquiries of the 1840s.

The condition of the streets also received only cursory attention from the council. Under the 1842 Act it could insist that new streets were at least 30 feet wide, and there its power ended, so that by the mid-1860s it could be said that, 'there have not been a dozen straight streets of any great length laid out within the last thirty years, though the population has increased sixty seven per cent in that period'.[18] The power to order streets to be made up was neglected during this period. A report from one of the medical inspectors of the Privy Council in 1858 highlighted some of the areas of Leeds which had experienced expectionally high mortality rates from infantile diarrhoea. In most of the districts he described there was a mixture of streets described as 'well kept' and 'in good condition' and streets 'in a bad state', 'filthy in the extreme, being unpaved, undrained, uncleansed and infected with effluvia from the privies'. Several of the areas in question were in fact places which had been singled out for condemnation 30 years before. One was the Leylands, where, in the words of the council's statistical survey of 1839, 'the condition of some of the streets and dwellings is proverbial'; another contained the Blue Bell Fold, where cholera had first appeared in Leeds in 1832, and which contained streets whose condition created 'a great sensation' when described to the council in 1839.[19] Clearly, in the intervening decades the council had done little to remedy some of the worst conditions which had existed at the time of the passing of the Improvement Act. Further evidence of neglect came to light in the select committee stage of the 1866 Improvement Bill, by which the council hoped to absorb the powers of the surveyors of highways. One of the council's witnesses, the distinguished civil engineer Rawlinson stated that in walking around Leeds he found the paving 'exceedingly defective in many of the bye streets: many of the undedicated streets are in a very defective condition'.[20] These were, however, the very streets which the council had powers to improve, and were thus evidence of its negligence. Another witness confirmed that there were 511 private streets still in existence and that 'several of these streets were actually scheduled in the 1842 Act'.[21]

The detailed code of bye-laws which the council finally introduced in 1866 showed that in at least two important respects it was not prepared to interfere with the established practices of the local building trade, however harmful they might be. The local press and enlightened public opinion might rage against the back-to-back house, 'the most unhealthy buildings which human perversity ever invented, with the rapidity of construction and ingenuity of disorder unequalled since the confusion of the tongues at Babel',[22] but the council refused to prohibit them. Instead it introduced a slight departure from existing practice by ordering that they were to be built in blocks of no more than four pairs, with each block separated by a space 'free from any erection above the level of the ground, excepting privies'.[23] Later regulations increased the minimum air space between blocks, and improved the ventilation requirement for the houses, but the standards laid down in 1866 remained essentially unmodified for over 40 years. The council even persuaded the Commons select committee which examined its Improvement Bill of 1893 to allow a clause which safeguarded its powers to allow the continued building of back-to-backs in the face of strenuous opposition from the Local Government Board, and protests from its own medical officer who in his evidence had condemned the building of such houses as 'utterly wrong'.[24] The council had indeed, as one M.P. complained in the House in 1901, 'obtained power to set aside the almost universal law of this country against the erection of back-to-back houses'.[25] The council remained the unabashed apologist for this type of house; indeed, it hoped to rehouse some of its slum clearance evacuees in purpose-built back-to-backs, and later petitioned against the section in the Housing and Town Planning Act, 1909 which prohibited further building of them.

The Local Government Board had no greater success in the 1870s when it tried to persuade the council to forbid the use of the privy-and-ashpit system in new houses. Following the Public Health Act, 1875, the Board, on receiving the annual submission of the council's bye-laws, asked it to adopt the 'model' clauses then being prepared. In reply, the council asserted its right to make bye-laws under its local Acts and was 'so alarmed at the suggestion that their position as an ancient corporation should be made subservient to a Central Authority' that the clerk was instructed to gain a personal interview with the Board.[26] There was a slight unbending when the council realized that it could benefit from the Board's technical expertise over minor matters, but it was not prepared to acknowledge the 'necessity for the revision of the entire series' for which the Board was pressing. In particular, as one official noted, the bye-laws 'contemplate in fact, the perpetuation in Leeds of a form of privy-and-ashpit which has again and again been shown to be the prime source of some of the greatest sanitary evils in Leeds'. If the revised version of the bye-laws which emerged in 1878 was, as an official minuted, 'such as the town council will accept and the Board may safely confirm' the concessions had come from the latter rather than the former. The failure to proscribe the privy-and-ashpit in the building bye-laws produced an anomalous situation once the sanitary committee's campaign of conversion began. Whilst the sanitary committee was abolishing privies in the poorest areas of the town, houses were being built in the suburbs provided only with privy middens, and the building clauses committee felt powerless to intervene. Despite the protests of the press in 1889 that the council should 'see to it that the Building Clauses Committee does not sanction the creation of evils to be dealt with subsequently by their colleagues on the Sanitary Committee', it was not until 1899 that the council obtained powers in an Improvement Act to require that all new buildings should have water closets. Nevertheless, by the turn of the century Leeds was well on the way to abolishing the privy-and-ashpit. In 1902, only 15,000 of the 100,000 tenants supplied with water had no water closet; only two years before nearly one quarter of tenants had been in this situation, and by 1904 the town clerk could assert that 'to-day Leeds is practically a water closet town'.

One of the major deleterious influences upon the environment in Leeds, as in other industrial towns, was the prevalence of atmospheric pollution caused by industrial smoke. The harmful effects produced by the almost universal use of coal in industrial processes in the 'one hundred and seventy mills and manufactories in different parts of the borough',[27] were made worse by the intermingling of factories, houses, and workshops, as manufacturers had no legal restraints upon their choice of location. For example, in the mid-1860s the council's smoke inspector noted that one of the worst cases to come to his attention arose from a firm in business in a yard in Briggate, in the very centre of the town, and he could do no more than enter an ineffectual protest that a tobacco-pipe make was building premises in another heavily-populated location where 'the smoke is sure to be a very great nuisance to the people in the vicinity'.[28]

A significant expression of public opinion came in January 1842, when a public meeting was organized to complain of the 'smoke nuisance' and establish a committee to investigate the various designs for smoke consumption apparatus then available. The meeting had a more important short-term aim, which was to influence the contents of the new Improvement Bill, which it did, but with only partial success. The smoke abatement clauses which were included in the bill were the cause of the only serious opposition to be heard before the Commons select committee. They were strenuously contested by the woollen dyers, who claimed that no smoke consumption machinery then in use had been successfully used in their trade. Although it was not disputed that it was possible to control the smoke produced by steam-engine furnaces, the dyers argued, in a lengthy and cogent presentation of their case, that they ought to be excluded from the proposed restrictions since such methods were not applicable to dyeing vats. A compromise was agreed whereby legal proceedings could not be taken against dyers until the practicability of smoke consumption in their business had been proved to the satisfaction of a local magistrate. The practical immunity which the dyers obtained for themselves was only one of the restraints upon the effectiveness of the smoke

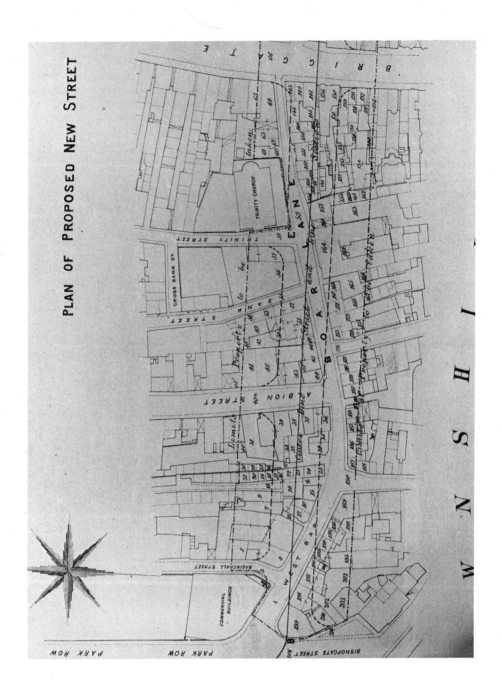

Figure 1. The redevelopment of Boar Lane proposed in the Improvement Act of 1866 (by courtesy of the West Yorkshire Record Office).

abatement clauses of the Act. Another was the unsympathetic attitude of the magistrates towards prosecution, and a third was the division of opinion in the council itself. Under pressure from public opinion which gathered around the smoke abatement committee of 1842, the council appointed an inspector in 1844, but after his death two years later, the office was allowed to lapse. It required a further concerted effort on the part of Edward Eddison, a councillor, and secretary to the smoke abatement committee, and the committee itself, before the council agreed to appoint a replacement in 1853.

The scavenging and nuisance committee favoured a policy of conciliation. Firms which attracted the disapproval of the inspector were invited to send a representative to attend a committee meeting, and it seems that for a short period persuasion was effective, although by the winter of 1855 the press complained that 'reform now decidedly flags'. The next year saw a further set-back to the faction on the council which favoured control. The improvement bill of 1856 contained proposals to regulate the pollution produced by the iron industry. The iron masters, however, adopted the dyers' tactics and won explicit exemption from interference. Their case was greatly helped by the select committee which decided that it did not think the Leeds proposals justifiable as a current government bill on smoke pollution was proposing to exclude the iron industry from its provisions. The result was predictable: as the smoke inspector observed in 1858 'the dense smoke complained of is principally made by those trades which are said to be exempt from the late amended act'.[29] The conciliatory policy continued, culminating in 1864 in the provision of a 'substantial tea and dessert' in the town hall for 500 engine men and stokers paid for by the committee chairman and several others. Its effectiveness, however, was very limited, and in 1865 the physician to the House of Recovery claimed that 'it is notorious that any attempts to control the smoke and other nuisances in Leeds are a mere pretence, and indeed, rather hollow even for a pretence'.[30] The magistrates continued to look unfavourably on prosecutions, and in November 1861, for example, the smoke inspector informed the nuisance committee that the magistrates had 'repeatedly adjourned the cases at the request of the defendants' and for this reason he had not taken any further steps in other outstanding cases. The council's unwillingness to regulate the activities of manufacturers on its own initiative was shown in the way in which smoke abatement clauses found their way into the 1866 Improvement Act. When the text of the bill was published in 1865 it was discovered that the council did not propose to acquire any additional powers over smoke pollution. Public response was the reconstitution of the smoke committee, which obtained the insertion of fresh powers into the bill. The committee was not wholly successful, for the dyers and iron manufacturers were again able to protect their interests, but it was able to obtain powers to enable the council to order chimneys to be raised to a minimum height of 90 ft. This allowed for the removal of a source of complaint which Robert Baker had voiced more than 25 years before. The strength of public opinion must have come as a revelation to the council, for after the bill became law there followed a spate of prosecutions. But the council's equivocal attitude soon reasserted itself: in 1872 the town clerk told a Commons select committee that 'we try to enforce the (regulations), but Leeds is so dependent for its prosperity upon its industry that we are anxious not to do too much'.[31] On the same day the committee was also told that one of the reasons for the probable potential of the Roundhay Park estate (about three miles from the town centre), as a new residential area was that 'there is no place within the same distance which is so free from smoke'.[32]

Twenty years later, scientific investigation showed that soot deposits fell over an area which extended almost nine miles from Leeds, by which time, according to the author of the research, prosecutions for pollution had become 'ludicrously few' in the borough.[33] Local opinion mobilized itself again: the Sanitary Aid Society urged the council's sanitary committee to take more effective action, and the Leeds Smoke Abatement Society began its investigations of the scientific evidence on pollution to support proposals for changes in national legislation. Neither were successful. The smoke inspector's researches into methods which had been tried to reduce the volume of smoke in iron and steel works elsewhere in Yorkshire, and in Scotland, forced him to conclude that only indifferent results had been obtained, and the sanitary committee could only reiterate in its own defence the claim that 'the powers of the inspector are confined almost entirely to boiler furnaces. The worst offenders in Leeds, however, are the protected trades'.[34] On the national level, the Smoke Abatement Society's attempts, in conjunction with similar bodies in Manchester and Sheffield, to press the Local Government Board for stricter controls met with no response.

The care of the sick throughout this period remained predominantly the concern of private semi-charitable institutions and of the poor law. In Leeds as in most other towns there were several types of hospital supported solely by public subscription and by fees charged to those who were capable of paying for medical attention. The oldest of these was the General Infirmary, founded in 1767. It did not accept those suffering from infectious diseases and the need for such a hospital, made increasingly necessary by the growth of insanitary conditions through urbanization, was met by the establishment of a fever hospital. The optimistically-named House of Recovery was located first near the Kirkgate market and then in 1846 was moved to new, more secluded premises, in Burmantofts. The medical care provided by these two institutions was supplemented by the Public Dispensary, established in 1824, the Hospital for Women and Children opened in 1853 and a small Convalescent Home set up in 1868. Initially the only public body to have any responsibility towards the sick was the poor law union, and since sickness was an important cause of pauperism, the medical services provided by the board of guardians became a significant aspect of their functions. By the late 1860s medical relief was costing the Leeds guardians more than £2,000 a year, and about 200 people a week were on their medical relief list. In 1874 the union built an infirmary at a cost of £18,000 to accommodate 456 patients. The council had no responsibilities in this direction until the Sanitary Act of 1866 allowed local authorities to provide hospital facilities. Its acceptance of this new responsibility was hesitant, grudging, and parsimonious, and was only undertaken as a result of pressure from other bodies and the regular recurrence of epidemics.

The issue was first forced on the attention of the sanitary committee by a smallpox epidemic in the winter of 1871–2. As an emergency measure the council hoped to persuade the workhouse infirmary to take non-pauper patients at municipal expense, but the guardians replied that their existing facilities were insufficient and advised the council to build its own hospital. The council then decided to exercise its discretionary powers under the Act of 1866, and granted the sanitary committee £1,000, a small sum but adequate for the modesty of its plans. It was decided to extend the 'cholera sheds' on land belonging to the guardians, a hasty improvisation which received a setback when the March winds came and blew them down. Municipal interest ebbed with the recession of the epidemic and, angered by this procrastination, the guardians in 1878 informed the council that they would not allow the use of their buildings in future. The council then cast around for alternative accommodation, without much effect, despite the medical officer's reminder that it was 'totally incapable of isolating effectually a single case, far less in dealing with the disease in an epidemic form'.[35] The reminder was in fact a prophetic warning, for a year after it was made, another smallpox epidemic began.

Despite their previous statement, the guardians gave assistance, but made it clear that this was only a temporary concession. The sanitary committee hurriedly advertised for a two-acre site, and by September had erected a 'temporary wooden building' at a cost of £3,000, which the medical officer of health regarded as possessing every defect imaginable. By the summer of 1883 the epidemic was still raging, and the committee was obliged to purchase a tent to house convalescent patients. At this time the trustees of the House of Recovery announced their decision to have the charity wound up. Fees from private patients, subscriptions and investments were proving inadequate, forcing them into heavy dependence upon fees from poor law unions, which made the charity into a mere adjunct of public provision for the sick. Negotiations began between the sanitary committee and the trustees, and despite the medical officer's damning criticisms of the buildings the council decided, in April 1884, to purchase the House of Recovery for £6,000. Even when the council owned both the fever hospital and the shedding built in 1882, a severe epidemic could put a serious strain on its resources. The sanitary committee was, moreover, not making any long-term plans to solve the problem, and the purchase of the House of Recovery, initially presented to the council as only a stop-gap, came to be seen by the committee as an excuse for shelving the problem.

Temporary crises recurred throughout the 1890s, as epidemics filled existing premises to capacity and forced the adoption of desperate expedients of corrugated iron and canvas. An outbreak of both typhoid fever and smallpox in 1891 obliged the council to build 'two pairs of galvanised corrugated iron cottages' on land in the east end of Leeds township. In 1892 more iron cottages were put into commission and in the following year, convalescents were being housed in marquees. After the epidemic of 1893 had receded the smallpox hospital of 1882, a supposedly temporary structure was finally dismantled and burnt. By this time the council had purchased a site for a permanent hospital, for in 1892 it had agreed to pay £10,000 for the 97½ acre Manston Hall Estate at Seacroft, which was outside the borough on the east. By June 1894 the sanitary committee had decided upon a design, and recommended the council to apply to the Local Government Board for a loan sanction for four hospital pavilions. The Board, however, objected to the plan to isolate all patients suffering from infectious diseases together, refusing to approve the treatment of smallpox patients on the same site. Despite representations the Board refused to waive its opposition and the council had no alternative but to agree to its stipulation. In 1896 contracts were let for a 160-bed general isolation hospital and two years later it was decided to build further wards to increase the capacity to 400 beds in all. At the same time the Local Government Board's insistence on separate facilities for smallpox victims was answered by the purchase of the 144-acre Killingbeck Estate for £21,250.

As the council was proudly aware, the formal opening of the two hospitals in September 1904, marked 'an epoch in the sanitary administration of the city'. The Seacroft isolation hospital had cost almost £250,000, and that of Killingbeck about £70,000 and the sanitary committee, with a certain antiseptic logic, hastened to reassure the public that 'the desire of the corporation has been to make the (Seacroft) hospital complete and perfect from the administrative standpoint, but as infectious hospitals are not usually visited for pleasure there has been every desire to minimise outlay on the architectural side'.[36]

In his discussion of the contribution which public health legislation made to the 'elimination of the causes of preventable mortality' in nineteenth-century Britain, Professor Flinn has argued for the existence of two chronologies, the customary and comforting chronicle of commissions and Acts of parliament, and the real and far less reassuring story of the progress of public health when measured by the only criterion which ultimately matters, namely the trend of mortality rates: 'in 1875 the death rate stood at almost the same level as it had in 1838 when civil registration began . . . In short, there was very little real improvement in public health before the last quarter of the nineteenth century . . . The two chronologies – the legislative and the mortality scales – moved forward only with a substantial time lag between them'.[37] In this respect, events in Leeds followed the national trend fairly closely. In the 1850s the crude mortality rate averaged 27.7 per 1,000, but rose slightly in the next decade to 29.7. From the mid-1870s a downward trend, arrested but not reversed in the early 1890s, is clearly discernable.

Table 7   Crude mortality rates in Leeds, 1865–1914 (five-yearly average)

1865–9	28.9	1890–4	21.1
1870–4	27.9	1895–9	19.7
1875–9	24.6	1900–4	18.4
1880–4	22.9	1905–9	16.3
1885–9	21.1	1910–14	15.3

Some of the reasons why the mortality rate failed to fall before the mid-1870s have been traced in the preceding pages. The recurring inefficiency of public cleansing, whether by contract or direct works, continued for 30 years, from the late 1850s when the service was inaugurated, up to the end of the 1880s. The sewerage system had little impact upon sanitary conditions until the 1880s, when the number of water closets in use began to increase considerably. Undoubtedly, the council's spirited defense of the privy-and-ashpit system did nothing to hasten the change. In many respects Leeds, with its privies, its dilatory record of sewage disposal, and its epidemic victims lying under canvas was not unique, but simply presents an exaggeration of the worst features to be found in many other towns. Under such circumstances, it is not at all difficult to appreciate why the aims of the public health propagandists of the 1840s took so long to achieve.

4   Urban amenities

Amongst the amenities which the council provided, the most famous was the town hall, the cynosure of 'civic pride' in the 1850s. This example of municipal munificence is the subject of a well-known study, and need not be further considered here, except to note that it was far from typical as an instance of council policy in this sphere. On the whole the atmosphere of economy which pervaded public health administration was not dispelled when projected public amenities – parks, libraries, baths, markets, and street improvements – came under discussion.

Although there was already a widespread recognition of the need for parks and recreation grounds in urban areas by the 1830s, little was achieved in this respect in Leeds until 30 years later. Before the 1870s, the only sizable areas of open space available for public use were the unenclosed commons or 'moors' in the townships of Leeds, Hunslet, and Holbeck. Woodhouse moor, on the north western boundary of Leeds township became municipal property in 1856, but through the force of circumstances rather than municipal initiative. The moors, although used for all kinds of public events, were nevertheless still in the private ownership of the lords of the manor. By the 1840s, the continuing growth of the central urban area began to create doubts over the future of these surviving vestiges of common land, and the possibility of the council acquiring an interest in Woodhouse moor to prevent its enclosure was raised, but not acted upon, in 1845. Five years later, the lords did in fact offer a portion of it for sale as building lots, and then withdrew the offer, only to renew it in 1854. Public opinion, tepid in 1850, was now strongly opposed to the sale, and the council decided to buy out the lords of the manor's rights. A year later it had been agreed, subject to parliamentary approval, to purchase both Woodhouse moor for £3,000 and Holbeck for £1,000; the council later obtained an option to buy Hunslet moor for £1,200. Provisions to approve these purchases were included in the 1856 improvement bill, but opposition from the township at Bramley to being rated for this purpose forced the council to abandon its hopes of buying any but Woodhouse moor. For many years, however, the purchase price was the only money which the council spent on the moor, for in 1871 the press was moved to complain that the moor was 'a standing disgrace to Leeds, being little better than a foul quagmire, decorated by all the diseased cattle in the town'.[38]

The promise of an active policy on open spaces was contained in the 1866 improvement act which allowed the council to spend up to £50,000 in providing recreation grounds. Although the council purchased land in the east end of Leeds township in 1869 and in Bramley in the following year, it was apparently found difficult to procure suitable sites and little more was achieved until the 1880s. In the meantime, the council made a remarkable acquisition. In 1871, the Roundhay Park estate, comprising a mansion house, extensive landscaped grounds and farm land in the township of Roundhay was offered for sale by auction. A month before the sale took place, the grounds were opened to the public, and a movement began, to urge the council to purchase a substantial part of the estate. The leading advocate of the purchase was the mayor, John Barran. In September 1871 the council considered the proposition and Barran spoke at length in its favour. Drawing an explicit parallel with the major prestige project of the 1850s, he claimed that 'if they got Roundhay Park, it would be as great a credit to them as their town hall. It would give them a status in a way few things would, and he thought they should take pride in trying to obtain it'.[39] Ranged against this, however, were practical objections of distance, size and cost. Roundhay was three miles from the centre of Leeds township and much further from the industrial suburbs south of the river. Public transport, moreover, was as Barran himself admitted, 'not what it ought to be', and this obstacle led one councillor to object, with reason, that 'Roundhay park was very well as a park, but not suitable as a people's park'.[40] The size and consequent cost of the park was also open to criticism. An integral part of the scheme was to set aside about 350 of the 773 acres which Barran hoped the council would buy for 'first class residences', so that part of the cost could be defrayed by encouraging suburban development. Barran saw the 'magnates of Leeds' competing eagerly to purchase sites, but not everyone accepted his sanguine judgment.

Nevertheless the ratepayers seemed, for once, strongly in favour of the expenditure proposed, and at a large public meeting at the Corn Exchange, organized for the day on which the council met to consider the question, there was unanimous support for Barran's project. The council agreed, and in October 1871 he attended the auction and paid £139,000 for the land he had hoped to acquire. An Improvement Act promoted in the following year gave the council the power to spend £150,000 on recreation grounds, so retrospectively legitimizing the purchase, and to sell part of the estate for building purposes. The venture was a personal triumph for Barran, but in a wider perspective, of dubious value to the borough, at least in the short term. The accuracy of Barran's belief that the park 'would be a great advantage to the working classes, by promoting their health, improving their morals, enlightening their judgment, and making them in every way better citizens',[41] is, in the nature of things, hardly susceptible of proof. In fact, the working classes would have had some difficulty in putting his faith to the test, for the park remained almost inaccessible by public transport until the beginning of a regular electric tram service in 1890. It took even longer for Barran's plans for suburban development to materialize, and again poor transport facilities seem to have been to blame. Auction sales in 1876 and 1877 disposed of about 60 acres, but many lots were withdrawn and no sales at all were made at an auction in 1879. No further sales were made until 1902. The financial implications were, of course, that the cost of the park was much greater than had been expected, but the miscalculation, given Barran's persuasive advocacy and the enthusiasm of the electorate, cannot simply be blamed on the council. It is significant, in terms of municipal priorities, than when Barran had claimed that the park, after sales of surplus land would cost 1⅛d. in the pound, 'a sum which would not be felt heavily by anybody', neither ratepayers nor council had objected, whilst a few years before the council had cavilled at the proposal to adopt the Public Libraries Act, with its maximum rate of one penny.

In the same decade the council also began to buy up the remnants of common land in the borough. But if the purchase of Roundhay Park was an example of patrician influence at work, the municipal acquisitions of common lands were made as the result of plebian pressure. The first eruption of local protests over encroachments happened at Woodhouse Ridge where, in 1875, rioters demolished the foundations of several houses which a builder had laid in defiance of alleged common rights. Twelve defendants, labourers, gardeners, and blacksmiths, were bound over at the August assize, and a month later the council agreed to purchase some 17 acres of the Ridge from the lords of the manor. In 1878, part of Holbeck moor was quietly purchased, more than 20 years after it had first been proposed; Hunslet moor, however, came into public ownership in the following year, only after local opinion had mobilized itself into a protest movement over encroachments by the Middleton Colliery Company. From the 1880s, the council began to make regular purchases of land to create recreation grounds in all parts of the borough, and by the turn of the century had nearly two dozen such sites, ranging in size from three to 80 acres well distributed within, or within easy reach of, the expanding urban area.

A far less popular proposal than Roundhay Park which came, hesitantly, to fruition a few years before it, was the founding of the borough's public library. The prospect of a municipal library was first raised in March 1861 when the council received a petition with nearly 2,000 signatures, obtained 'by a few working men on two or three nights'. In May one councillor proposed the adoption of the Public Libraries Act of 1856, but the motion was heavily defeated: 'to refer this question to the burgesses' one councillor claimed, 'would be asking the majority of non-ratepayers to say what the middle classes should pay'. Another, in the same vein, remarked that 'the memorial which was presented . . . was got up by a section of the working classes and did not represent the large ratepayers or the shopkeepers'.[42] Seven years later the question was raised again. Supporters of the measure could point to the fact that the town hall cellars held 2,500 volumes of patent specifications given by the Patent Office in 1855 for use 'in a free public library of the borough' and files of local newspapers which had been accumulating since 1841. Opponents could claim that existing voluntary provision was sufficient – 16 libraries with stocks of 300 to 13,000 volumes, and 18 Wesleyan schools with libraries of up to 1,000 books – and might indeed be injured by a free library. The council decided to allow the statutory town meeting necessary under he 1856 Act, and this, no doubt to the chagrin of the council, decided in favour of a free public library by a small majority. The council then prevaricated from March to August 1868, until only the town clerk's legal advice that it was bound to implement the decision of the town meeting forced it to formally adopt the Act.

The library committee hired rooms in mechanics' institutes in Wortley, New Wortley, and Holbeck for use as branch libraries. John Barran, in expansive mood, protested that 'a town which had the finest hospital in Europe, and one of the finest and most complete of town halls, should not be content with other than a noble building for a free library'.[43] There was justice in the reply that the libraries were located amongst the people for whom they were intended, and not in 'the neighbourhood of Boar Lane or the railway stations, which was the centre round which Mr. Barran moved'. By the mid-1880s, 25 branch libraries had been provided, all housed in police stations, the need for which was not in dispute, and it was not until 1902 that the first purpose-built library was opened. Nevertheless, a large book stock was gradually acquired which made the city's libraries one of the major library systems in the country by 1914.

Another area in which, after initial evasions, the council acted creditably was in the provision of public baths and wash-houses. In 1846, shortly after the enactment of the Baths and Washhouses Act, the council appointed a committee to consider its adoption in Leeds and in the following year one of the borough's M.P.s offered a site if the council was prepared to provide the buildings. Thirty years later, in 1878, the council adopted the Act, and created a committee to make recommendations. The recommendations were rejected, and it was not until 1886 that the first baths – swimming baths at the New Wortley recreation grounds – were actually built. It was not until the early 1890s, however, that the council accepted that the advantages for public health that baths might have outweighed the warning of the chairman of the sanitary committee that 'he could hold out no hope of the scheme paying',[44] and began to build a series of public baths which by 1914 had cost £115,000.

The most important of the assets which the council inherited from the improvement commissioners in 1842, was the public market in Kirkgate. Except for the cloth halls, there were no market places in the town until the 1820s, apart from those traditionally held in the public streets. This decade, however, witnessed the beginning of both public and private enterprise in this field. In 1823 the improvement commission purchased the vicarage and its gardens, and turned Vicar's Croft, Kirkgate, into a public market. Within a few years it was complemented by several joint-stock company ventures. A 'bazaar, new shambles, and fish market', opened in 1826, the Central Market opened its doors in the following year, and the Corn Exchange began business in 1828. By the 1840s both the new and traditional markets were the cause of complaint. The *Leeds Mercury* claimed that 'it is notorious to all our readers that for fair and market accommodation there is not a town in the kingdom in so bad a condition as Leeds'.[45] Kirkgate market had become too small, and the holding of street markets, for fruit and vegetables in Briggate and for horses in the Upper Headrow especially, were the cause of traffic congestion, 'accident, and even loss of life'. When the council took over from the commissioners it quickly set about to remedy the worst deficiencies. In January 1843 it approved the plans of the market committee to enlarge Kirkgate market by the demolition of adjacent property, so as to more than double the area available, and in October 1845 rented a field on the north-west edge of the town to provide a site for a horse and cattle market.

The markets were not only a public service, but a source of revenue to the corporation, realizing about £2,500 a year from the leasing of the tolls by the late 1840s. There were, therefore, tangible reasons why the council should wish to protect its franchise from possible competition. One minor challenge in 1843 was easily defeated, but a more serious threat came a decade later. In 1850, the council had considered the possibility of providing a fully-equipped cattle market, and of covering over part of Kirkgate market, but allowed both plans to lapse. In 1852, however, the Central Market Company promoted a parliamentary bill to enlarge its accommodation, and the council decided to oppose it in parliament. It did not have a very strong case, as the Company clearly offered superior facilities and in order to frustrate the Company's plans, the council had to make two pledges to the select committee. These were to build a covered market of its own, and to provide a proper cattle market to remove all such dealings permanently from the Kirkgate site. In accordance with the second of these promises, land for a cattle market was purchased and equipped in 1853 and in the next year £14,000 was spent on a glass and iron structure on part of the Kirkgate market site. Another major investment in market facilities followed a few years later when in 1859 it was decided that a site should be purchased for a corn exchange. Already subject to criticism in the early 1840s, active dissatisfaction with the privately-owned market led a number of factors, millers, and maltsters to petition the council for a municipal exchange in 1856. Three years later the council decided to buy out the shareholders and build new premises on an estate which it purchased from the trustees of the grammar school. The architect chosen was Cuthbert Broderick, the designer of the recently-completed town hall, and the finished structure 'a magnificent building of eliptical shape' cost £32,292.

By the time the visiting commissioner of the Royal Commission on Market Rights and Tolls visited Leeds in 1888, about £160,000 had been spent on improving Kirkgate Market, and the market area had increased from the original two acres to just over five, much of it under cover. There was little complaint over the adequacy of these premises, as is confirmed by the relatively trivial complaints voiced before the commissioner. The continuing growth of trading made market improvement a profitable enterprise, at least up to the late 1880s, by which time the borough accountant reckoned that the markets as a whole incurred a small deficit of £100 a year. This did not mean that every market, least of all Kirkgate, was operating at a loss: the sole cause of the deficit was the new cattle market and slaughterhouses, the establishment of which was one of the most contentious subjects of the decade. Promptings to establish public slaughterhouses came from several directions: to the RSPCA which petitioned the council on the subject in 1868 the motive was humane, and to the public health administrator, municipally-controlled slaughter-houses had two principal advantages over private ones. The latter were commonly in cramped, insanitary buildings, and the existence of nearly 300 such establish-ments in the borough made adequate inspection impossible. It was probably under the influence of Dr Robinson, the first medical officer, that in 1869 the council decided to seek powers to open public slaughterhouses when it next promoted an Improvement Bill. Such provisions were included in the bill of the following year but intense opposition by the butchers and others led the select committee to delete the clauses. The Public Health Act, 1875 gave the council the powers it had unsuccessfully sought five years before, and the market committee was instructed to investigate the matter. Six years of vacillation followed, until in June 1882 the council finally purchased 16 acres of land on the south-western outskirts of the town for a new cattlemarket, and three years later authorized the building of eight slaughterhouses. By 1889, the facilities there had cost nearly £40,000. The slaughterhouses, however, suffered from lack of interest by local butchers, and in 1898 the council capitulated to the trade and decided to build an abattoir and dead meat market near Kirkgate market. By this time the council was occupied in the planning of a new market hall to replace the piecemeal complex of buildings which had arisen over the previous 40 years. Contracts were let in 1901 and the completed building, 'designed in Renaissance style, with details of a classical outline', covering more than five acres, and costing about £100,000 was opened in July 1904.

Street improvements were one of the major functions of the improvement commission, and indeed one of the reasons for its existence. In the 1820s and 1830s the commissioners were intermittently engaged in schemes to widen and straighten the town's main thoroughfares, and the 1842 Act made considerable powers available for the compulsory purchase of property to enable many major improve-ment schemes to be carried out. Between 1844 and 1846 property was acquired to improve the approaches to Leeds Bridge, which was 'the great line of communica-tion with the railway stations and for the centre of the town':[46] a traffic census taken in 1842 revealed that on market days it was crossed by more than 16,000 pedestrians and almost 2,000 vehicles of all descriptions. Other improvements were undertaken elsewhere in the next few years, and plans were made to widen Boar Lane, Lands Lane and North Street. These, however, failed to materialize, for the streets committee found the cost of property in the central business district to be prohibitive, and moreover it wished to allocate as much of its budget as possible to its first priority, the building of the sewerage system.

The council obtained further street improvement powers in the 1856 Act, the most important of which were to make Boar Lane 36 feet wide along its entire course – although a major street, it was in places only 20 ft in width – and open up a new road for 'the purpose of improving the approaches to the town hall'. Neither was achieved, although proposals to begin work on Boar Lane were considered in 1861 and again in the following year. The 1866 Act, however, ushered in a period, albeit brief, of some activity in this sphere. The bill initially contained provisions which did no more than renew the plans for Boar Lane which had been included in the 1856 act, but when its contents became public knowledge, local opinion took the initiative. So strongly were the views of the public expressed at a meeting held to consider the bill that the council was 'almost forced' to plan a more ambitious scheme. In the late 1860s, therefore, the council carried out several major improvements: Boar Lane was finally re-aligned, involving the purchase of over £190,000 worth of property, £55,000 was spent on extending Briggate northwards and widening its route at its southern end, and £32,000 was spent nearby in Call Lane and in Kirkgate. At the same time, the council was consolidating its control over the borough's highways. The 1866 Act had authorized it to take over the powers of the borough's 13 independent boards of highway surveyors, and to remove the jurisdiction of turnpike trusts within the borough boundaries. As soon as the Act became law, the parliamentary committee began to negotiate terms with the bridge and turnpike trusts for the abolition of tolls, and by 1869 had spent almost £70,000 to this end. The money which the council was spending on highways, and its determination to become the sole highway authority in the borough influenced its attitude towards the gas and tramway companies, as will be seen in a later section.

The pressure of public opinion, then, was one reason for the council's decision to press ahead with long-deferred improvement schemes in the late 1860s and early 1870s; another was the adoption of a method already in use in Liverpool, Manchester and elsewhere, of reducing the cost entailed. In the 1866 Act the council had attempted to gain permission to buy more land than was necessary for the actual widening to enable it to resell the surplus so that the council rather than the private landowners 'get the benefit of the frontage'. The attempt in the 1866 Act failed, but a second attempt in the next local Act in 1869 was successful, and made a significant difference to the cost of the Boar Lane scheme: about £130,000 was recouped from surplus land sales, so that the net cost was around £60,000. Enhanced rateable values reduced costs still further. The property committee when reviewing the Boar Lane Scheme calculated that increased rate revenue would be equivalent to a rate of interest of $4\frac{1}{2}$ per cent on the cost of the improvement. No schemes on this scale were undertaken on the 1870s, although more than £60,000 was spent on street improvements in various parts of the urban area.

The major targets for the council's street improvement plans in the 1880s were the Quebec Buildings and the Coloured Cloth Hall, which occupied a strategic site close to the railway stations and near to the convergence of Wellington Street, Park Row and Boar Lane. By the 1830s buildings in this area were already a source of inconvenience, and the improvement commissioners had attempted to remove the worst obstructions. After abortive negotiations in 1882 with the Post Office, which coveted the Cloth Hall site, the council proposed to include the compulsory purchase of the hall in a new Improvement Bill, but found the opposition of the trustees far more fierce than it had expected. The issue was not reopened until 1888, when the purchase of the hall was agreed for £66,000. The owners of the Quebec Buildings, however, held out until 1892 before the council, anxious to remove the final obstacle to a major improvement in the area, agreed to their price. Part of the Cloth Hall estate was sold to the Post Office, and the remaining area was laid out in 1897 as a paved and ornamented area known as City Square. Private generosity gave it an incongruous equestrian statue of the Black Prince, and a group of attendant naked nymphs and Leeds luminaries. Leeds had acquired another monument to civic pride.

5   Public utilities, unemployment relief and 'municipal socialism'

The largest recurrent item in the accounts of the improvement commissioners was the cost of street lighting and this, even without taking into account the implications for the maintenance of law and order which the service had – 'a good lamp being equal to a policeman'[47] – gave them a close interest in the activities of the two local gas suppliers, the Leeds Gas Company established in 1828 and the New Coal Gas Company of 1834. The Improvement Bill of 1842 as originally drafted included powers to allow the commissioners to manufacture gas for their own use and for public sale, but the opposition of both companies led to this proposal being abandoned. In the following year the council took the opportunity provided by the Gas Company's bill to amend its constitution to instruct its parliamentary committee to intervene and secure 'the benefits of competition between the two gas companies'. The committee was successful in obtaining a clause similar to that which the council had managed to insert in the Waterworks Act of 1837 which restricted the dividend to a maximum of six per cent on new share capital. Seven years later, in 1850, the council appointed a committee to review the possibility of purchasing the gas and water works and all toll bridges within the borough boundaries. A few months after this a new stimulus was given to such discussions when the publication of a parliamentary return revealed that the cost of gas for public lighting was higher than in many other towns. Elsewhere it was usual to supply gas at cost price for this purpose but in Leeds the companies treated the council as merely another private consumer. The *Leeds Mercury* was moved to protest that 'a joint stock company has no right to calculate on deriving large profits out of a public rate'[48] and this view was echoed both in vestry and council meetings. In November, the council appointed a committee to negotiate with the companies with a view to purchase, and later decided to incorporate the proposal into the next local act. This stage was never reached, however, probably because the cost of the completion of the sewerage network and the imminent purchase of the waterworks seemed to be more urgent financial priorities.

The municipal ownership of public utilities, then, began with the waterworks in 1852. During the years of joint public–private control the company had extended its operations considerably and by the mid-1840s the directors found it necessary to consider annexing a new catchment area to cope with future demand. In 1846 they decided to apply for an Act to enable them to draw water from a source at Bramhope which had been discovered in the course of railway building. The supply promised to be plentiful and it could be relatively cheaply fed into the existing reservoir at Eccup. This decision involved the company in a conflict with both the Leeds and Thirsk railway company which, having discovered the source, planned to seek parliamentary sanction to exploit it itself, and with various landowners in the Bramhope area. Nevertheless, the water company was successful in its aim and by an Act of 1847 obtained authority to take water from Bramhope, build new works and increase its share capital from £91,500 to £250,000. But in the event it did not take advantage of the Bramhope supply, for subsequent investigation revealed that the cost of doing so was greater than anticipated. Whilst these abortive plans were being made, demand for water continued to grow and in 1851 the situation was made worse by a severe drought. The company quickly commissioned several professional opinions on the course of action it ought to take. J.W. Leather recommended it to adopt the river Washburn as a new source, but the plan was strongly opposed by a landowner whose acquiescence was essential. The directors approved this scheme, but only by a majority of one and in May 1852 it was decisively rejected by the shareholders. Instead, it was decided to draw further quantities of water from the river Wharfe.

Meanwhile the corporation had been considering the possibility of exercising its option to purchase the works and in August 1851 the committee created in the previous year reported at length, and strongly in favour. One one side there was the argument advanced by one alderman which represented the strict free-market approach to the problem, contending that

> there was a broad distinction to be drawn between the supply of water to a town
> and administering the ordinary duties of a town council, such as sewerage, police
> matters, lighting and paving, etc. A parallel had been attempted between the
> water supply and the sewerage; but there was this wide distinction – that the idea
> of profit had never been entertained as derivable from the construction of town
> sewers.[49]

In other words, the role of government was to perform only those functions which, while necessary, fell outside the ambit of private enterprise because of the absence of a profit motive. On the other side were ranged arguments which aimed to prove that 'town council was the proper body to manage the supply of water and that no principle of trade would be violated by their management of such works'.[50] The report considered the four choices which were available for the provision of a new supply of water. In the first place, the existing company could undertake the necessary capital investment; secondly, the council could seek independent authority to create another company; thirdly, private enterprise could be left to establish a new company to exploit new sources of supply; or finally, the council could take over the present works and carry out the necessary new investment itself.

The council could hardly apply to parliament for permission to form a new company when it had a substantial share in the management of the present one, and the creation of a second private company was undesirable. Resources would be duplicated and the result would probably be not competition, to benefit the consumer, but collusion between the companies to protect profits. The report here drew upon the experience provided by the operation of water companies in London, but no doubt the behaviour of the two Leeds gas companies provided a more immediate basis for judgment. If this argument were accepted, it implied that there should be only one company supplying water and the question then resolved itself into a choice between public and private ownership. The report preferred the former on two counts: the council could borrow more cheaply than a private company, lowering the cost of investment and hence the cost to the consumer and moreover it could be argued that 'if there must be a monopoly, and no doubt there

Figure 2. The Roundhay Park Estate, 1871 (by courtesy of Leeds City Libraries).

must, let it be placed in the hands of the government, or some public body responsible to the consumers'.[51] Public welfare also was an important consideration, since as alderman Hope Shaw, the advocate of municipalization, observed:

> tastes and habits of cleanliness in houses and persons did not grow up in men's minds, but must be created, fostered and encouraged, as most essential in a sanitary and moral point of view. Striking proofs had been given in official documents of the evils arising from want of water. Cholera had been traced directly to the want of good water in the dwellings of the poor. Well, then, was it not the duty of the municipal body to look to the welfare of the people they represented?[52]

His advocacy prevailed and in November 1852 the council purchased the company for £227,417.

The mere transfer of ownership did not, however, solve the problem of how the much-needed additional water supplies were to be secured. Two rival schemes were canvassed, Leather's proposal for the Washburn, involving extensive reservoir building was supported by J.F. Bateman, the waterworks engineer to Manchester corporation, Charles Tilney the borough surveyor, and Hope Shaw on the waterworks committee. The alternative scheme simply involved pumping more water from the river Wharfe. The financial aspects of both figured prominently in the council debate. The issue was complicated by technical considerations: pumping ensured that supply could be regulated according to demand, whereas the gravitational schemes adopted by Manchester, Bolton, Sheffield, Derby and Nottingham, for example failed to produce an ample supply of water at all seasons. Furthermore, there was some disagreement over the adequacy of the volume of water channelled by the Washburn to meet the demands of Leeds. The fundamental question however was financial. The report presented to the council calculated that an extension of pumping from the Wharfe would maintain the waterwork's profits, whereas the gravitational scheme, because of the cost of land purchases and reservoir building, would lead to considerable losses for at least the first decade of its operation. Hope Shaw protested against this myopic policy, maintaining that the growth of towns in Wharfedale would create pollution problems, and that the cost of pumping from the Wharfe would rise at a far greater rate than gravitational supply as future demand increased. The council chose the cheaper scheme, and in 1856 obtained an Act to allow it to take 2.5 million gallons a day from the river and a further act in 1862 to increase this to six million gallons daily.

By this time Hope Shaw's unheeded predictions were proving correct. Supply was insufficient for long-term requirements and there was growing concern over its purity. The solution the council was forced to adopt was essentially the same as that proposed ten years before. The borough surveyor advised the impounding of water from the Washburn and this was adopted as municipal policy in the Leeds Waterworks Act of 1867. The project was undertaken in three stages. The Lindley Wood reservoir with a capacity of 750 million gallons was constructed between 1869 and 1875, the Swinsty reservoir, to hold 960 million gallons was begun in 1871 and completed in 1877, and the Fewston reservoir, of 870 million gallons was built between 1874 and 1879. The overall cost was £508,173 which represented half the total sum, £1.18 million, which the council spent on the waterworks in the first 25 years of municipal ownership. In addition, the council obtained powers in the 1877 Improvement Act to enlarge Eccup reservoir to hold 1,400 million gallons representing half a year's consumption and sufficient to ensure an adequate supply under all conditions.

Even though the population of the Washburn Valley was small – 2,027 in 1861 – and declining, there was some fear that it could cause significant polution, and finally in 1896 the committee proposed that the council should follow the example of other major towns and purchase all the land in the area of the watershed. This provision was included in the local Act of 1897, and extensive areas of land were bought up in the following years. The Leeds Corporation Water Act of 1901 authorized the council to begin a second phase of reservoir-building which had become necessary because of the continued growth of the city's population and in its consumption of water. The Act sanctioned the purchase of land in the North Riding for the construction of the Leighton, Carlsmoor, Colsterdale and Laverton reservoirs, and ten years later expenditure on this major project had reached £846,000.

After the abandonment of the proposal to purchase the gas companies in 1851, it was not until 1868 that the purchase was mooted again, and this time with positive results. There were three arguments in favour of buying out the shareholders. By superseding the surveyors of the highways and the turnpike trusts in the borough, the council by the late 1860s was establishing an absolute control over the highways and in one respect the merging of the two companies under municipal ownership was an extension of this policy since 'there would not be that breaking up of the roads and streets which now prevailed for the purpose of laying pipes first by one company and then by another'.[53] Financial considerations also played a part: the prospect of being able 'to supply cheap gas and realise at the same time a handsome revenue'[54] was as attractive in the late 1860s as it had been 20 years previously. Although the price per 1,000 cubic feet had over that period fallen from 5s. to 3s. 6d., it was believed that the price might be reduced still further. Thirdly, it could not be said that the unification of the gas supply under public ownership would offend against economic orthodoxy by supplanting the benefits of competition for 'there was virtually no competition between the gas companies at present, nor had there been since the new company had obtained for itself a firm footing in Leeds. Those who were connected with the lamp committee would know very well that the prices charged by one company was exactly what was charged by the other; in fact the two companies seemed to have an understanding as to what they would charge all around the town'.[55] Negotiations were completed in late 1869, and ratified by an Act obtained in the following year. The transaction cost the council £263,245 which represented a very generous deal for the shareholders. Much of the plant acquired was obsolescent. At the Meadow Lane works the condition of the retorts, engine house, boilers and purifiers filled the council's inspector with gloom. The New Wortley plant, built by the Gas Light Company in 1857 was extensively rebuilt over the years 1871 to 1884, and the York Street gasworks, which possessed gasholders built in 1818 had undergone almost complete reconstruction by the 1880s. Nevertheless, except in 1873 and 1874 when exceptionally high coal prices caused considerable losses, the new municipal utility was financially sound. Indeed by 1877 the deficit of £27,509 of the 'coal famine' years had been liquidated, and the price of gas was progressively reduced, until in 1881 it had reached 1s. 10d. By that time the consumers were becoming concerned not over the price but over the quality of the product: 'the gas supplied though undoubtedly cheap, has been decidedly nasty',[56] remarked the *Leeds Mercury*, a judgment in which others concurred. The twin problems of purity and illuminative strength were the direct result of the gas committee's new policy. When in 1885 the committee asked their harassed engineer to explain why the yield of gas per ton of coal was low in Leeds compared to other towns, he pointed out that the committee chose coal giving high yields of tar and ammonia but which had 'almost contemptible' gas-making qualities. Given the cheap gas policy, however, the choice of coal was a logical one, since the by-products from a given weight of coal produced more income than the gas obtained from it. We can see here an obvious parallel between the council's approval of cheap, but poor quality gas in the later 1870s and 1880s, and its decision to opt for a cheap but inferior water supply in the 1850s.

Two of the motives which influenced the council's decision to purchase the gas companies – the need for undivided control over the highways and public ownership of renumerative utilities – also appeared in the initial discussions over the introduction of tramways. Discussion was stimulated by the news which the council received in October 1869 that a private company intended to promote an act to enable it to operate tramways in Leeds. The council decided to oppose the application to parliament, and to promote a bill on its own account if it was found to have public support. The arguments in favour of this course of action were compendiously expressed by alderman George, who maintained that

> if there was a great benefit derived from laying down tramways, and if there was to be great profit derived from tolls for the passage of carriages, the inhabitants of Leeds ought to have the benefit. The corporation had spent £60,000 in the purchase of the tolls, and had expended a good deal of money in the improvement of the streets; they were at present asking parliament for powers to take over the gas companies, so that the streets might be under no control but their own, and it would be hardly consistent to allow the promoters of these tramways to assume the powers over the highways which they wanted.[57]

Further action, however, was forestalled by the government's Tramway Act, 1870. This gave local authorities powers to construct tramways and lease the right to operate them, or to approve a private company's plans to build and run a tramway. But it expressly forbade any local authority to provide the service itself, although the track and rolling stock could be purchased from the private operators after 21 years. In November 1870 the council voted to support a private application to construct and manage a service in the town. No reason for this change of heart was made explicit, and a plea for municipal ownership by one councillor went unanswered. After initial difficulties, a limited company was incorporated in 1872.

In the early 1890s, as the 21-year veto on municipal ownership was coming to an end, a familiar problem drew the attention of the council to the company's activities. The culprit was 'that most objectionable of urban complaints – the steam tram',[58] which, introduced on lines designed to carry the lighter horse-drawn vehicles, was making road surfaces hazardous. Despite repeated admonition the company did nothing to improve the 'shameful state of repair' of its permanent way, and in late 1892 the council finally decided that it had no option but to exercise its right of purchase. After arbitration the council paid £112,226 to the company and came into formal possession in February 1894. The highways committee created a sub-committee to manage the undertaking temporarily, for at this time the council certainly had no intention of doing so on a permanent basis. Nevertheless, in November 1894 the council decided to apply for an Act to allow it to operate the tramways, but in the debate it was stressed that this was simply a permissive measure and did not imply a conversion to the idea of public ownership. In the event, however, it proved impossible to find a suitable leasee, and the council was obliged, unwillingly, to move from provisional to permanent management. To commuters, municipalization meant a progressive reduction in fares – by about 60 per cent over the first decade of public ownership – made possible by the cheaper operating costs which came with electrification. Lower fares led to more passengers. In 1895 10.5 million were carried, and by 1914 the number had risen to 93.7 million. Nevertheless, the tramways still catered for the suburbanite rather than the working man. It was only towards the end of our period that fare concessions were introduced which noticably increased the proportion of workmen in the tramways' clientèle, despite the city engineer, in 1895, drawing the council's attention to 'the sanitary or health aspect of the question, the enabling the artisan to live in more airy surroundings than he does at present'.[59] Workmen's cars were run every morning up to 7.45 a.m., but workers returning home in the evening had to pay the same fare as other passengers. Transfer ticket facilities were also restricted, and it was not until 1911 when more generous terms were introduced, that the percentage of workers using the trams showed a marked increase. Even so, only slightly more than 7 per cent of passengers were availing themselves of workmen's fares in 1914.

Electrification had first appeared in Leeds in 1890 when the council made an agreement with the Thomson-Houston International Electric Company to run electric cars on a corporation-built line from Sheepscar to Roundhay. Once the council had bought out the tramway company, electric traction was introduced onto other routes. Leeds had been the first town in the country to possess an electric tramway when the Roundhay line was opened in 1890, and 20 years later, in June 1911, the city was the first to operate trackless electric cars, or 'trolley buses' as they became known.

By 1914 the 22 miles of tramway track the council had acquired in 1894 had become 114 miles and capital expenditure had reached £1.5 million. The financial return was unmistakably healthy, for the net surplus of under £5,000 had grown into £70,000 by 1914. Apart from its record on workmen's fares, municipal trams in Leeds were an unquestionable success, essentially because the opportunities offered by electric power were recognized and fully exploited. But in contrast, the council was far more hesitant in its attitude towards the potential of electricity as a source of lighting.

During the early 1880s there was a national boom in the promotion of electric lighting companies, and in August 1882 the council was asked to support a private application to the Board of Trade to obtain a provisional order under the Electric Lighting Act, 1882 to authorize a firm to begin business in Leeds. A committee set up to consider the matter reported that there were eight applicants in all with hopes of supplying electricity in Leeds, and suggested that the council should seek a provisional order itself. In May 1883, the electric lighting committee was allowed by the council to begin experimental lighting. Six years later, it felt sufficiently confident to recommend to the council that it should be allowed to obtain plant and equipment to light town centre properties as a beginning. The committee urged the council to retain control over 'what may prove eventually a very important business'.[60] It reiterated the argument that no other body should be allowed to interfere with the streets and contended that consumers would benefit from a municipal supply, since it would be about half the price which would be charged by a private firm. The report, presented in July 1889, was firmly rejected. The venture was regarded as highly speculative, and one speaker, doubtless voicing the opinions of many council members, pithily remarked that 'they need not have any fear that the town would not be provided with electric light. As certain as the summer brought them new potatoes, there would be fools who would invest their money in electric lighting'.[61]

The committee reported again in the following year, but failed to move the council from its earlier scepticism, and in April 1891 the council gave its assent to a Board of Trade order in favour of the Yorkshire House-to-House Electricity Company. To the *Leeds Mercury* the council's decisions were deplorable, and tantamount to 'declaring itself incompetent to take upon itself an essentially municipal responsibility'.[62] It is true that in the 1880s development of electric lighting was indeed uncertain in both commercial and technological terms. But as far as technology was concerned, the committee seems to have taken a perverse pride in neglecting to make use of professional advice, in a situation where it was very much needed, in order to keep its costs to a minimum. In its first report it informed the council that it was 'buying the engines, dynamos, and other materials in the open market, and employing ordinary workmen on the installations, thus avoiding not only excessive trade profits on the material, but all profit on the labour, as well as high professional charges'.[63] At the very same time, a leading professional journal, putting a different gloss on the committee's claim, dryly expressed the hope that 'the forthcoming installation . . . may give as much satisfaction to the inhabitants, in a practical sense, as the confidence which the committee have in their own ability, without the aid of professional assistance, to carry out the same successfully, does to that body. Something must have been learned in six years'.[64]

Indeed, as events proved the council had taken a short-sighted attitude, and in 1897 the question of public ownership was re-opened. The speculative element which had created wariness eight years before had disappeared, and an old complaint was raised when one councillor observed that 'no-one . . . could have observed the state of the public thoroughfares along which the House-to-House company had recently laid wires without feeling that the entire control of the streets should be vested in the corporation'.[65]

The council paid dearly for its earlier lack of nerve. Under the terms of the Board of Trade order of 1891, if the council purchased the company before ten years had elapsed, substantial compensation was to be paid in addition to the value of the capital assets. The capital value of the works in 1898 was estimated as £154,409, but the price paid was £217,420, or 40 per cent more. In the following years the scale of operations expanded rapidly. By April 1914 capital expenditure had reached just over one million pounds and the number of consumers had risen from 980 to 12,900, or slightly less than two per cent of total population, which was about average for the early twentieth century.

Along with its utility companies the council acquired an accompanying labour force, of which the gas and tramway workers were the most numerous, so that by the end of the century the council had become an employer on a large scale. Its unhappy experiences in industrial relations, witnessed most dramatically in the major strikes of 1890 and 1913, have already received detailed analysis, and so need not be considered here.[66] A closely-related aspect of municipal activity, the involvement of the council in schemes for the unemployed is, however, a less familiar subject.

In the last decades of the nineteenth century, unemployment was beginning to be recognized as an important social issue, and Leeds corporation, like many other local authorities, became involved in schemes designed to alleviate the problem. In a national context, the 'Chamberlain circular' issued from the Local Government Board in 1886 has often been interpreted as a significant advance in the recognition of the need to make some public provision for the unemployed which was distinct from that offered by the poor law. The importance of the circular has, however, recently been contested, and it would certainly appear to have had no influence on the pattern of events in Leeds.

The council first participated in a large-scale unemployment relief scheme eight years before the circular was issued. The project began as a voluntarily-organized 'distress committee' with a relief fund of £5,717 to distribute in the winter of 1878–9. Grants from the fund were made only after the applicants' circumstances had been thoroughly investigated by a visitor from the ward committee, who was usually a member of the Benevolent Society or the Charity Organisation Society. Certain candidates were automatically ineligible, as in cases where the family income exceeded 10s. a week, where distress was caused by 'extravagance or intemperance', or the individual classed as 'unworthy', where distress was not 'temporary' but 'chronic', or where poor relief was being received. Despite disagreement on the committee it was decided to enforce this last proviso, since although on one hand it seemed unfair that 'persons obtaining a miserable pittance by test work should be refused relief, while others received it on condition as it seemed of remaining idle . . . it seemed . . . that every effort should be made to keep respectable persons from resorting to poor law aid, and so making themselves paupers'.[67] By February 1879 the committee had decided to try to introduce relief work as a condition of assistance, since the ward organizations had collapsed under the strain of their vetting activities. It approached the corporate property and sewerage committees of the council for help, and these agreed to find employment for those referred to them while the relief payments remained the responsibility of the distress committee. This arrangement lasted until the end of March when, with the voluntary funds nearly exhausted and the unemployment situation still urgent, the council agreed to take on the financial obligation also, leaving the distress committee still in charge of the administration. The scheme continued until the end of June, by which time between 700 and 1,000 men had been employed. They had received credit notes for 1s. 6d. for each five-hour shift worked, with no-one being allowed to work more than three shifts in a week. By the late 1870s, then, it was already locally agreed that the poor law was an inappropriate, and indeed degrading method of dealing with 'respectable persons' who temporarily found themselves without a livelihood. To this end it was necessary to ensure that relief funds were directed solely towards this group, and hence the committee employed the members and the methods of the Charity Organisation Society with the implicit assumption that the problem of unemployment was to be treated merely as an aspect of voluntary charitable work, and within the context of current economic, social, and moral orthodoxies. The transfer of the project from private to public

responsibility did not, of course, change the criteria: the *Leeds Mercury* emphasized that 'so long as the council only pays for the work actually done, there is no
violation of sound economic principles; and so long as work is not created, there is
no danger of the theories of socialism being reduced to practice'.[68] Privately-
mobilized funds had been shown to be insufficient to cope with the alleviation of
unemployment on a regular basis, and where the private sector failed, the initiative
then lay with the local authority. Thus some years before the issue of the LGB
circular the basic principle of the organization of relief schemes had been
established in Leeds. The municipal authority was the only body capable of
providing a viable alternative to the poor law in the alleviation of a cause of poverty
for which the traditional agency was increasingly seen as inappropriate.

But in fact for more than a decade the council paid no further attention to the
issue. In the 1880s it was raised only once, when in November 1887 the council
received a memorial from an unidentifiable source asking it to provide work during
the winter months. In February of the following year it was reported that no action
had been taken. But early in the next decade municipal relief works in Leeds were
suddenly revived. In the winter of 1892-3 the Labour Department of the Board of
Trade reported that 'the most important relief works carried out by English local
authorities were undoubtedly those provided by the corporation of Leeds'.[69] In
November 1892 the council decided to allocate £10,000 to be spent upon relief
works, and a register of the unemployed was opened in the city engineer's office.
Applicants were questioned on their family and financial situation, and enquiries
were made of the applicant's last employer, but no further selection was attempted
and there was no systematic co-operation with the guardians or the voluntary
societies as there had been on the previous occasion. Between December 1892 and
March 1893, 1,874 men had registered. Of these, 771 were rejected as ineligible, or
withdrew their names and the remainder were employed in 'spade labour' at six of
the municipal parks. Each worked a nine-hour day for three days a week, for 11s.
3d. In addition men were employed by the scavenging and highways departments in
moving snow. In the following year, 1893-4, similar schemes were re-introduced. A
total of 2,486 men registered with the corporation of whom 1,665 were found work
of the same kind, and on the same conditions, as before. In the winter of 1894-5
only snow-clearing work was offered by the council, although this was supplemented by relief provided by a voluntarily-organized distress fund. It adopted
the procedure formulated by the committee of 1878-9, and like their predecessors
the ward committees found 'ample scope for the exercise of their charity, and also
of their discretion'.[70]

How is the re-emergence of municipal relief activity in Leeds in these years to be
explained? The Local Government Board circular of 1886 had produced no local
response, and although its re-issue in 1892 is mentioned as a contributory course in
the Board of Trade *Report*, we can assume that, taken in isolation, it had no
appreciable influence on the council. The importance of economic conditions alone
is also debatable. Although there are no local employment figures, national figures
provided by the trade unions which made monthly returns to the Board of Trade
show that unemployment was just as severe in the winter months of 1886-7, when
the council took no action, as in the winter of 1892-3, when it was busily promoting
relief works. If these were contestable influences on the actions of the council, it is
clear that working class pressure was of decisive importance. As the Board of Trade
Report observed: 'there were a few centres, such as Leeds . . ., where . . . the

'unemployed' agitation attracted a special amount of public attention. . . . A series of meetings were held in the Town Hall Square, demanding work, before the corporation undertook extensive relief works'.[71] Following the success of 'new unionism' in Leeds with the 1890 gas strike the new spirit of the Labour movement was obviously exerting itself in matters concerning the unemployed as well. The local trades council, which had ignored the 1890 strike, was now itself involved in the agitation for relief works, as were other groups, including the Independent Labour Party. The spirited organization of the unemployed, and vigorous tactics deployed grated on the sensibilities of the middle class. The mayor observed dismissively that 'the decision . . . not to allow the unemployed to assemble in the crypt of the town hall . . . provided the labour Leaders with another topic for the exercise of their oratory', and at a meeting of the distress committee 'fear was expressed by more than one speaker lest some intemperate language on the part of the unemployed might prejudice intending subscribers against the fund'.[72]

In April 1895 the council decided to appoint a committee to discuss with the trades council and the Independent Labour Party the best methods of dealing with future unemployment crises, and the chamber of commerce and the poor law guardians were invited to co-operate. An interim report in October recommended the establishment of a permanent register of the unemployed, and the council decided to do this. The attitude of the labour representatives was luke warm: it was felt that the value of a register was questionable, and it posed the threat of being a means of mobilizing non-union labour during strikes. The final report of the committee was not sympathetic to innovations in methods of unemployment relief. It assigned a minimal role to municipal participation and advocated reliance on the poor law in all but 'times of very exceptional trade depression'. This was very far removed from the policies of the trades council and the Independent Labour Party which were proposing the general introduction of the eight-hour day, the creation of a municipal direct works department, and a more efficient municipal relief scheme. Municipal relief works were not resumed until January 1902, and they followed the now familiar pattern: 3,758 men registered, of whom 1,625 were selected to work a three-day week for 11s. 3d.

Once the Unemployed Workmen Act, 1905 came into operation the council applied to the Local Government Board for an order to establish a 'distress committee' under the Act, the provisions of which enabled the committee to register and provide work for the unemployed, supported by the product of a $\frac{1}{2}$d. rate. The Act did little more than give a definite statutory sanction to informal practices which had already been evolved in Leeds and other towns, and the hope of the local Liberal press that 'the very limited powers granted by the grudging government measure . . . will doubtless be exercised to the full in Leeds',[73] was scarcely realized, for it made little difference to the management of the relief schemes. In the first year after the Act, 1906–7, work was found for about 40 per cent of those who applied, who were employed on afforestation work in the Washburn valley, the construction of filter beds at Headingley, laying out cricket pitches and bowling greens and building a bathing pool at Roundhay Park. Thereafter the distress committee were faced with two problems: the rising number of unemployed and the difficulty of finding suitable work for them which increased year by year. By 1908–9 the number of persons registered had reached 6,819 and work could only be found for under a third. This proportion remained constant as the worst of the trade cycle passed: only 532 out of 1,758 could be found work in

1911–12. The 1905 Act had formally brought in the poor law and charitable organizations into the running of the relief schemes. The Leeds committee consisted of 18 members of the council, 14 poor law guardians and eight others 'experienced in the relief of distress'. With them came, not surprisingly, a return to the full-blown procedures to ensure that only those 'of good character and deserving of assistance' were considered for relief work.

The preceding outline of the council's policies on public utilities and unemployment provides the basis for a brief consideration of the meaning of 'municipal socialism' in the context of the history of a major municipality. The term itself is a coinage of Sidney Webb,[74] and is a highly idiosyncratic one: in the company of his wife, he later claimed to have discovered at least one of the principles of communism exemplified in the establishment of isolation hospitals.[75] In the Webbian sense, socialism was defined (for the purposes of *Socialism in England*) as merely the gradual restriction of the rights of private property through taxation or state regulation. In a widely-quoted passage in this book, Webb described the 'unconscious permeation' of councillors by 'socialist' ideas and mocked the intellectual inconsistencies unconciously held by the shallow-minded 'Individualist Town Councillor'.

Webb's contention that there were no principles involved in the definition of relevant areas of municipal policy might indeed seem to be given support by the council's parliamentary committee. In May 1900 after discussing the implication of the recent appointment of a parliamentary joint select committee on municipal trading it decided that

> the principle heretofore followed by each case being decided by inquiry into the merits thereof in relation to the particular facts has worked to the public advantage, as attested by the results attained in the various matters undertaken by the municipalities, whether considered from the point of view of the consumer and user or that of the ratepayer, and that it is not desirable in the public interest that any hard and fast line of limit should be drawn, but that, on the contrary, the principle and practice which have worked well in the past should continue to be followed, and each particular question considered and decided on its merits.[76]

Yet in fact as far as the municipal purchase of public utilities was concerned, there were no inconsistencies in the council's position. On the evidence already presented it can be seen that the reasons for its incursions into the private sector were clearly-articulated and consistent ones. The 'benefits of fair competition' which the council hoped to secure by amending the Leeds Gas Company's bill in 1843 were not to be obtained through legislation, either for gas or for water companies. Experience showed that where there was no obvious monopoly, there was collusion rather than competition. The existence of a local monopoly of supply applied also in the case of tramways and electricity. Contemporary canons of economic orthodoxy were thus not offended by the transfer of these enterprises from the private to the public domain.

A second motive was that the operations of all four utilities impinged upon the councils statutory responsibilities for the highways. The importance of this prosaic motive ought not to be underrated: as table 6 shows, expenditure for this purpose was the second largest item of capital expenditure. Financial considerations were also a significant motive, but policy in Leeds differed from that pursued in many other towns, as will be seen later. It is ironic that at the very time that the concept of 'municipal socialism' was being popularized, the council was turning away from further municipal involvement in economic affairs. The enthusiasm which trade union and socialist groups showed for the municipalization of the tramways was sufficient to cause the council to hesitate; in its administration of relief schemes there was 'no danger of the theories of socialism being reduced to practice'; and the rejection of proposals to build the new reservoir complex by direct labour was influenced by a fear that 'those who advocated direct administration . . . regarded this as only a stepping stone to the abolition of the capitalist class'.[77] The refusal of the council to encroach upon private enterprise in housing, and the complications this created, is one of the themes of the following section.

6 Slum clearance

In January 1869 a sub-committee of the scavenging and nuisance committee visited Liverpool to examine sanitary conditions there, and came back impressed by the pioneering slum clearances which the corporation was undertaking under its local act of 1864. When in the following year the council promoted a new Improvement Bill, it included in it powers explicitly based on those in the Liverpool act to enable it to purchase and demolish property in 'any court or alley or any premises' which the medical officer certified as unhealthy. In this perspective, slum clearance was conceived solely as a problem of public health: the subcommittee's report of 1869 had specifically advocated demolition 'to admit a free circulation of air in the courts'.[78] This attitude was not uncommon, for street improvements and railway construction were often applauded for this very reason, as for example in Leeds in the late 1860s, when in reporting the new railway building going on in the east end, the press remarked that 'in opening up many of the slums in this district, the North Eastern Railway Company has proved a most effectual sanitary reformer. The works in connection with the new line to Marsh Lane have cut right through some of the dismal recesses where fever was bred and disseminated; destroying over-crowded courts by wholesale, and spreading the blessings of ventilation and light in all directions'.[79] Such a point of view ignored the fact, known to more discriminating observers, that although slums may be demolished, slum dwellers remain, and if no alternative accommodation was provided, the result was often to increase the overcrowding in nearby housing. It was, not unexpectedly, a poor law officer who, speaking of the very same railway scheme, and apprehensive of tougher regulations against cellar dwellings, told Dr Hunter that 'we are going to have a worse job than ever through the new railway, and if cellars are against the law you must send down 3,000 tents from London'.[80]

For the same reason, the council was informed, the sanitary committee 'had not pushed the extinction of cellar dwellings to the extent to which they might have pushed it, for the very simple reason that houses at such a rent as such poor persons could afford to pay were not available, and that therefore to turn those persons out of cellar dwellings at a greater rate than had been done would have simply been to turn them on to the streets without houses and without homes'.[81] The problems of the homeless were also exercising the board of guardians who in January 1876 urged the council to adopt the Artisans and Labourers Dwellings Act of the previous year since the 'great deficiency' of working class housing in the town was so severe as to force people to apply for entry to the workhouse. The prospect of municipal participation in the housing market had been raised once before by the passing of the Common Lodging Houses Act in 1850, to be condemned out of hand by the *Leeds Mercury*:

> we do not say that a municipal corporation . . . might not erect one or two model lodging houses if no-one else could be induced to undertake the experiment; but we would much rather they distributed widely the information which the General Board of Health offers them in proof that well-constructed and well-managed lodging houses will pay better than lodging houses of another description. As to their becoming builders to such an extent as to provide 'substitutes' for a large proportion of the existing lodging houses, we apprehend no body of ratepayers will ever permit such a use of their money . . . The true parties to provide houses for the poor, as well as for the rich, are private capitalists.[82]

When the question was reconsidered by the town clerk in 1876 on being asked by the council to provide a report on the question which the guardians had raised, the sovereignty of market forces was still acknowledged, but he justified his recommendation that the council should provide some form of accommodation by a more subtle argument than that produced by the *Leeds Mercury*. The role of the council, he claimed, was to cater for the needs of the 'very poor', that is, those earning less than 25s. to 30s. a week. Such people exerted no effective demand in the building industry because the rents they could afford to pay would yield too low a rate of return on capital to attract private investment. There would, therefore, be no conflict between public and private enterprise. But if there was no prospect of profit to attract speculative builders, the council would, because of the lower rate at which it could borrow, be able to obtain a reasonable return on such expenditure if low-rent property was built on cheap land on the outskirts of the town. The sanitary committee accepted these recommendations, and advised the council to obtain powers to achieve this object. The council agreed, and in the 1877 Improvement Act gained powers to build, directly or by contract, houses for leasing to 'the labouring classes'.

Very little came of the housing and slum clearance powers of the local acts of 1870 and 1877. The provisions of the 1870 Act were invoked in only three instances: in April 1871 the council approved a scheme to demolish 60 houses and 21 cellar dwellings with about 600 inhabitants in the east end; in October of the same year it approved plans to clear another small area nearby, this time consisting of 163 houses and 46 cellar dwellings, housing about 1,000; and finally in 1884 a yard in Holbeck with 24 cottages was condemned as unfit for human habitation. The housing provisions of the 1877 Act were never implemented. Of the £800,000 spent on slum clearance by 1914, only about £50,000 of it had been spent in the 25 years up to 1895. Expenditure in the 1870s and 1880s represented the cost of acquiring some 300 houses and cellar dwellings with a total population of perhaps 2,000. In complete contrast, the council schemes in the subsequent 20 years affected more than 13,000 people, the overwhelming majority of whom lived in the Quarry Hill area in the east end of the city. The Quarry Hill project cost more than £700,000, and in the same period the council spent a further £50,000 on other demolition or

Figure 3. The York Street and Quarry Hill Insanitary Areas, 1896 (by courtesy of Leeds City Libraries).

improvement schemes. A large proportion of the inhabitants of Quarry Hill seemed to fulfil exactly the criterion laid down by the town clerk in 1876 for defining the 'very poor'. In 1896, when the council was beginning the legal processes to purchase the property at Quarry Hill, the *Yorkshire Evening Post* observed: 'Slum property seems to be still popular, owing to the small rent. To-day, in consequence of the increased cost of land, labour and building material, and greater restrictions imposed by the authorities, a house cannot be erected which will yield a return to the owner if let at less than 2/6d. a week'.[83] At about this time, of 500 houses in one district of Quarry Hill, 41 per cent were let at under this sum, and 57 per cent of houses in the adjacent Marsh Lane area owned by the Leeds Industrial Dwellings Company let at rents which ranged from 9d. to 2s. 6d.

The immediate cause of the council's interest in the Quarry Hill area can be dated to 1890, when an outbreak of typhus fever occurred there. The epidemic lasted about three months and produced 46 cases altogether, and there were two main disturbing features about it. The first was the nature of the disease itself. As the medical officer of health observed in exculpating his colleagues in private practice from any charge of negligence in not alerting attention to the disease earlier, 'there seems to be a certain amount of difficulty on the part of many medical men in recognising typhus fever. This is not very much to be wondered at, considering how improved sanitary conditions have almost banished this disease from England'.[84] In the second place, all the victims lived in the north east ward, and as many as one third lived in Allison's Buildings, Quarry Hill. The medical officer reviewed the history of epidemics in this area since 1867 for the benefit of the sanitary committee, and concluded that 'infectious diseases are more or less habitually present' in the neighbourhood. Only two years before this, the streets and sewerage committee had actually visited Allison's Buildings and had advised the sanitary committee that demolishing the property would be a significant improvement, but no action had been taken. Dr Cameron, the medical officer now proposed that two intersecting streets should be driven through the northern part of Quarry Hill as 'to do so would enable you to destroy a considerable number of unwholesome dwellings. It would give more air to the streets around, and would do some little towards relieving this neighbourhood from the opprobrium of being a hotbed of fever'.[85] The sanitary committee however, was prepared to consider a more comprehensive project and instructed the medical officer to consider the whole of the Quarry Hill area 'with recommendations as to what property should be demolished for sanitary improvement'. At first, then, the committee hoped to make a series of minor clearances, as they had previously done under the terms of the local Act of 1870. Prolonged examination forced them to the conclusion that the whole area would have to be dealt with, and considering the sheer size of the area involved it is not surprising that it took the committee, and the council, some time to acclimatize to the scale of expenditure which would be involved. The ratepayers also needed reassurance and thus when in January 1892 the mayor broached the subject in public, he observed cautiously that 'the time might come, though he did not think that it would come just yet, when the corporation would see its way to apply for powers to purchase the insanitary property . . ., pull it down, and provide for the erection of habitations fit for people to live in. In doing this, however, it must not be forgotten that those who might enter upon the enterprise would require a fair return for money invested'.[86] As Professor Hennock has shown, slum clearance came to figure prominently in the intensifying inter-party rivalry in Leeds in the early 1890s, and no doubt the political motive helped to ensure that clearance plans would be carried into effect.[87] Another undoubted influence upon the council was the fact that the changes in the law of compensation contained in the Housing of the Working Classes Act, 1890, by making compulsory purchase less expensive, eased the acceptance of the financial implications of the Quarry Hill scheme.

The law of compensation, codified in the Lands Clauses Consolidation Act, 1845 allowed specifically authorized bodies to take property by compulsion, but in return ensured that the dispossessed owners were to receive the most favourable compensation terms. Whilst this practice might be legitimate where a commercial concern, such as a railway company, was involved it could not have any but an inhibiting effect upon any scheme where commercial criteria were inapplicable. For this reason the council had failed to adopt the Torrens Act of 1867 and the Cross Act of 1875. In a discussion on the former, one councillor observed that 'the value of property was to be arrived at under the Lands Clauses Consolidation Act. Everybody knew that that was a tedious and expensive process . . . corporations buying under it generally had to pay double the value of what they purchased'.[88] Similarly, on the subject of the 1875 Act, the town clerk wrote to the home secretary informing him that 'practically the present measure was valueless because of the enormous cost involved'.[89] The fact that the revision in the law effected by the 1890 act was of crucial importance in Leeds was attested many times at the hearings held at the various stages through which the council's scheme progressed before receiving parliamentary approval. The chairman of the sanitary committee declared that 'as to dealing with the properties . . . under the Lands Clauses Act, such a course would mean the 'killing' of the scheme on account of the enormous additional cost that would be entailed'.[90] The property owners who petitioned against the scheme also testified, by implication, in support of this and similar statements in claiming that their own properties should, for various reasons, be purchased under the terms of the 1845 rather than the 1890 Act.

It was decided to purchase the property in the Quarry Hill area in two stages, the first of which, approved by the council in October 1895, was known as the 'York Street insanitary area'. This was a 16½ acre district with a population of around 4,000. The Local Government Board agreed to the scheme, and the confirming act became law in August 1896. Four years later arrangements had been made to purchase all the properties involved. By the time all the negotiations were completed in June 1900, the council was pressing ahead with plans to acquire the far larger remaining area – 50 acres with a population of over 10,000 – originally certified by the medical officer in 1895. This scheme, the 'Quarry Hill insanitary area' received parliamentary approval in 1901, and purchasing began in the following year. In 1909 the engineer in charge of unhealthy areas calculated that £191,000 had been spent on property purchases in the York Street area, and £565,000 on the not quite completed purchases at Quarry Hill.

In allowing the council the right to acquire all these properties for slum clearance, the Local Government Board also stipulated, as the law required, that a certain proportion of the working-class residents of the district were to be rehoused. In approving the York Street scheme, the Board specified that the work of clearance was to proceed in four stages, and that after each some housing provision should be made before the next stage was begun. Similarly, the 1901 Act embodied provisions for phased rehousing. Two thousand inhabitants were to be catered for under the terms of the 1896 scheme, and 6,000 under those in the 1901 scheme. These conditions resurrected the problem which had been discussed in Leeds 20 years before, that is, the admissibility of municipal enterprise in the housing market. In 1897, the Board approved the plans of the council to build homes for 1,000 persons on the Ivy Lodge Estate which had been purchased in 1886 for recreation grounds. Each was to have a living room, scullery, cellar, pantry, two bedrooms, attic and outside w.c. It was then decided by the sub committee responsible for the slum clearance schemes that instead of the council providing this accommodation, the land would be sold to private builders who were to construct the houses to the standards laid down by the Board.

This decision generated a major debate on policy, which while rehearsing some long-standing arguments, contained some new elements. The supporters of municipal housing returned to the point of view put forward by the town clerk 20 years previously, contending that the council could provide low-rent housing for the poor through the advantage which it had over private builders in the borrowing of money at low rates of interest. A new feature of their case was the claim that housing was another service which could be added to an already lengthy list of municipal functions. As one proponent of municipal housing observed: 'some members might object to the corporation entering into what they considered the domain of private enterprise; but its possession of the gasworks, the waterworks, and many other works for the public benefit showed that it was already a great trading concern, and he could not see that it would enter into any new departure in building suitable dwellings for the people in question.' The Conservative chairman of the subcommittee replied that 'it was not the duty of the corporation to compete with private traders; they had no right to use public money for the purposes of such competition, even if it could be shown to produce a profit to the city'.[91] This argument could, however, no longer be countered, as it might have been in the 1870s, by the assertion that the council would provide houses only for the 'very poor', those whose incomes were too low to influence the speculative builder. A new factor had been introduced unwittingly into the debate by the Local Government Board. The standards which it set for the housing to replace the slums was such that, unsubsidized, it could not be let for under 5s. 6d. a week, a sum twice as high as many in the clearance areas were paying. As a result, municipal housing would not be able to cater for the poorest, and could not now avoid entering the preserve of the private builder. It was presumably with these difficulties in mind that in November 1898 the council approached the Board to try to persuade it to allow back-to-back houses to be built in the York Street area when cleared; predictably the Board refused to agree. Some cheaper accommodation became available when in 1900 the council sanctioned the building, again by private enterprise, of a tenement block of two and three-room flats to house 198 people. But it never adopted part III of the 1890 Act, which would have allowed it to build working-class lodging houses. The hardship which this attitude undoubtedly inflicted on the residents of the insanitary areas – the press claimed that the Ivy Lodge estate 'did not provide for a single person displaced by the clearance'[92] – was mitigated by the council's lack of enthusiasm for wholesale clearance. In 1902, the chairman of the sanitary committee made it clear that the schemes would take 25 or 30 years to complete, and whilst demolishing the worst property the committee was also rehabilitating houses 'not required for immediate demolition', a policy which yielded around £20,000 a year in rents. By the end of the period, on the basis of the number of residents displaced, about two-thirds of the York Street area and only one quarter of Quarry Hill had been cleared to make way for a wide street which was to be driven through the centre of the area. Municipal determination to avoid becoming involved in house-building, which would have entailed the equally unwelcome alternatives of subsidizing the rents of one group in the community or of offering houses at an economic rent, so competing with the private builder, and the absence of a viable alternative policy, ensured that the major slum areas of the east end of Leeds survived into the inter-war years.

7 Financing municipal government

The remarkable development in the role of the corporation over the 80 years between 1835 and 1914 surveyed in the preceding sections of this chapter had, not unexpectedly, unmistakable financial implications. The most obvious implication for the ratepayers can be seen in table 8. Several different types of rate were levied in this period, and something must be said of these to make the table comprehensible. Under the Municipal Corporations Act, the council was empowered to levy a 'borough rate' to meet the cost of the obligations the Act imposed, the most important of which was the maintenance of the police force. The acquisition of the powers of the 1842 Improvement Act gave the council the right to make two additional assessments, the improvement rate, levied on each township separately according to the cost of the services provided for each, and the lamp rate. The local Act of 1848 enabled the council to impose a 'main sewer rate' on any area which it designated a drainage district, served by the main sewerage system. The first such district, declared almost immediately, was that comprising the townships of Leeds, Hunslet and Holbeck. With the exception of the small district of St John's, New Wortley in 1866, no further drainage districts were created, and when the sewerage system was extended in the post-injunction period, the cost was recouped from the townships' improvement rates. The fifth and last rate to be added to the list was the highway rate, when, as a result of the local act of 1866, the functions of the highway surveyors in all the townships were transferred to the corporation. Up to 1893, the council, therefore, made 16 separate rate assessments every year: the borough, lamp and highway rates, of a uniform amount throughout the borough, two separate main sewer rates, and an improvement rate for each of the 11 townships. However, in the local Act obtained in that year, the council, with the aim of equalizing the cost of municipal government between the townships and rationalizing the rating provisions, received the authority to amalgamate the improvement, main sewer, and lamp rates and thereafter a single assessment for these purposes – the 'consolidated rate' – was made for the borough as a whole.

Major increases in the borough rate took place in the 1860s and 1880s. In the 1840s and 1850s the rate hovered around an average of 6d., but in the next decade it more than doubled, then remained at its new level in the 1870s, and then almost doubling in the 1880s. These developments were brought about by two major items of legislation. The County and Borough Police Act of 1856 was responsible for altering the pattern of policing in Leeds. Up to that date, only Leeds township, and parts of Hunslet, Holbeck, Wortley and Potternewton had been patrolled. The Act offered a substantial subsidy to local authorities to meet the cost of policing, but on the condition that the Home Office inspectors certified a force as efficient. In order to qualify for the grant, Leeds corporation was obliged to police the entire

Table 8   *Rates levied in the borough of Leeds, 1850–1914 (decadal averages in old pence)*

years	improvement and main sewer rates				lamp rate	highway rate	consolidated rate	borough rate
	Leeds	Hunslet	Holbeck	others				
1850–9	10.3	8.4	8.2	0.9	5.3			5.7
1860–9	18.6	12.8	18.0	1.8	4.5	16.6		12.2
1870–9	28.6	19.6	26.3	8.7	4.5	12.4		11.7
1880–9	26.8	19.8	25.3	21.2	2.9	10.0		21.8
1890–3	30.3	22.5	28.8	26.2	4.0			
1894–9							35.3	
1890–9						9.0		25.3
1900–9						8.4	51.3	20.4
1910–14						10.5	50.7	26.4

borough, which entailed a considerable increase in the size of the force. The Education Act, 1870, was the cause of the increase in the poundage from the 1880s. The school board obtained its funds by a precept on the borough rate and, to the chagrin of many councillors, the amount of the precept increased rapidly. In 1875 it was £13,000, by 1880, £49,000, and by 1896 it had reached £81,500.

By this time, the size of the borough rate had been eclipsed by that of the improvement rate and its associated levies. In Leeds, Hunslet, and Holbeck, where urban development was most advanced, this had already taken place by the 1850s. At first the main sewer rate was the largest of these, exactly equal, on average, to the borough rate in the 1850s, but it was soon outpaced by the growth of the improvement rate. In Leeds township, the improvement rate more than doubled in the 1860s compared to the decade before, and in the 1870s, as the main sewer rate declined, it doubled again. After only a fractional increase in the 1880s, the rising trend resumed in the next decade. The impact which an extension of 'improvement act' services, particularly sewerage, had upon poundages in the outer townships from the 1880s is unmistakable. In this perspective, we can see that implementing the provisions of the Leeds Improvement Acts entailed a commitment to hitherto unexperienced levels of local government expenditure. This commitment, however, was not, in many quarters, readily or graciously given.

The group most actively antagonistic to proposals of increased expenditure was the shopocracy. There is much evidence, largely impressionistic but persuasive, that the electorate contained a highly-influential body of small shopkeepers whose political vigilance was particularly directed towards maintaining economy in local government. Robert Baker, the local pioneer of sanitary reform, was an early, and conspicuous, victim of their influence. After four years as chairman of the streets and sewerage committee he stood down from the council, and in 1847 the secretary of the south ward sanitary association threw some light on the reason for the termination of his municipal career when he recalled that 'Mr. Baker was turned out of the representation of the south ward because he wanted to spend £20,000 in making a sewer to drain the ward. The shopkeepers now saw the matter in a different light'.[93] Two years later, in the course of one of the debates over the sewerage question, one councillor presented a memorial from electors in the Kirkgate ward, expressing satisfaction at the recent decision to postpone the letting of contracts: significantly the petitioners were 'mostly shopkeepers'. Similar instances could be quoted from many debates in subsequent decades. In 1879, for example, during a debate on officers' salaries, a proposed increase was opposed by one councillor who claimed to speak 'for a class he represented, the shopkeepers of the town, who felt that if ever there was a time that pressed upon them it was the present,' and by another who 'sympathised with the shopkeepers, who could scarcely make ends meet'.[94]

Several reasons combined to make the shopocracy a significant political factor. Many were particularly susceptible to the effects of economic fluctuations as this affected the purchasing power of their customers. As Robert Baker himself observed in a different context: 'few persons know better than the grocers and tea dealers of the town how general trade is moving; the demand for the luxuries of life is a correct barometer of the means within the power of consumers'.[95] The rise of an expenditure-conscious group in local politics was by no means unique to Leeds. Professor Hennock has shown it to be characteristic of other local authorities once the electorate had its first experience of the cost of improvement.[96] However, perhaps in Leeds this factor assumed an exaggerated importance brought about by the vagaries of the law on municipal franchise. The Act of 1835 gave the municipal franchise to all inhabitants who were rate-payers of three years standing, but in practice the possession of a municipal vote was complicated by the existence of local customs relating to the compounding of rates. The uncertainty of the law on this question, and differing local interpretations of the law, created anomalies. In the case of a leasehold where the tenant paid his rates direct, there was no doubt about his entitlement to vote. But a difference of opinion arose when rates were paid by the landlord, particularly where there was compounding, that is, when the rating authority allowed a landlord a rebate upon his rate payments in return for collecting one sum from him rather than many small sums from his tenants. Appropriately, it was Edward Baines senior of Leeds who, according to his son, had proposed an amendment to the 1835 Act which would have ensured compounders of the right to vote. Baines junior then went on to observe that 'by this practice of compounding, many thousands of small occupiers lose their municipal votes; and to such an extent does this prevail in Manchester, that the municipal electors of that city are fewer in number than the parliamentary electors, though in Leeds the former are more than double the number of the latter'.[97] The Leeds municipal electorate appears to have been unusually large and, in containing a relatively high proportion of poorer voters, was particularly sensitive to increases in local government expenditure. The implication which this had for municipal policy-making hardly needs stressing. As the mayor observed during the public debate on the excessive local mortality rate in 1865, 'they needed a public opinion to back them, for so long as the public were crying 'economy, economy' and upbraiding the council for spending money on what they deemed most advantageous, they made the council what they were . . . if public opinion had supported the council, they would not now have only one inspector, but three or four inspectors of nuisances'.[98] It is important also to remember that initially the ratepayers were liable for virtually the entire cost of local government. The corporation had none of the resources which some other boroughs possessed to cushion the impact of increased expenditure, and there was a 'great difference between Leeds and many other towns, such as London, Liverpool etc. where there were large incomes derived from borough and corporate property; but in Leeds the corporation possessed no property and had to levy upon the burgesses rates for the smallest improvements'.[99] Supplementary sources of finance, however, gradually became available. One of these was the income derived from the trading profits of the water, gas and electricity works and the tramways. The prospect of having such resources at its disposal to provide subsidies for municipal projects had, not surprisingly, been an attractive one to the council from a very early date. In the discussion over the purchase of the gas companies in the late 1840s the example of Manchester, where the gasworks profits had for a long time contributed to the commissioners' and then the council's revenues, was cited as a precedent. Part of the income of the waterworks was diverted into the borough fund, and in 1872 the town clerk could tell the Commons select committee that 'we have built the town hall out of the profits of the water within twelve years; or at least we have paid £120,000 to the credit of the borough fund out of the water'.[100] The municipalization of the gas supply in 1870 created a new source of income, and up to the late 1870s the council treated the two utilities as a source of income in the conventional manner. Municipal policy, however, abruptly changed after the improvement act of 1877 which contained detailed provisions for the financial management of the gasworks, and waterworks, and powers to fund the borough debt. Profit from the utilities was no longer diverted into the relief of the rates. In giving evidence before the select committee on the electric lighting bill in 1882, the town clerk, when asked if the council looked upon the gas profits 'as a means of improving the town', replied: 'the opinion which has been acted upon since 1877 has been, not to pay into the Borough Fund any profit, but to give to the man who consumes the gas within the borough the best possible gas at the cheapest possible price'.[101] From 1877 until they lost their majority on the council in 1895 the Liberals ran the utilities for the benefit of the consumer, and shunned cross-subsidization. The policy operated both ways, for the fear that unprofitable tramways would require subsidizing by the ratepayers inhibited the council from taking over the tramway company. The Conservatives in the late 1890s reversed this policy, and income from the utilities began to be paid into the borough fund again: the waterworks began to contribute in 1898, the gasworks and tramways in 1899, and the electricity works in 1901. The Liberals, consistent with their previous approach, opposed the practice, but when returned to office in 1904 decided to continue it, for to do otherwise would have entailed considerable rate increases.

In addition to rates and profits, grants-in-aid from central government became, by the end of the period, an important source of income. Government funds became available to subsidize municipal functions in 1856 when the County and Borough Police Act authorized the government to defray a quarter of the cost of the pay and clothing of efficient forces. Further financial aid came from central government in 1874 when the contribution to police finances was raised to one half, and the nationalization of the prisons three years later meant that the cost of maintaining the borough goal passed from the council to the Home Office. The Local Government Act, 1888 also increased the amount of nationally-raised taxation channelled into local funds, but as can be seen from table 9, by the later 1890s, government grants from all sources met less than 10 per cent of the cost of municipal government in Leeds. Indeed, the amount received in grants barely exceeded the council's income from market stall rents. The table clearly demonstrates, however, the change brought about by the Education Act of 1904, and the consequent transfer of the Board of Education grants from the defunct school

Table 9   City fund income from rates, grants and trading profits, 1895–1914 (five-year averages in £s; percentages take no account of other sources of income)

| period | rates | grants | | | profits from utilities |
		education	other	total	
1895–9	394,570 (86%)	6,684	28,665	35,349 (8%)	27,832 (6%)
1900–4	498,282 (82%)	7,268	30,499	37,767 (6%)	72,459 (12%)
1905–9	665,004 (67%)	185,015	26,521	211,536 (21%)	116,683 (12%)
1910–14	730,232 (68%)	210,726	34,453	245,179 (22%)	102,948 (10%)

board to the corporation: in percentage terms the importance of grants increased by more than three times, and in monetary terms by almost six times. The present-day structure of local government finance was beginning to emerge.

BIBLIOGRAPHY

The research depended heavily upon the records of the corporation currently held not in the District Archives Department but in the Civic Hall, Leeds; I am most grateful to the officers of Leeds corporation, as it was up to April 1974, for being allowed access to them over a long period. The principal record groups comprise the proceedings of the council from 1835, the report books (from 1842), the minutes of the committees and sub-committees, and the series of annual reports of committees which begins in 1879. Council proceedings were not printed until 1897, but the annual reports of committees were printed from the beginning. Annual abstracts of accounts appeared in print regularly from 1870, but apart from those for 1867, 1870–2, 1875 and 1877, the medical officer's annual reports appeared annually only from 1890. All these printed sources are held in the reference department of the Leeds headquarters of the Leeds District Libraries, as are copies of the major newspapers, the *Leeds Mercury* and the *Leeds Intelligencer*.

Volumes 263–5 of the Webb Local Government Collection, housed in the British Library of Economic and Political Science (at the London School of Economics), contain the research on Leeds corporation done by the Webbs and their research assistants around 1900 as part of their projected, but sadly unwritten, history of English local government since 1835. The letter books of the Local Government Board, containing correspondence between the Board and Leeds corporation from 1871 to 1896 are held at the Public Record Office (Kew office), call numbers MH 12/15244 to 15274. The House of Lords Record Office possesses the manuscript minutes of evidence occasioned by the local bills promoted by the corporation.

All secondary works which are directly relevant to the research have been mentioned in the notes. On municipal politics, in addition to the work of E.P. Hennock, there is D. Fraser, *Urban Politics in Victorian England* (1976). On public health issues there are articles by the council's first medical officer, M.K. Robinson, 'The sanitary improvement of Leeds', *Trans. National Assoc. for the Promotion of Social Science* (1871); J. Braithwaite, *An Enquiry into the Causes of the High Death Rate in Leeds* (1865); A.W.W. Morant. *Description of the Leeds Sewage Works, and of the Various Processes which have been tried for the Purification of Sewage* (1876) and J.B. Cohen, 'A record of the Leeds Smoke

Abatement Society', *J. Royal Sanitary Inst.*, xxvii (1906). On housing there is, G.F. Carter, 'Operation of the Housing of the Working Classes Act in Leeds', *J. Royal Sanitary Inst.*, xviii (1897) and an article with the same title in volume xxx (1909) of the same journal by W.T. Lancashire. Both Carter and Lancashire were employers of the corporation; a hostile view of municipal slum clearance, and a chronicle of the work of the Leeds Industrial Dwellings Company, by its secretary can be found in E. Wilson, 'The housing of the working classes'. *J. Society of Arts*, xlviii (1899–1900). A modern perspective on Quarry Hill and its redevelopment is provided by A. Ravetz, *Model Estate: Planned Housing at Quarry Hill, Leeds* (1974).

One aspect of municipal enterprise, in Leeds and several other towns, is discussed in G.C. Dickinson and C.J. Langley, 'The coming of cheap transport – a study of tramway fares on municipal systems in British provincial towns, 1900–14', *Transport History*, vi (1973).The present state of knowledge on the growth of Leeds is summarized in the collection of papers in *A History of Modern Leeds*, ed. D. Fraser (1980).

NOTES

1 Quoted in B. Keith-Lucas, *The English Local Government Franchise* (1952), 47.
2 J. Fletcher, 'Statistics of the municipal institutions of the English towns', *J. Statistical Soc.*, v (1842), 101.
3 First Report of the Commissioners appointed to Inquire into the Municipal Corporations in England and Wales . . . Part III, (Parl. Papers, 1835 [116.] XXVI, 1620). The whole of the report on Leeds occupies pp. 1617–24.
4 Annual Report of the Finance Committee, *Annual Reports of Committees, 1913–1914.*
5 For which see M.J. Cullen, *The Statistical Movement in Early Victorian Britain* (1975), 126–31; and M.W. Flinn, (ed.), *Report on the Sanitary Condition of the Labouring Population of Great Britain* (1965), 50–1.
6 F. Clifford, *The History of Private Bill Legislation,* I (1885), 493.
7 B. Keith-Lucas, 'Some influences affecting the development of sanitary legislation in England', *Economic History Rev.,* 2nd series, vi (1953–4), 296, and reiterated in his *English Local Government in the Nineteenth and Twentieth Centuries* (1977).
8 I.C. Taylor has discovered a similar chronology, and motivation, in Liverpool: see his 'The insanitary housing question and tenement dwellings in nineteenth century Liverpool' in *Multi-Storey Living,* ed. A. Sutcliffe (1974), 45–6.
9 See R. Lambert, *Sir John Simon 1816–1904, and English Social Administration* (1963), 434.
10 J. Vetch, *Report . . . on the Sewerage of Leeds, under the Improvement Act* (1843), 16.
11 J. Smith, 'Report on the condition of the town of Leeds', *Second Report of the Commissioners on the State of Large Towns*, ii (1845).
12 *Leeds Mercury* (hereafter cited as *LM*), 20 Jan. 1849.
13 Streets and Sewerage Committee minutes, 22 May 1857.
14 'Report by Dr. Henry Julian Hunter on circumstances endangering the public health of Leeds', *Eighth Report of the Medical Officer of the Privy Council* (1865), 233.
15 *LM*, 5 Dec. 1865.
16 J. Hole, *The Homes of the Working Classes, with Suggestions for Their Improvement* (1866), 129.
17 *LM*, 9 Feb. 1865.
18 Hole, *op. cit.,* 142.
19 *LM*, 2 Nov. 1839.
20 House of Lords Record Office, House of Commons Select Committee, Evidence 1866, vol. 24, 24 April, f. 51.

21 *Ibid.*, col. 24, 14 June fos. 97–8.
22 *LM*, 20 Nov. 1859.
23 Bye-laws as to New Streets and Buildings, etc. 1870, no. 8.
24 House of Commons Select Committee on Police and Sanitary Regulations. Leeds Corporation (Consolidation and Improvement) Bill, 20 April 1893, Qu. 1157.
25 *Parliamentary Debates*, 4th series, xcv (14 June 1901), col. 392.
26 PRO, MH 12/15247, item 11754/76 and subsequent correspondence and memoranda in this volume and in MH 12/15248.
27 Figure for 1844 from *LM*, 13 April 1844.
28 Sub Scavenging and Nuisance (Smoke) Committee minutes, 5 May 1865.
29 *Ibid.*, 27 Oct. 1858.
30 *LM*, 16 Sept. 1865.
31 House of Lords Record Office, Select Committee of the House of Commons, Evidence 1872, vol. 39, 25 April 1872, f. 44.
32 *Ibid.*, f. 52.
33 J.B. Cohen, 'A record of the Leeds Smoke Abatement Society', *J. Royal Sanitary Inst.* xxvii (1906), 71–3.
34 'Report of the Sanitary Committee' *Annual Reports of Committees, 1899–1900.*
35 Sanitary Committee minutes, 11 April 1881.
36 *Leeds City Hospitals: Seacroft and Killingbeck September 29 1904,* 17, (brochure produced for the official opening).
37 M.W. Flinn, Introduction, 7–8, to A.P. Stewart and E. Jenkins, *The Medical and Legal Aspects of Sanitary Reform* (1969).
38 *LM*, 30 Sept. 1871.
39 *Loc. cit.*
40 *LM*, 14 Oct. 1871.
41 *Loc. cit.*
42 *LM*, 2 April, 1 June 1861.
43 *LM*, 1 April 1870.
44 *LM*, 6 April 1893.
45 *LM*, 5 Sept. 1840.
46 *LM*, 8 Feb. 1840.
47 *LM*, 22 Oct. 1842.
48 *LM*, 26 Oct. 1850.
49 *LM*, 16 Aug. 1851.
50 *Loc. cit.*
51 *Loc. cit.*
52 *Loc. cit.*
53 *LM*, 2 Jan. 1868.
54 *LM*, 12 Aug. 1869.
55 *LM*, 2 Jan. 1868.
56 *LM*, 14 Aug. 1879.
57 *LM*, 10 Feb. 1870.
58 'Leeds electric tramways', *The Electrical Rev.*, xiv (1897), 275–9.
59 Report Book, Jan. 1895.
60 *Ibid*, July 1889.
61 *LM*, 4 July 1889.
62 *LM*, 7 Oct. 1890.
63 Report Book, July 1889.
64 *The Telegraphic J. and Electrical Rev.*, xxv (part 2), 19 July 1889, 71.
65 *LM*, 2 Sept. 1897.
66 See E.P. Hennock, *Fit and Proper Persons* (1973), 237–42; E.P. Thompson, 'Homage to Tom Maguire' in *Essays in Labour History*, ed. A. Briggs and J. Saville (1960), especially 299–301; J.E. Williams, 'The Leeds Corporation strike in 1913' in *Essays in*

Labour History 1886–1923, ed. A. Briggs and J. Saville (1971), 70–95, and
A. Greenwood, 'The Leeds municipal strike', *Economic J.*, xxiv (1914), 138–45.
67 *LM*, 1 Aug. 1879.
68 *LM*, 7 June 1879.
69 Board of Trade (Labour Department), *Report on the Agencies and Methods for Dealing with the Unemployed* (1893), 219.
70 *Second Report of the (Commons) Select Committee on Distress from Want of Employment* (1895), 44.
71 Board of Trade (Labour Department), *op. cit.*, 183.
72 *Report of the Central Committee, for the information of Subscribers to the Fund* (1895), 6.
73 *LM*, 20 Oct. 1905.
74 S. Webb, *Socialism in England* (1890).
75 S. and B. Webb, *A Constitution for a Socialist Commonwealth of Great Britain* (1920), 11–12.
76 'Report of the parliamentary committee' in *Annual Reports of Committees, 1899–1900.* See also the evidence of the town clerk, W.J. Jeeves to the Joint Select Committee, qu. 3036–3226.
77 *LM*, 2 Feb. 1905.
78 Scavenging and Nuisance Committee Minutes, 29 Jan. 1869.
79 *LM*, 9 Feb. 1869.
80 'Report by Dr. Henry Julian Hunter on the circumstances endangering the public health of Leeds', *Eighth Report of the Medical Officer of the Privy Council* (1865), 238.
81 *LM*, 16 Jan. 1877.
82 *LM*, 22 Nov. 1851.
83 *Yorkshire Evening Post,* 14 Jan. 1896.
84 Sanitary Committee Minutes, 6 May 1890.
85 *Loc. cit.*
86 *Yorkshire Post,* 15 Jan. 1892.
87 Hennock, *Fit and Proper Persons,* 254.
88 *LM*, 26 March 1867.
89 *LM*, 3 Jan. 1876.
90 *Yorkshire Post,* 20 March 1896.
91 *LM*, 2 Sept. 1897.
92 *Yorkshire Post,* 5 Sept. 1901.
93 *Leeds Intelligencer,* 1 May 1847.
94 *LM*, 2 Jan. 1879.
95 'Report upon the condition of the town of Leeds and of its inhabitants', *J.S.S.* ii, 422.
96 E.P. Hennock, 'Finance and politics in urban local government in England, 1835–1900' *Historical J.,* vi (1963).
97 *LM*, 7 April 1849.
98 *LM*, 3 Feb. 1865.
99 *LM*, 23 Nov. 1850.
100 House of Lords Record Office, Select Committee of the House of Commons, Evidence, 1872 vol. 39, 25 April 1872, f. 46.
101 Report of the Select Committee on the Electric Lighting Bill, 1882 (227.) X, qu. 817.

Municipal government in Bradford in the mid-nineteenth century

ADRIAN ELLIOTT

Municipal government in Bradford in the mid-nineteenth century

ADRIAN ELLIOTT

1 Introduction

The essay which follows is based upon 'The establishment of municipal government in Bradford, 1837–57', a doctoral thesis submitted to the University of Bradford in 1976. The major objectives of the research upon which this work was based were fourfold; firstly, to consider the circumstances which led to the granting of a charter of incorporation to Bradford in 1847, secondly to review the creation of local government administration, thirdly to examine the early activity of the new corporation and fourthly to investigate municipal politics in mid-century.

The Municipal Corporations Act passed by the Whig government in 1835 merely reformed corporations already in existence; it failed to provide a new form of government for towns such as Sheffield, Manchester or Bradford which were administered by institutions more suited to seventeenth-century villages than expanding industrial towns. Proposals to incorporate such places were often the cause of bitter political controversy. In Bradford, the social problems created by its extra-ordinary growth in the early nineteenth century were accompanied by a developing political conflict, particularly after 1832, when the town elected its first members of parliament.

An analysis of the party rivalry in the 1830s and 1840s was crucial to the early part of the research. It became clear that this conflict was fought out across a wide range of local institutions rather than merely at the time of parliamentary elections. Research revealed that the heightened political rivalries of the 1830s led to a climactic struggle in the next decade for control of the town's political life. The eventual Liberal victory in this conflict led to the incorporation of the borough and the election of the first town council.

The research continued by investigating the work of the new council and the somewhat limited areas open to it including public health and law and order. Apart from the setting up of the machinery of local government, aspects of municipal administration examined included the financing and expenditure of the corporation and its relationship with central government.

The final part of the research involved consideration of the political and social context of reformed local government and comprised sections on the wards, electorate and elections, and council members. It included a socio-economic analysis of the populations of the various municipal wards based upon a sample survey of households taken from the census of 1851. The voting habits of a number of occupational groups were also examined. Examination of council membership involved a detailed study of its social and political composition in this period.

The present work follows approximately the same pattern as the original thesis but contains major shifts in emphasis. The period under review has been extended slightly to 1860. In several areas municipal activity was only initiated with the passing of the Bradford Improvement Act of 1850 and so examination of the first decade of municipal government in Bradford should properly extend to 1860. The difference in length between this work and the original thesis has obviously necessitated much compression. Well over a quarter of the original work was devoted to the political conflict in Bradford which preceded incorporation as well as the social and economic conditions out of which this conflict grew. This section has been here drastically reduced as a result of the publication in 1979 of my article 'The incorporation of Bradford', in *Northern History*. Other material omitted from the present work includes the sections on the finances of the corporation and an analysis of contemporary voting habits which in the absence of municipal poll-books had to be based on voting in parliamentary elections.

The objectives of the present work although largely dictated by the original research have resulted in a fresh approach to the topic. Certainly the first chapter, albeit in abbreviated form, examines once more the political and social background to the incorporation of Bradford. But reconsideration of the evidence from the post-incorporation period has suggested that the first eight years of the corporation's existence were dominated by debates over the very nature of local government, i.e. what a municipal corporation was, rather than merely what it should do. Hence the council's endeavours over the Improvement Act of 1850 and its acquisition of the town waterworks four years later are here presented as questions of political principle rather than examples of local sanitary activity as had been the case in the original thesis. Such activity is here discussed in a separate chapter. The fourth chapter of this work seeks to analyse the relationship between central government and one local authority in the middle of the nineteenth century whilst the last three chapters will, it is hoped, help to set municipal activity in Bradford in a wider social and political context.

2 The incorporation of Bradford

The first half of the nineteenth century saw the population of Bradford increase eight-fold as the town grew from little more than a village to one of the largest textile centres in the world.[1] Economic growth, however, was accompanied by crises as the existing local government proved inadequate to deal with the severe social problems which had arisen from industrialization. Furthermore, the 1830s and 1840s witnessed growing political conflict in the town as liberal non-conformists sought to wrest control of local affairs from the tory-anglican establishment. Their eventual aim was the creation of a municipal corporation, although this was preceded by a campaign against the local church rate.

The government of Bradford prior to incorporation in 1847 was chaotic. Six separate bodies, whose rights and responsibilities were a cause of confusion even to contemporaries, exercised authority within the town. None of these bodies, which included the vestry, lord of the manor, magistracy, highway surveyors and after 1837, the poor law guardians, were equipped to deal with the disease and social disorder which were so rife by 1840. The major local authority was the Improvement Commission formed by a local act of 1803. The Commission's 58 members, who filled vacancies by co-option, were responsible for the cleansing, lighting and watching of the main streets. But the act applied only to what was, by 1840, little more than the town centre. The Commission's legal powers were, moreover, restricted and its members largely indifferent.

The population explosion in Bradford in the early nineteenth century was accompanied inevitably by crises in two areas in particular: public health and the preservation of order. Inadequate housing, sanitation, water supply, appalling atmospheric pollution and a particularly noxious canal all contributed to Bradford having the lowest life expectancy in Yorkshire,[2] and the fifth-highest infant mortality rate in the country.[3] There were two distinct aspects to the maintenance of order in the town. First there were the sporadic outbursts of mob violence, 'the propensity to riot'[4] such as the demonstrations against the new poor law in 1837,[5] and secondly the ever present round of drunken violence and petty thieving. Significantly, one of the first acts of the new council after incorporation in 1847 was to be the establishment of a police force.

But if the impetus for incorporation arose from the social consequences of industrialization, the campaign which brought it about was a political affair deriving from liberal antagonism towards irresponsible government in the years after the passing of the Reform Act. Nationally, of course, muncipal reform had been seen by provincial liberals as an essential sequel to the reform of parliament. It was inevitable that Bradford liberals would eventually seek the opportunity offered them by the Municipal Corporations Act.

Certainly the decade following the enfranchisement of Bradford in 1832 was the most dynamic period in the town's political history.[6] Four general elections and a by-election were contested, the town's first successful newspaper, the Liberal *Bradford Observer*, was founded and a number of political societies were formed, including the Reform Society (later amalgamated with the Radical Association as the United Reform Club), and the Operative Conservative Society, dedicated to ridding the town of its reputation as a 'hotbed of Whiggery and Socialism'.[7] Although largely pre-occupied with parliamentary politics, the political societies became increasingly involved in local issues. After 1837 the new office of poor law guardian was the focus of bitter party rivalry,[8] and by 1841 even such a minor office as constable of Horton (a Bradford township) was contested with such determination that carriages were hired to bring in voters from outlying districts.[9]

But the first truly local issue to arouse political controversy in Bradford was the Liberal Dissenter campaign against the compulsory payment of church rates which was to be closely linked with the attempts to set up a corporation. Bradfordians knew that whilst both issues were part of wider national questions they could be settled in the town to an extent to which corn tariffs and factory reform could not. A further similarity between the corporation question and church rates was that in both campaigns a vigorous Liberal party was attacking the Tory establishment.

Liberals frequently claimed that the consequences of reform would be the removal of unjustified privilege, first ecclesiastical and then secular, and certainly feeling against the Church of England, which led to the national controversy over church rates, ran deep.[10] The issue came to a head in Bradford in 1839 when the newly installed Vicar Dr William Scoresby presided over a stormy meeting of 3,000 ratepayers in the churchyard.[11] Despite a show of hands against the levying of a church rate that year, tory-anglican leaders demanded a poll. In the week which followed political activity in the town reached a frenzy as a Church Rates Abolition Society was founded by the same liberal-non-conformist industrialists who were to later lead the campaign for a charter of incorporation. Victory in the poll for the opponents of the rate was greeted by a jubilant *Bradford Observer*, 'in the dullest and darkest times what glorious events occasionally burst upon us to cheer and re-animate by their splendour.'[12] Two years later the churchwardens obtained a writ from the archbishop of York making the rate compulsory. When the wardens brought a test case against John Dale, a radical printer, for non-payment of rates, the liberal non-conformists retaliated by securing Dale's election as churchwarden.[13] Although the case against Dale was to drag on six years before he was ultimately successful, his election signalled the abandonment by Bradford anglicans of their attempts to levy church rates. The Tories were shortly to face attack on another front, however, as the Liberals encouraged by the experience of a successful political campaign were to challenge their domination of local government.

As early as 1839, William Byles, liberal editor of the *Bradford Observer* had stated that, 'it has long been clear to us that Bradford must soon apply to the Queen for a charter',[14] but it was 1843 before the campaign began in earnest. In March, the Vestry agreed to adopt a provision of the Highways Act of 1835 which allowed boards of surveyors to be elected in the larger towns.[15] The ensuing elections gave ten of the 13 places to the Liberals who were to use the board as a political arena in the campaign for incorporation. The Liberals also infiltrated the improvement commission. Although this body was not elected, Tory apathy allowed the Liberal entry. At the November meeting in 1843 only eight commissioners were present out of a total of 41 and seven of them were were Liberals.[16] The meeting co-opted 15 new members, 12 of whom were Liberals, including Joseph Farrar, a draper, who was to organize the campaign, Henry Brown, the town's second mayor, and William Byles of the *Observer*.

Within a week the commissioners had resolved to call a town meeting to discuss local government. The Liberals intended that this meeting should call for incorporation but they were defeated in this by the Tories, supported by Chartists, who saw incorporation, with some justification, as a means of making working-class ratepayers pay for the removal of environmental problems largely created by the Liberal industrialists themselves. But to the *Bradford Observer* the vote at the meeting against a charter was 'a declaration that the town shall remain as it is – exposed to the burglar, covered with dirt and wrapt in pestilential diseases'.[17]

The political struggle was to continue for three years. Both sides formed committees to propagate their views in handbills and placards and to canvass support for rival petitions to the Privy Council.[18] The *Bradford Observer* argued bitterly with its rival, the tory *Leeds Intelligencer*, over the merits of municipal reform. As in Manchester, in 1837, an alliance of Tories and Radicals emerged united in opposition to a police force and increased rates.[19] The Tories certainly fought a vigorous counter offensive, capturing control of the board of surveyors which had earlier petitioned the Privy Council in favour of a corporation and reasserting their influence in the improvement commission.

In January 1845, a number of petitions on incorporation were presented in London, including two from the ratepayers in general. The petition supporting incorporation had 8,715 signatures and the opposing one 10,716.[20] In August 1845, an indignant *Bradford Observer* announced that the Privy Council had rejected the petition for a charter of incorporation. As a matter of course the paper gloomily prognosticated 'bad will become worse',[21] but in fact the Tory victory was short lived. In July 1846, Peel resigned following the repeal of the corn laws and Russell took office at the head of a Liberal ministry. Bradford Liberals expected and received their small share of the spoils. After a hurriedly renewed campaign, Bradford's charter was granted at a Privy Council on 24 April 1847.

Analysis of the political affiliations of the improvement commissioners who signed the opposing petitions revealed, as all the contemporary evidence suggested, that divisions over municipal reform ran overwhelmingly on party lines. Twenty-two of the 26 commissioners who petitioned against incorporation were Tories and 27 of the 30 who supported it were Liberals. Samples taken from the two general petitions further indicated that the ordinary voters, as opposed to party activists, also saw the issue as a political one. The votes of over 200 enfranchised signatories of the pro-incorporation petition and those of 100 opponents were analysed as shown (table 10).

Table 10   Analysis of votes of pro-incorporation petition signatories and opponents (figures in percentages)

	Tory	Liberal	cross vote[22]
pro-incorporation	24	72	4
anti-incorporation	78	17	5

Even assuming that canvassers concentrated on known party supporters, these totals do suggest a remarkable degree of solidarity. It is evident that municipal reform was seen by most Bradfordians in the 1840s as a party issue. To support incorporation was to seek an increased share in local government for the Liberal party, not merely to demand action over disease and drunkenness. The Municipal Corporations Act under which Bradford was governed from 1847 was primarily a political, rather than a social or administrative, reform. A measure of democratic control over local government was achieved by household suffrage and annual elections and certainly the establishment of responsible municipal government in Bradford had, in itself, been a major aspiration of local reformers in the 1840s. The Act, however, had done little more than construct the machinery of local government: it gave the new corporations little to actually do, particularly amongst those social ills which in Bradford and elsewhere had provided that hard evidence of the need for change which had sustained the rhetoric of political reform.

This lack of direction on the administrative functions of the new corporations meant that the struggle over the government of Bradford was not to end with incorporation. Whereas until 1847 the question at issue was whether Bradford should have a municipal corporation, for at least seven years afterwards controversy was to rage over the form that corporation should take. Battle was joined between those who demanded that the council should carry out only its minimum legal responsibilities and those who sought for it an active role in attacking urban evils. In particular in the period 1847–53 attention was focused on two issues – the acquisition of powers by the new corporation to tackle longstanding threats to public health in the town, and the proposal to place control of local water supplies in the hands of the corporation.

3   The establishment of municipal government

The first municipal elections were held in Bradford in August 1847. The new Liberal council soon moved to the creation of the trappings of corporate government as a mayor, the merchant Robert Milligan, and aldermen were installed and committees established. But the weakness of the new council was soon clearly demonstrated, for, as already stated, incorporation had not in itself bestowed any power upon the council in the area of public health or improvement. In 1849, following an outbreak of cholera in Bradford which caused over 400 deaths, the council resolved to apply for a new Improvement Act which would enable it to pave and drain streets, dispose of refuse and sewage, clear polluted streams, and regulate abattoirs. Joseph Farrar, the author of the bill, like many local politicians of the period was opposed to central government involvement in municipal affairs and rejected the adoption of the 1848 Public Health Act as a possible solution to the problem.

But Farrar's bill was attacked by the Tories as expensive and motivated by Liberal greed for patronage. An anonymous correspondent of the *Bradford Observer* attacked the Liberals' motives,[23] 'Violent political changes had not given them all the patronage which profit and pride had hoped for. This Bill was a scheme for . . . making places for the dependents and creatures of Liberals.' Certainly the council's first year had seen the Liberals busy with the spoils system as party supporters were installed as aldermen, on the newly-created borough bench, and as paid officials of the council, including of course, the town clerk.

Ironically opposition to the bill arose from Liberals who were liable to lose places if it became law. The bill would allow the council to take over the responsibilities of the board of surveyors and render it defunct. A split developed within the board, with those surveyors who were also councillors, or about to become so, supporting the bill and five Liberal surveyors who were not councillors opposing it.[24] The spoils system had apparently broken down on this occasion as a surveyor such as Cousens, a barber, realized that his office, probably the highest to which he would ever aspire, was to be cut from under him. Such opposition led to the bill being promoted privately by a group of leading Liberals, Joseph Farrar, William Rand and Henry Brown; this device, although transparent enough, effectively stifled discussion in the council chamber and provoked fury amongst Tories like Joshua Pollard, ironmaster, who engaged counsel to oppose the bill in the parliamentary committees.

When the Bill came before the Commons committee in April, 1850, Knowles, counsel for the Tory interests opposing the bill, made an effective attack on Liberal motives.[25] He claimed, as had Bradford radicals before incorporation, that the town's manufacturers were seeking to use the ratepayers' money to resolve social problems largely of their own making. The town clerk, William Hudson, admitted under cross-examination that a number of prominent manufacturers on the council (most of whom were Liberals) had recently defeated an attempt to suppress smoke pollution. Alderman John Ramsden, a promoter of the bill, revealed that privies from his own mill emptied into the beck. Knowle's reply crystallized Tory opposition to the Bill, 'You keep on fouling the brook and then you come here to make it clean'.[26] The committee accepted the need for the bill in principle but enforced widespread changes in it. In particular the bill was to incorporate most of the 1848 Public Health Act with the council constituted as the local board of health under the supervision of the General Board of Health in London.

Within Bradford the political furore reached a climax between May and July 1850 when the bill was considered by the Lords in committee. Placards were posted throughout the town, the Tories were imaginatively labelled 'the minority of muck' by their opponents and council meetings turned into near riots.[27] The dispute now centred on the devious manner in which the bill was being promoted.

Although the Improvement Bill had been originally discussed both in full Council and the General Purposes Committee, it had come before the Commons as a private affair, although clearly promoted by Liberal leaders on the council. In June 1850, Tory leader Joshua Pollard, infuriated by this 'gagging' device, demanded in council that a town meeting be held to allow discussion of the bill. His motion was lost in a straight party vote, by 24 votes to eight. When further discussion was ruled out of order, which was of course the reason for promoting the bill privately, Pollard insisted on speaking. He was shouted down by Liberal councillors, and when, he raised the issue again later, the *Bradford Observer* reported 'it is wholly impossible to dispose in a parenthesis of the prolonged and deafening tumult which followed.'[28] Despite the Liberals' chicanery, the bill passed the Lords committee. Pollard and his supporters made a last-ditch attempt to stop the Bill. A petition with over 7,000 signatures was sent to the General Board of Health, requesting that the Public Health Act be applied to Bradford.[29] This desperate ploy was clearly a choice of the lesser of two evils and it was doomed to failure. A hurried letter to the board, from the solicitors of the improvement bill's promoters, pointed out that the petition 'came from parties who opposed the improvement bill in the House of Commons and are continuing their opposition'.[30] The general board agreed to suspend proceedings on the petition and the bill was safely enacted in July 1850. The machinery of the new act, including a Building and Improvement Committee to inspect plans was quickly established, and new officers responsible for highways, lighting, and scavenging appointed.

Within two years of the passing of the Improvement Act, yet another conflict raged in Bradford over the course of municipal government. The campaign to place the town's water supply under control of the corporation was accompanied with much of the rancour of the earlier struggles over incorporation and the Improvement Act. The issue at stake was a basic one. Public ownership of water would not only represent a vast extension of local government but would mark the first step on the road to municipal socialism which would lead to government involvement at local level in education, housing and transport by the end of the century.

Although the political argument in Bradford was often lost amidst a welter of technical and financial disputes, many townspeople saw the issue as more than a wrangle over the relative merits of a number of civil engineers, or the potential of various moorland springs. When Councillor Whitehead maintained in March 1854 that the water supply should be under public ownership because the 'ratepayers were delighted with self-government',[31] he clearly saw corporation control of essential services as a necessary outcome of municipal reform.

Naturally the issue was also central to the debate on public health. It was clear, by 1852, that the provision of a pure and regular water supply was essential to the solution of the sanitary problems of the industrial towns. Indeed the failure of private water companies to provide a cheap and reliable supply had been exposed at least 30 years earlier when a Commons committee had noted that 'the public were at the mercy of companies subject to no control or regulation.'[32] The excessive profits and poor service of private water companies, aroused public indignation throughout the country. Long and expensive legal and political battles resulted in many places, including Liverpool, Exeter and Sheffield.[33]

Bradford's first water works had been opened in 1744 but, although enlarged in 1790, it was clear by the 1830s that the supply had failed to keep pace with the increase in population.[34] Customers received water on three days a week for 30 minutes and only then 'at the caprice of an old woman who pleased herself whether she turned the water on or off'.[35] Despite the creation of a new joint stock company in 1839 with a capital of £40,000 the majority of the population still depended on water sellers, wells, or springs. Nor were the new company's customers satisfied with their service. In Leeds Road, the water was described as 'very hard and in scarce supply',[36] whilst in Manchester Road, the supply was switched off completely on Saturdays, the local washing day. Elsewhere in the town the water was apparently 'red as a fox' and 'dirty, hard and muddy and not fit to cook in'.[37]

Mindful of such public disquiet, the company decided, in August 1852, to seek parliamentary powers to enlarge their works and take water from new sources at Denholme and Hewenden Moor. Within a month the council had thrown down the gauntlet in resolving to seek powers to buy out the company, and take water from Oakworth and Keighley Moors. A committee was set up consisting of two aldermen, including the active Joseph Farrar and four councillors: all were Liberal and all regarded as radicals. In council, Farrar had attacked the failure of the company to supply the town adequately, contrasting the meagre 44 gallons of water per household received in Bradford with the 120 gallons at Preston, Wolverhampton, and Glasgow. Alderman Beaumont, a Whig surgeon compared the handsome $9\frac{1}{2}$ per cent dividend recently paid to company shareholders with the scarcity of water over the previous three months.[38]

Farrar was supported by a public meeting in January 1853 which voted for municipal ownership of water despite a spirited defence of private enterprise by shareholder and director William Walker, Tory textile magnate: '[The shareholders] had invested their capital and were ready to go again and invest it for the same object. If the Corporation made the proposed works the ratepayers would not only be taxed for water but also for making their works . . . if they allowed the company to make their works they would merely have to pay for water.'[39] Walker was a Tory, but the company delegation at the meeting included leading Liberals such as Alderman William Rand and Henry Brown, both mayors in this period. The water question, unlike the previous political controversies of these years, was to create a rift in Bradford Liberalism, as a number of local party leaders placed self-interest before what the majority of Liberals saw as the needs of the community. Moreover, a further group of wealthy Liberal council members were to demonstrate a marked lack of enthusiasm for the proposed take-over, in contrast with the more determined stance of radical tradesmen and shopkeeper councillors.

In January 1853 the corporation and company published similar bills. In view of the likely cost of a parliamentary contest to ratepayer and shareholder alike it was hardly surprising that by the spring a strong body of opinion had emerged in the town in favour of an early settlement. This view was supported by the *Bradford Observer* acutely aware that leading Liberals were amongst the most vociferous supporters *and* opponents of municipal ownership. William Byles had, untypically, refused to commit his paper on this controversial issue: 'it will little concern the public whether their daily supply of the limpid fluid is conveyed in municipal or company's pipes.'[40] But moves to settle the dispute came too late, and both bills were scrutinized by the same Commons Committee in May 1853. Strong opposition to the corporation's plans came from the town authorities of Keighley, and landowners in the areas from where the corporation intended to draw its supply.[41] (One of the strongest objections, incidentally, even as late as this time, rested on the need for sufficient water in streams and becks to drive factory power wheels.)

In the event, despite evidence of the failure of the company to supply the town satisfactorily, both bills were rejected. The *Bradford Observer* was in no doubt that the Committee had been influenced by the failure of the two sides to settle: 'We believe no one regrets this double disaster unless it be the few persons on either side who had the management of the controversy. Everyone saw from the first that it was an unnatural dispute.'[42] The 'unnatural dispute' had already created tension within Bradford liberalism. In July 1853, employees of H.W. Ripley, a Liberal councillor and dyer, started to lay pipes in the streets of Bowling.[43] Ripley was shortly to apply unsuccessfully to parliament for powers to supply water to parts of Bradford. Ripley's support for the water company had already angered his Liberal colleagues on the council, which now resolved to seek an injunction to prevent Ripley's men digging up the streets. The Liberals present in the council split, with 13 voting to take Ripley to court and five supporting an accommodation with him. The issue was clearly seen as part of the larger contest over the town's water. Aldermen, like Henry Brown and George Rogers, who were conciliatory towards the company, also favoured compromise with Ripley, whilst radicals like John Sharp and John Moore, who were strongly opposed to the company, voted to fight Ripley. The injunction was, in fact, refused although Ripley's plan to form a third party in the water dispute came to nothing.[44]

In the meantime a more serious issue had arisen for the Liberals. At their July meeting, councillors had discussed renewing the application to parliament for a water bill. Shortly after, however, they learnt the disturbing news that William Walker had applied for an injunction to restrain payment of expenses for the first application, on the grounds that a number of irregularities had taken place. There was a distinct possibility of councillors having to share costs of over £8,000.[45]

Hardly surprisingly there was a lack of enthusiasm on the part of some members of the corporation, and a positive objection on the part of others to risk another expensive contest.[46] By September, any doubts had been confirmed by the corporation's defeat in the court contest with Ripley. At a poorly attended meeting that month, the rift between the Liberal establishment and the radicals was again evident.[47] Indeed, the threat of Walker's injunction had frightened some who had previously wholeheartedly supported the corporation. The meeting was surprised to hear even Joseph Farrar, architect of both the Improvement Act and the corporation Water Bill, admit 'I could not personally support an application to parliament against the present injunction'.[48] The Radicals were appalled. John Rawson retorted that Walker's application for an injunction, 'had frightened the leading gentlemen out of their wits.'[49] William Whitehead, a forceful exponent of municipal ownership of water, argued that 'The council would not act with dignity if it submitted to such terms as might ensure their own pockets'.[50]

A motion to renew the application, despite Walker's injunction, was defeated by nine votes to eight, with two abstentions.[51] The Liberals present were clearly divided between wealthy Whig Aldermen like William Rarl and Isaac Wright, both Anglicans, who opposed applications, and Radical craftsmen like the joiner, John Moore, whose election to the council had been welcomed by the Chartist *Northern Star*,[52] who supported the motion. Significantly Joseph Farrar and Thomas Beaumont both left before the vote was taken. Within a fortnight however the council had reversed its decision.[53] The municipal elections were only a few weeks away and public opinion clearly favoured decisive action. Walker was eventually to drop his injunction, when final agreement was reached between the corporation and the company.

The November local elections witnessed a striking success for the supporters of municipal control of water. All 14 successful candidates were Liberals. Meetings in five wards voted in favour of a take-over of the water and several candidates published addresses on the subject. In East Ward, after Councillor Whitehead had spoken the meeting condemned 'the unrighteous and factious attempt to fix upon the several members of the council the expenses incurred in their late efforts to procure Parliamentary powers to obtain water.'[54] There is no evidence of any strong 'economist' group opposing increased rates emerging amongst shop keepers and the like as one might have anticipated in this period.[55] The most fascinating contest was in Bowling Ward, where H.W. Ripley, opponent of his party's plans for water, stood for re-election. The Liberals rejected Ripley and nominated William Corless, a manufacturer, instead, and Robert Brownridge, a Radical butcher. The Tories put up only Charles Turner, manager of Bowling Iron Works. Ripley clearly sought and captured the other Tory votes, but was comprehensively defeated (table 11).

Table 11   Results of the 1853 Bowling Ward election[56]

candidate	no. of votes
W. Corless	382
R. Brownridge	392
H.W. Ripley	151
C. Turner	149

In March 1854, agreement was finally announced between the corporation and the company.[57] The corporation was to pay £40 a share, plus £23,000 for other assets and to take over the works and property of the company, including its proposed extension scheme now at Barden in Wharfedale, instead of Denholme. It was ten years before the scheme was completed, and H.W. Ripley must have enjoyed the situation in 1858 when he was asked to supply water, during a drought, to the corporation.[58]

In the final analysis, however, Ripley's individualism had to bow to the collectivism of Farrar, Rawson and Whitehead. Not all the Liberal leaders who had helped in control of the town's government between 1843 and 1850, evinced much enthusiasm for extending the boundaries of that government when it affected their own self-interest. With Radical determination, however, the Corporation Water Act signalled the completion of the process by which municipal government in Bradford was established as an influential force affecting the lives of all its inhabitants and not merely an arena for a political élite.

By 1860, local politics in Bradford had entered into a period of what the *Bradford Observer* described as almighty stillness,[59] whilst reflecting on 'the humane and sympathetic spirit on the part of not a few of the ruling class',[60] demonstrated since the dark days of 1848. Clearly, events in Bradford were largely reflecting the emergence of consensus on the national political stage. But locally also the late 1850s witnessed the resolution of disputes which had raged for 15 years over both the necessity for and later, the roll of, elected local government. Liberal supremacy in the town council by 1855 effectively concluded the debate over the nature of municipal government. It was now widely accepted that the corporation ought to assume responsibility for the preservation of order within the town and the maintenance of at least minimum standards of public health. Furthermore, it seems to have been accepted by many of the townspeople that the latter responsibility could lead to a considerable enlargement of local government through initiatives such as the take-over of the water supply, the laying of drains in public streets, and the regulation of building with the attendant consideration of planning applications.

Inevitably, opposition to this increase in municipal activity lingered on particularly amongst those who had most vigorously rejected incorporation in the first place. A reader complained angrily to the *Bradford Observer* that the first building by-laws were 'most tyrannical'.[61] Even radicals expressed doubts occasionally, as when Councillor Chris Wilkinson demurred at the financial imposition on the working class which might result from the acquisition of the water supply.[62] However, these were minority views in Bradford by 1855 and as noted earlier, nothing remotely resembling a ratepayers' revolt occurred in the town.

It could, of course, be argued that municipal activity was limited enough to satisfy the most stringent economist. Certainly the responsibilities of Bradford Corporation were narrow as compared with those of the late nineteenth century. In the short space of 15 years after 1884, Bradford Corporation resolved to establish or assume responsibility for an electricity works, a tramway network, an art gallery, public baths and parks, the Technical College and 700 acres of land on Baildon Moor; it also initiated a public housing programme and appointed Britain's second local authority architect.[63]

But if Bradford council were eager disciples of Joseph Chamberlain's civic gospel by 1890,[64] it is clear that the principle of municipal intervention in vital areas where private enterprise could not or would not act efficiently, had been established 40 years earlier. It is questionable whether there is any difference in kind between public ownership of the water supply, and an art gallery, even if the arguments used to justify the latter did propound a more comprehensive view of municipal government. Speaking at the annual conference of the National Association for the Promotion of Social Science in Bradford in 1859, the vice-president of the Board of Trade, W.H. Cowper, insisted that the state has a direct interest in guarding against the 'deterioration of the race'.[65] He did in fact go on to argue for the assumption of wider responsibilities by both central and local government than this rather narrow definition of the duties of the state could suggest – including the provision of recreational and cultural facilities from public funds. Although no park had as yet been provided in Bradford out of the rates by 1859, and St Georges Hall, the new monument to civic pride, had been built from private subscription, the wide acceptance of the proposals for water supply, drainage and building regulations suggest that battle for an active municipal government was over by 1860.

4 Municipal government at work

The practical effects of municipal reform in Bradford in this period were clearly most evident in the fields of public health, peace-keeping and improvement. Underlying the more serious complaints about disease and violence, the years prior to incorporation had witnessed growing concern over the need to regulate building and improve traffic flow in the town centre. By the time the Improvement Act was passed, Bradford was in the grip of a tremendous building boom encompassing housing, warehousing and commercial premises. It was to the resultant problems here rather than actual threats to public health that the council, dominated of course by commercial and textile interests, first paid serious attention. The town clerk wrote to the General Board of Health 'at present from the very great traffic along the narrow portion of Market St . . . the vehicles were frequently brought to a standstill for a considerable time and especially on market days.'[66] The council proposed to extend one of the town's main thoroughfares at a cost of £7,000. Robert Rawlinson, the eminent Victorian engineer who inspected the site on behalf of the General Board, agreed there was a problem: 'the old streets are generally irregular and narrow. Buildings project forward to the great inconvenience of the public and the serious interruption of cart-traffic.'[67] The extension was completed in a couple of years. Such a large undertaking, though, was not typical of council activity in these years. A glance at the work of a typical year, 1853, reveals many less ambitious operations. Three and a half acres of paving had been laid, the Building Committee had considered over 650 plans for new buildings in the town, covering around 2,000 shops, 45 warehouses, 18 mills and 132 shops.[68] The committee was clearly determined not to be a rubber stamp and had referred back over 500 housing plans for alterations. Even so, by 1854, the council had determined to tighten building regulations and drew up new by-laws. These were concerned with health as well as traffic flow, and laid down minimum standards for the width of streets, height of buildings, provision of lavatories, light, ventilation etc. The new rules produced considerable opposition from at least one local capitalist who asked 'Do the men in office want to drive capital out of the borough? . . . A man wanting to lay out money in building is not of necessity obliged to lay it out here.'[69] But the council was less unanimous in its attitude to another of Bradford's health hazards – atmospheric pollution. Numerous attempts in the nineteenth century to enforce by-laws against smoke, were defeated by the manufacturing interest on the council.

Industrialists were quite prepared to forget party differences and join forces on this issue. In 1850 a motion to enforce the by-laws was defeated by 21 votes to 16.[70] Ten Liberals and six Tories voted for the motion, and 13 Liberals and eight Tories against. Thirteen of all those opposed were manufacturers as against only four of those in favour.[71] The debate was lively. The Whig surgeon, Alderman Beaumont, spoke of Bradford one day enjoying an atmosphere as fine as Cheltenham, but councillor Golt, whose firm was amongst those offending, claimed that smoke kept off fevers, while John Ramsden, one of the architects of the Improvement Bill, maintained that carbon acted as an antidote. It was left to Joshua Pollard, Tory manager of Bowling Iron Works to expose Liberal hypocrisy in a devastating fashion. 'If you carry out one bye-law you must carry out another – if you carry out a bye-law against a poor man you must carry out another against a rich man.'[72] As late as 1855 not a single prosecution had been initiated in Bradford for atmospheric pollution. The problem was not to be solved for over a century.

The council was more active in other areas. By 1854 plans were under way for a comprehensive system of drainage costing £13,000 which would drain some of the worst areas of the town.[73] The council also actively supported the opening of the new cemetery at Undercliffe, now a magnificient, if overgrown, monument to the Victorian way of death, and demanded the closure of the parish church graveyard.[74] This was supported by an Inspector of Burial Grounds who visited the graveyard and took away a macabre souvenir of Bradford – a human jaw-bone![75] In 1859, the council took action over another notorious Victorian health hazard when it petitioned the Commons in favour of a Bill (ultimately unsuccessful) attacking the adulteration of food.[76] This followed an appalling accident in the town, when a sweetmaker inadvertently mixed arsenic into peppermint lozenges – 18 people died and over 200 were taken seriously ill.[77]

The same year this tragedy occurred, W. Hudson, the town clerk, made brave claims on behalf of the corporation's success in public health when he spoke at the conference of the National Association for the Promotion of Social Science.[78] The town's death rate had apparently fallen by six per 1,000 in the previous decade and according to Hudson, the primary cause of this was the sanitary action of the corporation.[79] But other evidence does not support his optimism. Marx quoted Dr Bell, the local poor law doctor, writing six years after Hudson's speech, describing cellars with nearly 1,500 inhabitants as 'dark, damp, dirty, stinking holes, utterly unfit for human habitation'.[80] Between 1858 and 1862, Bradford Corporation successfully initiated only 43 prosecutions for public health offences.[81] Sheffield, with a population less than twice that of Bradford, saw over 300.[82] Bradford appointed no medical officer until compelled to do so by the Act of 1875 and in the 1860s inspection of food and supervision of lodging houses was still deemed very inadequate.[83]

The fruit of council activity must surely lie outside the period under consideration here. The importance of the initiation of higher standards in drainage, water supply and housing to later generations is self-evident, but it may be unwise to attach too much emphasis to mere beginnings as far as contemporary townspeople were concerned.

The establishment of an effective police force lay at the heart of middle-class demands for the incorporation of Bradford. A correspondent of the *Bradford Observer* had maintained in 1843 that the town was 'infested with thieves and vagabonds, the doors of its inhabitants besieged with beggars whilst riot, drunkeness and street-fighting are carried on with impunity.'[84] The town's new commercial and professional classes were demanding protection from an urban subproletariat brutalized by the poverty and squalor of industrialization.

The original Bradford police force, created in late 1847, consisted of the Chief Constable, William Leveratt, a superintendent and two inspectors, four sergeants, and 48 police constables for night duty, and two sergeants and ten constables for the day time.[85] The new constables had to be under 30 years of age, literate, and at least 5 ft 7 inches in height.[86] They were to be paid 17s. a week, a wage hardly excessive when compared with the 26s. a week paid to woolsorters in the area a few years earlier.[87] However, both work and wages in the textile trade were uncertain and against this must be set the security which attracted so many young working-class men to the police force in the nineteenth century. Many of the new Bradford police were hand-loom weavers from surrounding villages, who saw little future in their declining trade.

The Watch Committee drew up detailed instructions on the duties of the constables. When appointed to a beat, for example, the officer was warned that 'disorder in the streets is occasioned either by women of the town or by drunken and quarrelsome men. With disorderly women the constable is to hold no communication whatsoever. He must behave towards them with a determined sterness of manner.'[88] Two detectives were appointed at £1. 5s. 0d. a week. They were informed, somewhat gratuitously, that they 'possessed a great advantage over their brother officers in uniform in watching the pursuits and haunts of suspected persons.'[89] The uniformed officers were also to watch for suspicious-looking people carrying crowbars, lucifers, gunpowder, pick-locks, or skeleton keys.[90]

But the first major challenge to the new force came not from professional criminals but in the Chartist disturbances of 1848. The depressed state of the textile trade led to Bradford becoming a major centre of physical force Chartism.[91] On 19 May the local magistrates wrote to the Home Office of 'the highly alarming state in which this part of the manufacturing district is at present placed . . . one street in the borough is virtually in the possession of the Chartists – the police dare not venture into it without being supported by the military.'[92]

The failure of the police to act against the Chartists is understandable. The whole inexperienced force numbered only about 60, and many of the officers must have lived in streets inhabited by Chartist sympathizers.[93] Nevertheless, an attempt on 27 May to arrest a number of Chartist leaders, particularly Isaac Jefferson, a blacksmith known locally as Wat Tyler, was a total fiasco.[94] The Bradford superintendent was ill and a force of about 100 police and special constables set off under the command of a superintendent Brigg from Morley. Unfortunately Brigg was completely drunk. According to *The Times,* the police were driven back by stones, attacked with bludgeons and poles and Mr Buckley, a surgeon, was so dreadfully cut and wounded that for a time his life was despaired of.[95] Later that day the magistrates launched a force of 800 regular troops, including cavalry and artillery, which had been brought in from Colne and Manchester against the working-class strong-holds of Manchester Road.[96] Arrests were made, but further set-backs followed for the police. In early June four policemen were driven out of the White Abbey area by a crowd which retreated only when confronted by sabre-swinging dragoons.[97] Tory magistrate and councillor Joshua Pollard gloated over the humiliation of the new 'Whig' police. He claimed, moreover, that he and his fellow magistrates had been 'thwarted in their measures by the police . . . and the sooner they were done away with the better'.[98] Naturally the Liberal Watch Committee rejected these allegations and later in the year were to express total confidence in the police.[99]

The ordinary duties of the new force mainly involved dealing with drunken disorder, prostitution, and petty larceny. Even today the efficiency of the police in reducing crime is difficult to assess. In a town such as Bradford in the last century, much petty crime must have gone unreported due to indifference, hostility to the police, or intimidation. Tobias maintained that 'improved policing . . . was effective in reducing crime in the nineteenth century.'[100] Whilst accepting the deficiencies of many forces, he points to the tendency of criminals to move from the newly policed towns to outlying districts. However, if this had been the case in Bradford it seems unlikely that the inhabitants of Manningham or Great Horton would so strenuously have opposed the extension of police patrols to their villages. The first Bradford police did have their successes. In 1856 Detectives Field and Shuttleworth apprehended a gang of thieves,[101] whilst four years later Sergeant Sugden was allowed to keep 10s. presented to him by a member of the public for apprehending a notorious burglar.[102]

Sadly, however, complaints leading to the dismissal or suspension of officers appear to have been more frequent than commendation. The first years of the force's existence saw dozens of policemen disciplined, usually for drunkeness.[103] In 1859 the Watch Committee even learnt that officers accompanying prisoners to jail in Wakefield were in the habit of stopping at public houses with them on the way.[104]

No independent view of the Bradford police appeared until 1857 when the first report of the new inspectors of constabulary were published following the passing of the County and Borough Police Act of 1856. The Bradford force was inspected by Lieutenant-Colonel Woodford who spoke highly of its state of general efficiency.[105] Moreover, the Bradford constables compared very favourably with their colleagues in Leeds, Sheffield and other Yorkshire towns.[106]

Perhaps, despite the complaints and dismissals, it was in the new police that the Bradford middle class was to see its hopes for incorporation first fulfilled.

5   The corporation and central government

To modern eyes Victorian antipathy towards central government may well seem excessive.[107] Viewed from the 1970s, which have seen the disappearance of entire counties, the amalgamation of borough police forces and fire brigades and the regionalization or water boards, the impact of central government on a town like Bradford in the mid-nineteenth century may seem light enough. Indeed, the use of the term centralization in this era is somewhat misleading, for as Gutchen has commented, although supervision by departments of the central government was being exercised, local government was never directly administered by agents or servants of the central government.[108]

Only two departments of government were to any extent concerned with the administration of Bradford at this time: the Home Office and the General Board of Health. It is doubtful, in fact, whether agents of the central government entered Bradford on official business more than a handful of times each year, in the form of

an occasional visit from a Factory Inspector or Assi
Law.

And yet opposition to centralization in Victoria
not confined to High Tories or *laissez-faire* Liberal:
government in Bradford, antagonism against the p
local communities was focused particularly upon th
the General Board of Health which it had created.
dozen clauses of the Public Health Act gave the Board any real measure of control
over the local authorities'.[109] The Act, however, and even more an unsuccessful bill
of 1847 appeared at the time to be an encroachment on local freedom. Opponents
of central government, like the lawyer, J. Toulmin-Smith, bitterly attacked the
Act: 'The fundamental principles of the Common Law . . . are altogether set at
nought by the Public Health Act . . . a central Board having no possible knowledge
of circumstances, presumes to arrogate power to dictate as to all those things which
. . . can only be well-understood and ordered by those immediately interested.'[110]
Not all the opponents of Edwin Chadwick and the General Board of Health were as
principled as Toulmin-Smith. Burn noted that in industrial towns 'what could be
paraded as opposition to centralization per se might well be no more than the
resentment felt by a self-made non-conformist manufacturer to centralization as
represented by an inspector who was an Anglican and a gentleman.'[111] The 1848
Act was certainly attacked in Bradford by the Liberal Alderman Joseph Smith, a
surveyor, who demanded that the council 'ought to take any and every step to
oppose the leading feature, that of centralization.'[112] Other councillors, however,
took a less blinkered view, and Burn's scepticism is not supported by the Bradford
resolution that 'the Bill possessed many very excellent details which cannot but
tend to the promotion of the physical well-being of the community.'[113]

In 1850, following the passing of the Bradford Improvement Act, Bradford
Council was designated the local board of health. Edwin Chadwick maintained
that, despite the outcry against the new powers of central government from a
variety of interests, tension between the General Board of Health and the local
boards was rare.[114] Such a claim is difficult to substantiate, but the following
analysis of correspondence between Bradford Council and the General Board
should clarify the relationship in one case at least.

Bradford Corporation and the General Board of Health
Between 1850 and 1858 when the General Board of Health was abolished, W.H.
Hudson, the Bradford town clerk, corresponded regularly with the Board, and
letters appear to have been exchanged at least once a month. It is clear from this
correspondence that the initiative, as the Act had always intended, rested
overwhelmingly with the local board. The image of an authoritarian Chadwick
bullying naive provincials into sanitary improvements is largely unsustained.
Bradford Council utilized the expertise of central government, while remaining
wary of any intrusion into what it saw as its own domain. Relations were,
nevertheless, amicable enough and if the advice sought was often on financial and
legal questions, Bradford at least never demonstrated Clitheroe's antagonism
towards the General Board of Health, where a fierce dispute arose over the local
board's efforts to sack its surveyor.[115] When the necessary permission was refused
in London, the local board retaliated by reducing the surveyor's salary to 25s. a
year – he resigned.

against
centralisation

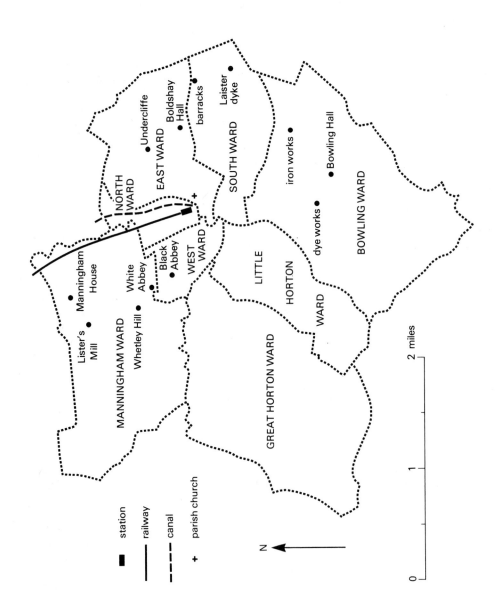

Figure 4. Bradford in the mid-nineteenth century.

Many of the early communications from Bradford to the General Board of Health concerned interpretation, often on trivial points, of the Public Health Act. In October 1850 Hudson asked if the council had the power to delegate its sanitary duties to committees.[116] Examples of such duties cited, include the sanctioning of building plans and the appointment of officials. The council was also much pre-occupied with the problem of rating. Hudson asked the board to sanction a new assessment of the whole borough.[117] The existing assessment had been made for the poor law before muncipal incorporation, as a result of which the four townships of the borough had laid rates at different levels. Hudson pointed out that 'since the poor rates were made for the different townships they have become clearly unequal and unfair because the overseers of one or two of the townships have interfered with the valuation and reduced it.'[118] The council obviously felt that an appeal to the board would avoid a bitter local conflict 'raising or reducing the amount by which people will be rated under the Act will be a very invidious duty for the council to perform and will tend to produce jealousy and ill-feeling between the ratepayers of the different townships.'[119]

The reply from Hudson's point of view was brief and unsatisfactory, the general board apparently having no power to interfere with ratings assessment.[120] Midwinter found that 'on the whole the General Board sent non-committal replies and shielded itself against a bombardment of complaints with its formula of having no power . . . to interfere.'[121] Certainly this was often the case with Bradford, at least on financial or legal issues.

Interest in rating was inevitable. New councils or boards were often uncertain about the law, and expenditure was the basis of most attacks on municipal activity in the field of public health. Councils were aware of the acute political dangers in apparent profligacy with ratepayers money. Following the decision to improve the thoroughfare in Bradford between Market Street and Kirkgate, Hudson wrote to the board 'the council are finding difficulty in the wording for laying a rate for £7,000 for . . . new streets. Your assistance is earnestly sought in obviating in the documents any objects which might be made use of to defeat or annul it.'[122] The fears expressed in the final lines were far from idle. In 1852, the Tory William Walker seized on a loophole in the council's handling of the application to parliament to take over the water company to try and prevent payment out of the rates of expenses incurred.[123] Hudson and the Liberal majority on the council were prepared to marshall the support of the General Board of Health against such determined opponents. In 1851, W.C. Haigh, a staunch local Tory who had bitterly opposed incorporation, attempted to summon a vestry meeting in Bradford to consider a council proposal to divert a footpath. The implications, of course, extended far beyond a right of way. Haigh was attempting to put back the clock, to return power to institutions which had lost it with the reform of local government. Hudson expressed his fears to the Board who supported him and the attempt failed.

Only occasionally was the General Board of Health able to take the initiative in its dealings with Bradford Council. When Hudson wrote for the Board's permission to raise the loan for the new street in the town centre, however, it was granted only after an inspection of the town by Robert Rawlinson, the eminent civil engineer. Rawlinson looked not only at traffic problems but at the 'confined courts, contaminated open water-courses, crowded cellar-dwellings, . . . middens crowded upon dwelling houses.'[124] He noted the very dirty and neglected market and the slaughterhouses crowded in amongst houses.[125] The reaction of the council to

Rawlinson's report was, perhaps, unexpected. Rather than taking umbrage at his criticisms and the parting shot that 'I beg that the board recommend these things to the notice of the Local Board,'[126] the council appears to have made a genuine attempt to improve sanitary conditions. Hudson had not communicated with the Board on a matter directly concerned with public health before Rawlinson's inspection. Afterwards, however, a number of requests for advice were made, in several instances about the very issues Rawlinson had raised.

In May 1851, Alderman Henry Brown even visited London to discuss proposed cellar dwellings in Bradford which the council wished to ban.[127] With the aid of the Board, the council was able to prevent the erection of the dwellings although, as Marx pointed out, such accommodation was still a feature of Bradford life nearly 20 years later.[128] The council continued to seek the assistance of the Board on such threats to public health as the failure of slum landlords to provide lavatories, and the state of the local beck.

In 1852, when a new drainage system was proposed for the town, the Board suggested that one of their own engineers, Henry Austin, should visit Bradford to advise the borough surveyor William Shaw.[129] The offer was accepted with enthusiasm by Hudson and, moreover, there seems to have been little evidence on Shaw's part of that professional jealousy towards the Board's engineers, which has said to have been one of the main obstacles to their work. Shaw wrote personally to the board on several occasions for technical advice. The new sewers were of course to be oval, as approved by Edwin Chadwick.

Despite this apparently harmonious relationship between Bradford council and the General Board of Health, the town was not one of the five which sent testimonials to London on Chadwick's behalf when he was replaced in 1854.[130] His successor, John Simon, rejected Chadwick's centralizing politics, at least until the 1860s,[134] but there seems to have been little change in the relationship between Bradford and the General Board of Health. However, the council did react sharply to two bills published in 1855 and 1857. Although both were aimed at extending and amending local powers over public health, they were seen in Bradford as moves to shift power from the local boards of health to town meetings and the magistracy. Naturally, local Liberals, entrenched in power by 1855, viewed with horror the prospect of rowdy meetings shouting down their enlightened sanitary proposals. The council petitioned the Board against the Public Health Bill of 1855 claiming that a proposal for annual ratepayers meetings to pass the accounts of every local board would 'only foment . . . discord and excitement,'[132] whilst a provision that every board had a bounden duty to keep their district free from nuisances was 'too general and too vague and might be made use of to embarrass Local Board'.[133] Although the petition briefly welcomed the decentralizing tendencies of the Bill, the council clearly regarded its own truculent ratepayers as potentially more formidable opponents than any central board.

The 1855 bill fell but the council's concern over a loss of authority to town meetings emerged in its attitude to a further bill two years later. W.H. Hudson noted it would be possible to appeal for part of a district to be excluded from the jurisdiction of the new act.[134] The prospect of say, Bowling, breaking away from the authority of the council in sanitary matters alarmed Bradford Liberals. 'This power', insisted Hudson, 'is undesirable in the case of a district of well-defined limits already formed under the Act of 1848'.[135] Furthermore, this bill would have denied councils or boards of health the power to force builders to deposit with it plans for new buildings which would mean that 'the Local Board in Bradford could never enforce compliance with their regulations or know when they were infringed'.[136]

Although this Bill also was never enacted, it appears that even a decade after incorporation, the authority of Bradford council was still far from secure. In 1858 the Conservatives, under Derby, came to power briefly and abolished the General Board of Health, transferring medical responsibilities, along with John Simon, to the Privy Council whilst town improvement was to be the concern of the Local Government Act Office under Tom Taylor. These changes did not fundamentally alter the role of central government in public health.

Bradford was one of those active authorities which continued to 'demand central aid',[137] which as has been shown, had always been taken on Bradford's terms. Whatever the original doubts of Bradford councillors about the 1848 Public Health Act, once the Act had been adopted in Bradford, Hudson and the council were prepared to co-operate totally with the General Board of Health and avail themselves of its financial and legal expertise. Obviously the board was seen primarily as an advisory body and any hint of control or unsolicited interference was resented. But although much of the advice sought by Hudson was over trivial points of interpretation, the technical assistance of the board was sought in major undertakings with apparently no hint of local jealousy.

Furthermore, despite the Liberal victory over incorporation and the Improvement Act, their opponents continued to resent the councils activities in public health and its association with central government. Clearly, glib assumptions about divisions between central government and local authorities are unsatisfactory, when conflict within the local community was so strong. The Liberal councillors in Bradford were eager to seek the support of the General Board of Health in their political battles at home.

The reform of the borough police 1854–6
According to the Municipal Corporation Act of 1835, all corporate boroughs were required to set up watch committees to supervise the policing of their towns. This other major responsibility of local government in the mid-nineteenth century, with sanitary improvement, was a focus of conflict between the municipalities, including Bradford, and the central government. Before 1856 local authorities had no obligations to the government in this field apart from an annual report from the chairman of the watch committee to the Home Office containing the barest details of the size of the force, equipment, pay and rules. However, concern in the Home Office about the state of borough police-forces, particularly the smaller ones, and the lack of police in several counties led to two attempts at reform in 1854 and 1856; the latter was successful.[138]

In 1854 Palmerston introduced a bill which would have compelled all counties to establish police-forces, within which those in towns of less than 20,000 people were to be absorbed. The home secretary would have been empowered to make rules for borough police-forces, and an inspectorate was to be established. The Home Secretary was to have the right of veto over the appointment of chief constables, who in turn were to have sole control over appointments and dismissals within their forces. Unlike the successful bill of 1856, it held out no financial carrot to the local authorities.

As an administrative measure, it would have entailed a far greater degree of central control than the 1848 Public Health Act. 'This serious encroachment on the traditional pattern of English local government',[139] aroused violent antagonism in towns throughout the country, not least in Bradford. The reluctant acceptance of the Public Health Act, followed by a determination to make use of it, contrasted sharply with the implacable rejection of central interference with the local police.

Representatives of various towns attended a meeting in York, presided over by the Lord Mayor, at which a resolution opposing the bill was seconded by Samuel Smith, Mayor of Bradford. Smith again attacked the Bill at a meeting in London of Mayors, watch-committee members and M.P.s, including both from Bradford, after which he was one of a delegation of three mayors chosen to meet Palmerston. On Smith's return from London, the full council condemned the bill with a rare unanimity.[140] Hudson, the town clerk, was convinced that the bill struck at the very roots of local liberty. Once the council had lost control over the appointment and dismissal of police-officers, the watch committee and the Municipal Act would become a dead letter.[141] Samuel Smith went even further, in raising the dramatic spectre of a national police-force becoming the tool of a despotic government. He claimed that the bill was 'an attempt to take power out of the hands of those who now hold it and place it in the hands of persons who might wield it against the liberties of England'.[142] He added that the only supporters of the bill in the provinces were rural chief constables, often ex-army men, who favoured a quasi-military role for the police.

Much of the fury over the Bill centred on Palmerston's expressed wish to see the provincial police eventually placed under direct central control as in the case of the Irish or Metropolitan police. The arch-enemy of centralization, J. Toulmin-Smith, had written three years before this that central control of the police would be the 'first step to bringing every corner of the land under the direct surveillance and armed control of the immediate creatures of the Home Office'.[143] Now in Bradford, Samuel Smith reported the Mayor of Kingston's description of the 'iron rule which characterized the centralizing system which prevailed in the metropolis'.[144]

The opposition of the boroughs, supported by the City of London, which has of course jealously guarded the individuality of its police-force to the present day, was such that the bill was withdrawn. Nonetheless government concern about the provincial police remained, and it was no surprise when Palmerston's successor, Sir George Grey, introduced another Police Bill in 1856. It was a milder measure than the earlier effort: small borough forces were not to be abolished and the Home Office was to offer grants of up to one quarter of the annual cost of clothing and equipment to local authorities whose forces had been deemed efficient by the inspectorate.

The *Bradford Observer* welcomed the new bill, voicing fears about the increasing use of modern communications by criminals: 'The electric telegraph is as open to the forger as to the detective and sharpers travel by express train. The time has come when our police system should spread its network over the entire country to entangle the feet of the lawbreaker'.[145] Grey was praised for striking the correct balance between local and central authority. In council, Alderman Rand, chairman of the watch committee, expressed similar views but the opposition was soon making itself heard. Another alderman, Thomas Beaumont expressed astonishment that his friend Rand 'should so completely ignore his own position and authority . . . to request that somebody should be sent by the government to look after the police'.[146] Samuel Smith again hinted at the dark purposes to which police-forces such as those contemplated might be put. A similar meeting to that which had helped destroy Palmerston's bill, was arranged in London, causing George Hadfield, Radical M.P. for Sheffield, to comment that 'boroughs up and down the country were in a very excited state upon the question of police reform'.[147] Alderman Beaumont, representing Bradford at the London meeting, claimed that Grey could not 'legislate for this country in the Austrian or Russian manner'.[148] Other opposition to the bill reached near hysteria. Captain Scobell, Liberal M.P. for Bath, declared in the Commons, 'Let the House pass the Bill and England would soon be overrun by twenty thousand armed police-men – perhaps Irishmen or foreigners – upon whom a bad government could rely for the perpetration of acts of oppression'.[149] But overall opposition was not as strong as to the 1854 bill, and with Grey dropping clauses which would have enabled the government to make regulations for the provincial police, the County and Borough Police Act of 1856 entered the statute book. There was a move in Bradford to register a protest against centralization by refusing the government grant awarded to efficient police-forces. Three boroughs actually did refuse: Doncaster, Sunderland and Southampton.[150] The proposal in Bradford emanated from a High Tory and an Anglican on the watch committee, both of whom, although for different reasons, objected to government influence over the police;[151] it came to nothing.

Bradford Corporation was largely free in this period of the supervision or control of central government, for all that these years saw the first tentative steps to establish a policy of selective interventionism. In practice there was a marked difference in attitudes locally to the growth of centralization in the field of public health and in the supervision of the police. Clearly, the much stronger opposition to reform of the police arose partly from the tighter central control envisaged there, as compared with public health. However, the council also accepted the existence of a need for technical assistance in sanitary affairs, which it did not recognize in policing. The widespread animosity towards Edwin Chadwick has perhaps obscured the fact that, if Bradford is any guide, interference with the local police touched a more sensitive nerve than any dictate of the General Board of Health.

In both areas, however, for all the resistance to centralization, there existed amongst Bradford councillors a willingness to work within the system once it was established, which was apparently lacking in many smaller boroughs. It is worth recalling that the Bradford police force passed its first Home Office inspection with flying colours.

Finally, it appears that whilst the question of the relationship between the corporation and central government was of such moment to local councillors, little interest was displayed by ordinary towns people. Not a single letter appeared in the *Bradford Observer* on the proposals to reform the police in 1854 and 1856; whilst the Improvement Act and the campaign over the water supply produced numerous letters to the press, public meetings and abusive placards, hardly a voice was raised in the town, either for or against the General Board of Health. The very remoteness of central government may have made its tentative moves to influence the administration of the town difficult for the ordinary inhabitants to grasp.

6 Municipal elections

The incorporation of Bradford in 1847, although partly the result of social factors, was a political event which ushered a new era into the life of the town. Five thousand townspeople were to vote annually to elect 42 councillors to run their local government. This innovation both accelerated the growth of political activity and widened its scope. Predictably it was the Liberals, flushed with their triumphs of the previous decade, who were first to grasp the opportunities offered by the municipal charter. Amongst Bradford Tories, however, there was a move to boycott the new council, as had happened in Manchester after incorporation. Thomas Ashworth, a solicitor and unsuccessful nominee for the office of town clerk wrote to the local paper, 'I feel there is much apathy and indifference existing amongst Conservative gentlemen of the borough as to their desire to form a part of the council . . . It would ill-behove such of you as are Conservative to stand aloof and neglect the best interests of your fellow-townsmen'.[152] The first municipal elections were held in August 1847 and, perhaps heeding Ashworth's plea, the Tories contested all eight wards. Thirty-two Liberals and ten Conservatives were elected. Several of the town's leading Liberals disdained the uncertainty of the hustings and awaited, with a justified confidence, the summons to the aldermanic bench. Thirteen of the 14 aldermen were Liberals and the political nature of these elections – the Liberals had actually printed a list of the first aldermen *before* the first council meeting – led to a protest from E.J. Mitchell, a Tory, who 'was sorry to see any consideration of politics should cause any of his brethren to act in this manner and he trusted that all colours be they yellow, green or blue would be wholly disregarded in the council room'.[153] The charter of incorporation had divided Bradford into eight wards, four in the old township of Bradford, North, South, East and West and the four outer wards of Bowling, Manningham, Little Horton and Great Horton. North and East wards covered the oldest residential areas in the town, East also including the parish church. South and West were the most industrial wards consisting largely of poor working class streets, mills, dye-houses, small foundries and rail-yards. All the outer wards included large tracts of agricultural land. Even today there are a surprising number of farms and small-holdings clinging tenaciously to the edge of Bradford. Industry, however, had already encroached substantially on the outer wards, particularly in Bowling with its iron-works.[154]

Apart from the first elections in 1847, November was the normal month for municipal elections. Two vacancies were filled for each ward except for Great Horton and Manningham, which had only one councillor each. The vast majority of municipal elections in Bradford in this period were contested on a party basis (table 12).[155]

Only in one election, November 1847, did the Tories win more seats than the Liberals and indeed their position deteriorated after that until the mid-1850s. Under the Municipal Corporations Act of 1835 all males who had occupied a warehouse, house or shop in the borough for two years and lived within seven miles of its centre were enfranchised.[156] Many small tenants compounded their rates, that is, included them in the rent to the landlord who was then classed as the ratepayer but after the passing of the Small Tenants Rating Act of 1850 this practice no longer disenfranchised the tenant. Voting was by signed ballot paper. Fluctuations in the numbers on the electoral roll were not due solely to population change. The fall in

134

Table 12   Bradford municipal election results, 1847–60 (excluding by-elections)[157]

		Tory	Liberal	cross	voter unknown
August	1847	10	32		
November	1847	8	6		
	1848	7	7		
	1849	5	9		
	1850	6	8		
	1851	4	10		
	1852	2	12		
	1853	0	14		
	1854	3	11		
	1855	1	11	1	1
	1856	2	12		
	1857	2	11		1
	1858	2	11		1
	1859	3	10		1
	1860	3	10		1

The numbers of voters on the municipal burgess list in this period are shown in table 13.

Table 13   Bradford municipal electorate, 1847–60[158]

Year	no. of voters
1847	5457
1848	4609
1849	4741
1850	5590
1851	8395
1852	10466
1853	11539
1854	11777
1855	12477
1856	14594
1857	15409
1858	15281
1859	15333
1860	15218

the total for 1848 resulted from disenfranchisement following non-payment of rates during the economic depression of the period. Between 1850 and 1852 the roll nearly doubled as a result of the Small Tenements Rating Act's enfranchisement of compounders. The decade 1850 to 1860 as a whole saw Bradford local politics become more democratic. Whilst the population rose by only 2 per cent, the municipal electorate increased more than $2\frac{1}{2}$ times.

The less rigorous residential qualifications for the parliamentary franchise resulted in some towns having a larger parliamentary electorate than municipal but this was not the case in Bradford (nor elsewhere in Yorkshire, in Leeds and Sheffield).[159] The parliamentary and local electorate in Bradford in general election years is shown in table 14.

Table 14   Bradford parliamentary and municipal electorate, 1847–59

Year	parliamentary electorate	municipal electorate[160]
1847	2083	5457
1852	2694	10466
1859	3599	15333

Any election was always an occasion of note in the town's life, fulfilling the function perhaps of a major football match today. Shortly beforehand, party leaders in each ward would meet, often in a public house, and choose a candidate. Frequently addresses to the votors would be placed in the press, but a common cause of complaint was the practice of concealing a candidate's name or even his existence until the last moment. In 1852 the *Bradford Observer* grumbled that 'perhaps prompted by a spirit of malice or mischief or perhaps with the simple idea that it was possible to "catch a weasle asleep" the Tories produced a candidate in several of the wards at the last minute'.[161] However, once election day dawned, the parties revealed a marked degree of organization. The most fiercely contested municipal elections of this time were probably in 1850, a year which had seen the furore over the Improvement Act. The *Bradford Observer* described the day at length: 'There was much of the machinery of a parliamentary election. Committee rooms of the rival candidates with their committees of canvassers and staffs of messengers and coaches and cabs, driving to and fro, conveying the burgesses to the poll gave to the contest an animated and excited character. Groups of working men and others congregated around the committee rooms and polling booths and watched the proceedings throughout – for want of a better occupation or why? Vehicles in the employ of the various committees were placarded with large bills bearing the names of the candidates'.[162] In North Ward the Liberal candidate, E.H. Parratt, was supported by a row of eight small boys, who marched through the streets, each exhibiting a coloured placard bearing the words 'vote for Parratt and eight small children'.[163] The *Observer* admitted to missing the point! There is abundant evidence of the sophisticated machinery available to the parties. In 1852 the *Northern Star*, commenting on the Little Horton election in which George White, the Chartist, was a candidate, reported that the Liberal candidate had a staff of paid canvassers at his disposal.[164]

Written propaganda played a large part in the campaigns, much of it in the spirit of contemporary politics, abusive and personal. In 1850 handbills were put out by three different Chartist groups in Little Horton ward. Chartists led by David Lightowler, who favoured an alliance with the Liberals, attacked Joshua Pollard, Tory magistrate and councillor by spelling his name backwards and reminding voters of his anti-Radical record. The language was to say the least intemperate: 'God forbid that either Jos Drallop or any of the emissaries of the Evil Spirit of the lower regions should ever again be allowed to have a seat in the Town council'.[165] Throughout the period the Liberals had the advantage of the whole-hearted support of the town's only newspaper. When Pollard and another Tory candidate, Coates, were defeated in Bowling Ward, the paper went so far as to observe that the voters in the ward 'be now permitted to take their rank among the free, honourable and independent'.[166] The burgesses had of course disproved the old charge that they were in the pocket of the Tory-controlled Bowling Iron Company.

The bias in the paper's political comment is further revealed in a leading article in November 1847 in which William Byles rebuked the electorate for returning more Tories than Liberals at the hustings. 'We cannot congratulate the burgesses of Bradford on their exercise of their civil franchise on the 1st of November'.[167] Bradford Tories did, however, receive occasional support from the nearby *Leeds Intelligencer.*[168]

Much of the material published at election time was printed after the event, in the hope of having the result overturned, rather than as political propaganda designed to sway the voter. Charges of bribery and corruption were as common-place as in parliamentary contests. The Liberals were so accused in 1852, after the election in Little Horton, where it was alleged 'scores of voters had been rejected by the presiding Liberal Alderman for trivial reasons and . . . some of the oldest inhabitants had been rejected . . . simply because their names had been misspelled'.[169] In 1848 the *Bradford Observer* launched a vicious attack on the Tories' conduct in the election: 'The franchise has been dishonoured and defiled and made an instrument of corruption . . . the chief arguments used to secure votes were beer and tobacco. Voters were inveigled into public houses and being well dosed with liquor were easily persuaded to vote for the man whose friends had so liberally entertained them. In Manningham, parties were induced to . . . deliberately declare themselves certain burgesses although they were not'.[170] Victorian elections were notorious for widespread drunkenness and violence. In 1853, an independent radical publican named Shackleton topped the poll against two Liberals in West Ward. The *Observer* sourly described the aftermath: 'Shackleton's supporters – a motley crew belonging to no party and caring for no principle – bore him from the polling booth to the Fleece amidst the loud applause and laughter of the rabble. Arriving at his house he delivered a ridiculous harangue . . . sneered at water-drinkers and teetotallers and expressed his desire for liquids of an opposite character as being . . . constitutional and destructive to the worms'.[171] But whilst many Bradfordians clearly saw elections as a vast free entertainment this is not necessarily an indication of genuine political involvement. The latter is best ascertained from the number of council seats contested and the percentage of the electorate which voted in municipal elections. The number of wards contested each year in the period are shown in table 15.

To modern eyes a total of 52.5 per cent of seats contested does not suggest a high degree of political involvement. Uncontested local elections are not unknown in our day, particularly in rural areas, but they are increasingly the exception and it would be unusual indeed for a ward in Bradford to be uncontested today in an election. However, figures from other northern towns suggest Bradford was not exceptional in the mid-twentieth century (table 16).

Moreover only in the twentieth century has the development of party-politics led to the virtual disappearance of non-contests in parliamentary elections – in 1852 only 34 per cent of parliamentary seats were contested.[172] These figures are, of course,

Table 15   *Wards contested in the Bradford municipal elections, 1847–60*[173]

year		no. of wards contested
1847	August	8
1847	November	6
1848		7
1849		3
1850		6
1851		4
1852		5
1853		5
1854		2
1855		2
1856		3
1857		3
1858		0
1859		5
1860		4
		63

Table 16   *Contested municipal elections*

town	years	percentage
Leeds	1835–67	61
Manchester	1838–67	29
Liverpool	1835–67	58
Sheffield	1843–67	51

only of limited value in assessing the political interest of the electorate as opposed to the political parties. The best indication of the involvement of voters would probably emerge from the percentage of enfranchised townspeople voting in municipal elections. Unfortunately the electoral system of the period makes the calculation of the turn-out in elections frequently impossible, if as in the case of Bradford, no poll-book has survived. Often there were only three candidates for the two vacancies. In these circumstances it is not possible to ascertain how many voters used both their votes and how many 'plumped' for a single candidate if he was the sole representative of the party of their choice. It is then, of course, impossible to know how many people voted. Only when all parties put up the same number of candidates, can one be reasonably certain of the number who polled, by dividing the total number of votes cast by the number of vacancies. It is true that even with the same number of candidates from the different parties one still cannot be certain that everyone used both their votes. However, the frequent closeness of the total vote for candidates of the same party suggests that any discrepancy was probably not very large; that is all but a very few voters voted for the party rather than an individual, as the examples indicate (table 17).

Table 17   Election results, 1850 and 1853

Election results	North Ward (1850)	Bowling Ward (1850)	East Ward (1853)
Liberal I	126	508	621
Liberal II	125	502	621
Tory I	108	439	205
Tory II	102	433	205

On this assumption the percentage of the electorate voting in municipal elections between 1847 and 1854[174] in which all parties nominated the same number of candidates was as shown (table 18).

Table 18   Electoral turnout in Bradford municipal elections 1847–54 (all figures in percentages)

	North	South	East	West	Bowling	L. Horton	G. Horton	Mann
1847	59	45	65	47	34	40	27	44
1847	84	83		58	74		51	
1848								48
1849			75		69			
1850	80	95			74	81	46	
1851			77				38	
1852			66				39	
1853			52			72	63	
1854						66	42	

Unfortunately there are too many gaps for these figures to offer anything but tentative conclusions. They do, however, suggest that voters turned out in proportionately greater numbers than in a modern local election.[175] It must be remembered, though, that the electorate was far more restricted than today and a higher percentage poll is likely where there are fewer voters.

As today, it was the likelihood of a close result or the existence of clear-cut issues, which turned out the voters in large numbers. When Bradford Tories put up a real fight as in 1847, or when the parties had been divided over a crucial question such as the Improvement Act in 1850, the electorate voted in numbers which matched those of a parliamentary election of the period.

As far as Bradford is concerned many local elections in the mid-nineteenth century were fought with a surprising degree of intensity and level of organization. Until the late 1850s at least, such elections engendered fierce rivalry. Certainly electoral organization was often *ad hoc* and wards fought fiercely one year would, as likely as not, be not contested the next. Nevertheless there is ample evidence that municipal elections occupied a most central position in the town's political life. When contested, the ward election excited interest both amongst political activists and the ordinary voter to a degree largely unknown today.

7   The political and social composition of the council

Political composition
In view of Bradford's reputation for radicalism in politics, it would have been surprising if the Liberals had had less than a comfortable majority on the town council in its early years. In the event the party all but monopolized the mayoralty and the aldermanic bench and dominated the council from the early days of bitter party-conflict in 1847 to the political calm of the late 1850s.

The political affiliations of men serving on Bradford council between August 1847 and November 1860 were as follows.

Table 19   The politics of Bradford council 1847–60[176]

	Liberal	Tory	split voter	unknown	total
mayors	7	0	1	0	8
aldermen	25	7·	2	0	31
councillors	108	45	1	4	158

The Liberal superiority was evident throughout the period. Only at one local election in November 1847 did the Tories win more seats than their opponents. The Liberals, moreover, used their majority to monopolize the office of mayor. Eight men served as mayor of Bradford during these years; they were

Robert Milligan	1847–8
Titus Salt	1848–9
Henry Forbes	1849–50
William Rand	1850–51
Samuel Smith	1851–4
William Murgatroyd	1854–6
Henry Brown	1856–9
Isaac Wright	1859–60

Seven were committed Liberals in both local and national politics and voted for Liberal candidates, including the Radical Colonel Thompson in all the parliamentary elections of the period. The exception was William Rand, the Anglican wool merchant, who came from a staunch Tory family. He had quit the Tory ranks over the corn law question but although supporting the Liberals over most local issues, normally voted for the moderate Tory and Whiggish Liberal candidates in parliamentary elections. Nevertheless in local politics he was clearly in the Liberal camp and was denounced vehemently as an apostate by Tory councillor George Lister when elected mayor in 1850.[177]

Hennock noted the willingness of Leeds Liberals to acknowledge the eminent position which some of their opponents occupied in the town by offering aldermanic places to leading Conservatives.[178] Such generosity was not to be found amongst Bradford Liberals (although even in Leeds it was short-lived). Only seven of the 34 aldermen elected before 1860 were Tories but even this overstates their representation. Only one Tory alderman was elected in the tense years before 1852 when the Liberals were as yet unsure of their ascendancy in local government. The other six were nominated between 1852 and 1860 when Liberal supremacy was beyond question. Even then, Liberal magnanimity was not all-embracing. It certainly did not stretch to Tory leaders such as William Walker or Joshua Pollard who led opposition to the Improvement Act or municipal control of the town's water. Indeed typical of Tory aldermen was John Gordon, a staunch enough Conservative at general elections but a supporter of several Liberal proposals in the council chamber. Liberal supremacy was thus secured at the highest levels of local government.

Social composition
Discussion of the social composition of the council must inevitably be based largely on occupation. Apart from analysing the range of occupation and social background represented within the council it is also of interest to consider occupational differences, if any, between both aldermen and councillors, and Liberals and Conservatives.[179]

The office of mayor was as one might anticipate, virtually the preserve of the textile trade. Four mayors were wool-merchants, one a manufacturer, one a dyer; Henry Brown was an exception, in that he was a draper. If, as Liberal Dissenters, the first mayors of Bradford were not sprung from the old gentry of the area, they had all nevertheless reached the top of their professions by the 1850s. Indeed, only a wealthy man could have accepted the office for the mayor was expected to pay for all municipal entertainment out of his own pocket, as well as support numerous local charities. Robert Milligan entertained over 200 guests at the first mayoral banquet in 1847 and when Henry Brown decided to waive the traditional dinner in 1856, he emphasized that the action was based on principle rather than parsimony by donating 100 guineas to a local society for the relief of decayed tradesmen.[180] Indeed the office became so expensive that for a time in 1861 no one was willing to accept it.[181] Even if the mayors had all achieved substantial wealth and social standing by the middle of the century, their origins had been mixed enough. Robert Milligan came of Scottish peasant stock, settled in Bradford in 1810, and created a vast wool mercantile concern. Henry Forbes, from Easingwold in North Yorkshire, began his career as a traveller for Milligan, whilst Henry Brown's mother had run a small drapery in central Bradford. Brown became one of the largest retailers in the town and the store which bore his name until recently (Brown Muff's) is today the best known in Bradford.

Only four of the first eight mayors were actually born in Bradford, an indication of the rapid growth of the town as a commercial and industrial centre. The four natives were Brown, Rand, Murgatroyd and Wright. Titus Salt was born in Morley, near Leeds, where his father Daniel was a woolstapler before moving to Bradford. Titus succeeded in business as a manufacturer of alpaca cloth in the late 1830s. Samuel Smith, the dyer, wealthy enough to sustain three terms of office as mayor, came from Halifax.

The spiritual centre of Bradford Liberalism in the nineteenth century was Horton Lane Congregational Chapel, under the ministry of the Reverend Jonathan Glyde.[182] The Congregationalists were the most political religious sect in Bradford and no less than five of the first eight mayors worshipped at Horton Lane. The only Anglicans elected mayor in the period were William Rand and Isaac Wright, the election of Rand drawing forth ironic surprise from one Tory councillor that a non-member of Horton Lane Chapel had been so honoured.[183]

The campaign for incorporation arose partly from the striving for political and social status amongst men already successful in commerce and trade. Seven of these men epitomized this phenomenon (again Rand, from a long established Bradford family, was the exception). Predictably, municipal office was only one outlet for the ambitions of this successful group. Two of the first mayors, Robert Milligan and Titus Salt, were eventually elected to parliament[184] whilst all eight played leading roles in various aspects of the town's commercial and social life. All were, of course, magistrates by virtue of their office and Salt became a deputy lord lieutenant of the West Riding. Other interests arose from commercial success. Rand and Murgatroyd were active in establishing Bradford's first rail-link, opened to Leeds in 1846, Salt was president of the town's chamber of commerce, and Wright was treasurer of the wool exchange.

Samuel Smith's initiative in bringing about the erection of St George's Hall was a valiant effort to fill a cultural vacuum in a town dedicated, or so Ruskin believed, to the creation of wealth.[185] Having built the hall, Smith founded the Bradford Festival Choral Society to sing in it and even helped organize the subscription concerts at which Charles Hallé's musicians were to entertain local music-lovers.

In electing aldermen, the council also deferred to the town's social leaders – or at least to those of Liberal persuasion. 'Our chiefs' wrote Joseph Farrar of 1847, 'were made aldermen'.[186] There existed a clear social gulf between aspiring aldermen and councillors which was bridged by few. Only 13 of the first 34 Bradford aldermen had previously been elected to the council. At least two Liberals, Joseph Farrar and John Ramsden, heald maker, originally lacked the wealth and social standing to become aldermen, but probably gained the office as a result of their sheer energy in municipal affairs. Farrar, who must have been the most active member of the council in its formative years, was elected aldermen in 1849 but only two years earlier his nomination for magistrate had been greeted by derisive laughter in the council chamber. Another Liberal, Thomas Ambler, had served quietly as councillor for Manningham for six years before becoming an alderman in 1856. The occupations of Bradford aldermen elected between 1847 and 1860 are shown in table 20.

The near monopoly of the office held by the textile trade is manifest. It is often difficult to specify occupations within the wool industry because so many successful capitalists moved easily between different fields of activity.[187] The 25 aldermen would appear to have fallen into three broad categories, however: merchants (12),

Table 20   Occupations of Bradford aldermen 1847–60

	Tory	Liberal	split voter	total
textiles	5	18	2	25
iron and engineering	1	1		2
professional and gentry	1	3		4
retailers		2		2
other		1		1
total	7	25	2	34

manufacturers (10), and dyers (3). The three dyers were Smith, the mayor, Edward Ripley, a politically inactive individual, and his son, Sir Henry, who was to quit Liberal Nonconformity for Tory Anglicanism in the 1860s. Merchant aldermen included the Tory William Cleeseborough who went spectacularly bankrupt in the mid-1850s. Most of the town's largest manufacturers were invited to become aldermen in the period, at least those who were Liberal or not ostentatious in their Toryism. Only four men described as professional or gentlemen were elected to the aldermanic bench, two surgeons, a surveyor and a gentleman. The figure would probably have been higher if more Tories had been invited to take office as so many Bradford professional men had Tory sympathies. Occupations of councillors elected in this period may be broken down as shown below (table 21).

Table 21   Occupations of Bradford councillors 1847–60

	Tories	%	Liberals	%	cross voter	unknown	total
textiles	12	26.7	50	46.3	1		63
iron, engineering and coal	5	11.1	6	5.5			11
professional and gentry	16	35.6	14	13			30
other manufacture	1	2.2	0	0			1
craftsmen	0	0	15	13.9		1	16
retailers	5	11.1	19	17.7			24
drink trade	5	11.1	2	1.8			7
others	1	2.2	1	0.9		1	3
unknown	0	0	1	0.9		2	3
total	45	100	108	100	1	4	158

These figures do reveal a striking difference in the occupations of aldermen and councillors. Over 70 per cent of aldermen were in the textile trade compared with only 40 per cent of councillors. The total of 63 councillors in textiles was distributed amongst the various occupations as follows: 31 manufacturers, 22 merchants, seven agents, and three dyers. Whereas merchants outnumbered manufacturers amongst aldermen, the reverse was true amongst councillors which perhaps confirms an impression that merchants enjoyed a higher social standing at the time. Representatives of the professions included solicitors, surgeons, auctioneers and an architect. Councillors in the iron, engineering and coal industries included ironmasters, machine-makers and mine-owners, the latter in this period not necessarily the large-scale entrepreneurs one might anticipate.

Bradford politics were never dominated by a 'shopocracy', the shopkeepers, craftsmen and innkeepers who so often appear to have been major force in Victorian municipal government.[188] Nevertheless retailers and craftsmen were always a powerful minority on the council, representing about one quarter of councillors elected in the period. Craftsmen councillors included watch-makers, printers, cushion-makers, basket-makers, plumbers and a heald-maker. It must be remembered that to qualify for the office a man had to possess property to the value of £1,000 or be rated at £30 *per annum*. Such men would normally have been employers of labour although this, of course, does not preclude the possibility of their having risen in trade quickly, particularly in view of the buoyant state of the local economy after 1848.

Shopkeepers on the council were involved in retailing quite a wide variety of products as is shown by the following list of a total of 24 councillors in retail trades, 1847–60:

Grocers	9	Confectioners	1
Drapers	1	Ironmongers	2
Booksellers	3	Glass sellers	1
Chemists	3	Pawnbrokers	1
Butchers	2	Unspecified	1

The predominance of grocers is predictable as they were by far the largest retail group in the town (392 of a total of 1,475 shopkeepers).[189] Some of these men were clearly in trade in a large way. The Roman Catholic Liberal, George Alderson, described himself as a grocer and tea-dealer and regularly took two-column advertisements on the first page of the *Bradford Observer*. Other retailers like the ex-Chartist pawnbroker Joseph Hudson, who joined with the Tories in attacking Liberal improvement plans, were probably very different social animals.

Bradford laid claim to be the centre of the temperance movement and it was perhaps this which led to the drink trade's small representation on the council at this time. Only seven persons from the trade were elected to the council between 1847 and 1860, five of them Tories. It was not until the Liberal Licensing Act of 1872 that the liquor trade fell in solidly behind the Conservatives, but the strength of the temperance movement amongst Dissenters in towns like Bradford, probably led many innkeepers to favour the Tories long before then.[190] If so, this would be a further reason why the drink trade was apparently under-represented in radical Bradford, as a comparison with other industrial cities in two years of the mid-nineteenth century indicates (table 22).

Table 22 *Percentage of council in drink trade*[191]

	1852	1856
Bradford	3.5	1.7
Birmingham	7.8	14.0
Leeds	3.1	9.4

In discussing the take-over of Leeds council by the Liberals in 1836, Hennock has written 'it is as if the opposing team had gone into bat. The rival merchants, the rival bankers, lawyers and doctors, even the rival flax spinners'.[192] He was speaking of the council leaders and, as has been shown, in Bradford also, one set of wealthy textile magnates had wrested control of the town's affairs from their political opponents. Figures of occupations represented on the whole council tell a rather different story though, and distinctions do emerge between the two parties. Even in Bradford, deference, however covert, played its part and Liberal mayors and aldermen were chosen from a class which could maintain the rank with the requisite dignity. In choosing their councillors, however, Liberal voters could and did allow more radical sentiments to surface.

The various occupations were represented on the whole council in the following proportions according to party affiliation (table 23).

Table 23   Occupations in party groups on whole council 1847–60

	Tories (52) %	Liberals (133) %
textiles	32.7	51.1
iron, coal and engineering	11.6	5.2
professional and gentry	32.7	12.8
other manufactures	1.9	
craftsmen		11.3
retailers	9.6	15.8
drink trade	9.6	1.5
others	1.9	1.5
unknown		0.8

In comparing the composition by occupation of the two party groups on the council it seems that significant differences existed in a number of categories – although in both parties the textile trade is the largest occupational group, not only was the proportion of Liberals in textiles greater, but their representation drawn from a wider circle in the trade. Only an exclusive group of the most wealthy merchants and manufacturers stood in the Tory interest, whilst the Liberals included loom-makers, a moreen manufacturer and on a more humble level, three yarn agents. On the other hand, Tory representation was strong in the iron and coal industry. Joshua Pollard, Edward Turner and Edward Onions were all Bowling Iron Works directors elected to the council. Mine-ownership often indicated a long standing link with the land and Tory councillors David and Abraham Baxandall who sold coal to the local iron industry, came from a long established local family.

It is amongst the craft and retail groups, however, that the clearest differences between the parties are evident. Whereas 15 Liberal craftsmen sat on the council there were no Tories: there were 19 Liberal shopkeepers and only five Tories. Moreover, whilst the Liberals included grocers and ironmongers, the Tory group consisted of three chemists, a confectioner and a draper, all in the town centre and presumably serving a somewhat socially restricted clientèle.

It would seem that Bradford Tories made little attempt to seek candidates for the council outside a fairly narrow circle of wealthy manufacturers and professional men. This had certainly not been the case in Leeds in the early 1840s, when over 18 per cent of Tory councillors had been craftsmen or retailers as against 3 per cent of Liberals.[193] Apart from the fact that the Leeds figures are drawn from the heyday of Tory Radicalism when one might have expected many small traders to support the Tories, the different figures for the two councils probably arose from the varying strengths of the parties in Leeds and Bradford. After 1848, Bradford Tories were fighting a losing battle in local politics. Elections with a chance of victory were luxuries too rare for nominations to be offered to plumbers or butchers. It was the very failure of Bradford Toryism that made its representation on the council so socially exclusive.

It is commonly assumed that some years after the incorporation of the large boroughs, power shifted in many of them from the large manufacturers and professional men to shopkeepers and traders.[194] The reasons for this trend are thought to have been first a growing disdain for municipal affairs on the part of the urban upper middle-class and secondly, reaction by smaller ratepayers against alleged extravagance in municipal government. Certainly the *Bradford Observer* feared such a move in the town, in 1858, when the editor urged local men of substance not to neglect their public responsibilities: 'there has been a growing complaint that municipal honours are not valued as they once were. We have heard too much of late as to what this unpatriotic desertion of civic duty has brought about in American politics'.[195] It must be said, however, that as far as evidence from occupations of council members is concerned, there is no real sign of any change taking place in the composition of the council before 1860 at least. In the last years of the 1850s, as in the late 1840s, the council was dominated by men with what appear to have been substantial business or professional interests in the town. Councillors in textiles, the iron and coal trades and the professions, never represented less than 70 per cent of total membership of the council. The *Observer* may well have been concerned with the quality of councillors rather than social or financial standing, but this is in any case impossible to assess except in individual cases. What *is* certain is that the growth in municipal government, the planning of expensive projects and a massive increase in the electorate had not weakened the grip of the town's establishment on local government, nor had municipal office lost its appeal for the wealthy merchants and manufacturers of Bradford.

8 Municipal politics in Bradford 1847–60: a review

The first 13 years of muncipal government in Bradford may be divided into three distinct stages. The first three years were a time of bitter party conflict as the Tories, despite their defeat over incorporation, still hoped to win the control of the council lost to the Liberals in the first elections. After 1850 the Tory cause was effectively lost and the next four years were a period of growth in local government as the Liberals embarked on various municipal enterprises, particularly in the field of public health. The third phase commenced about 1855 as Bradford local politics, like those of the nation generally, entered a period of tranquility – 'the great peace of the fifties'[196] – no great issues were debated, no principles were at stake. Local government became a drainage and pavement affair.

1847–50

It was totally untrue, as the *Leeds Intelligencer* claimed, that Bradford Tories were unable to provide any real opposition in the first municipal elections because they were unaware until the last minute which wards the Liberals were contesting.[197] The Tories actually fought every seat in the borough, nominating a large number of well-known local personalities, including W.H. Horsfall, one of the largest manufacturers in the town, who was in the event unsuccessful. Elsewhere defeated candidates included a mine-owner, two surgeons, a solicitor and a surveyor. The early municipal elections were hard-fought as the violent clashes and never ending flow of beer testified, and in these first years the council chamber resounded constantly to invective and innuendo. But the elections of 1850 marked a turning point in local politics. Up to that year the Tories had won 36 per cent of seats contested in the annual municipal elections – hardly a triumphant performance but respectable enough. But 1850 had, in fact, seen the party at its zenith and in the decade which followed they were to capture only 18 per cent of seats on the council. It was not that their performance in 1850 was so disastrous, for their successes were one more than the previous year. The real blow was the defeat of the Tory registrar George Coats, and Joshua Pollard in Bowling Ward. The failure of the local party agent and one of the most prominent Tories in the town in a ward regarded as an invincible stronghold was a shock from which the party never recovered in this period. Pollard was found a 'safe' seat in East ward but over the next few years his voice was to be an increasingly isolated one and in 1855 the Tories actually failed to win a single seat at the November elections.

The Liberal success lay largely in the increase of the municipal electorate. The years of the Tory rout followed quickly upon the enlargement of the electorate by the Small Tenements Rating Act. Even in 1847, though, the municipal electorate was three times as large as the parliamentary (5457 to 1966) The percentage of the vote gained by each party in the two elections (parliamentary and municipal) in Bradford in 1847, was as follows.

	Liberal	Tory[198]
parliamentary election	53	47
municipal election	62	38

It is true, of course, that the following year saw the Tories gain their only majority of seats contested in municipal elections. Significantly, however, this 1848 electorate was also the smallest in the period, following whole-sale disenfranchisement due to non-payment of rates in the economic slump. Results from individual wards also show that the Liberals performed better in areas with a high proportion of working-class households such as West ward whilst the Tories gained seats in the older, more middle-class districts such as North ward.[199] It appears that despite the upsurge of Tory radicalism in the 1840s, within a few years it was their opponents who were benefiting from the enfranchisement of the new working-class voters.

These early years also saw the beginning of the process of sharing the spoils of office. Victorian government rested on a system of overt patronage which reached to the most lowly social rung, as was demonstrated in the appointment of an active Liberal, the butcher William Bakes, as inspector of nuisances by the new council.[200] Nonetheless, it was soon clear that more exalted offices such as town clerk were to be allocated on a party basis. The first town clerk was J.A. Cooper, who had been secretary of the committee which had organized the campaign for incorporation, but his sudden death a few months after the first municipal elections led to a fierce struggle for the office between the two parties, the office eventually passing to the Liberal nominee John Rawson.[201]

However, the true prize was the magistracy, which Vincent called 'the small change in which debts between local notables and the national party were adjusted. By this means men were led to undertake . . . work in the local levels of a national party in exchange for local power and social eminence'.[202] The creation of a borough magistracy in Bradford and appointments to it cannot be viewed solely as rewards for services in national politics. The appointments were seen in the town as 'the spoils of incorporation', yet another manifestation of the assumption of power locally by the Liberals, assisted by the election of a friendly government at Westminster.

Bradford Liberals had already long been aware of the political bias of the existing bench of West Riding magistrates, all but one of whom were Tories, and demands for the creation of a borough magistracy were heard at the first council meetings.[203] The Lord Chancellor eventually selected 12 names for the new court, only three of whom were Tories, none of them politically active at the time. Furthermore the Tories charged that Robert Milligan, the mayor, and Joseph Smith, a Liberal alderman, had actually gone to the Lord Chancellor's office to ensure that the leading Tory, William Walker, was not placed on the list. According to Joshua Pollard, 'it was only with a bad grace that those who charged the County magistrates with being partisan should appoint party magistrates for the borough and that the mayor should go to London for the purpose'.[204] However, over the spoils of office, as in the electoral battle, the Tories had lost and by 1850 there had ended the last organized resistance to the Liberal campaigns which had occupied the town's political life for the previous 13 years.

1850–5

By the early 1850s the nonconformist industrialists who made up the leadership of the Bradford Liberal party were entitled to feel a good deal of self-satisfaction. Apart from their political success, they were acutely conscious of the newly-established commercial and social prominence of the town. It was of Bradford textile mills that Baines was speaking when he referred to 'splendid works . . . which count in the first rank of the palaces of industry'.[205] Bradford was proud of its showing at the Great Exhibition,[206] whilst the *Morning Chronicle* praised the example of progress it had given other West Riding towns.[207] As Hobsbawm pointed out, St George's Hall was one of the first of the great civic monuments so characteristic of the age.[208]

Such success accompanied a more peaceful approach to politics; although there was conflict it lacked the angry intensity of the 1840s. The early 1850s were dominated by Liberal attempts to municipalize the water supply, and the electoral weakness of the Tories, coupled with the unpopularity of the water company, prevented any effective opposition to the council's plans.

These years did, however, see the emergence of a Radical Liberal group on the council. That there was no major split within the party was the result of the left-wing nature of Bradford Liberalism. The local party leaders had themselves been regarded as Radicals in the late 1840s when men like Milligan and Salt had demonstrated strong sympathies with moral-force Chartism.[209]

The Radicals could be divided into two groups, on the one hand middle-class respectables who were close to the Liberal leadership, on the other hand ex-Chartists with strong working-class connections who had little contact with the wealthy mill-owners and merchants on the aldermanic bench. The first group was led by men like Joseph Farrar and the cotton spinner John Rawson, who made an unsuccessful attempt in 1848 to persuade the council to vote in favour of the principle of universal suffrage.[210] Even before 1850, however, representatives of a more extreme political philosophy had been elected to the council; James Diggles, a grocer, who won a seat in Little Horton in 1848 was said by the *Leeds Intelligencer* to have lost the support of many Liberals because of his strong Chartist sympathies.[211]

Clearly some difficulty exists in determining the extent to which Bradford Radicals should be regarded as a separate party. Significant elections in this regard took place in Little Horton in 1850 and 1851. Two Chartists, John Hudson, a pawnbroker and John Moore, a joiner, opposed the official Liberal candidates against the advice of David Lightowler, a leading Chartist turned Liberal, who had been arrested and imprisoned in 1848. The two Chartists fared disastrously, coming bottom in the Little Horton election of 1850:

Liberals		Tories		Chartists	
Booth	392	Wade	337	Moore	52
Hill	368	Stowell	317	Hudson	42

According to the *Bradford Observer,* the majority of Chartists led by Lightowler supported the cause of Hill and Booth,[212] and the following year his policy of co-operation with moderate liberalism was accepted without protest by local Radicals. Moore, Hudson, John Sharp, a loom-maker, and John Glover, another prominent ex-Chartist, were all duly elected to the council on the Liberal ticket in Bowling and Little Horton wards. In 1852 the Chartist paper, the *Star of Freedom*, claimed of Bradford that 'there is little doubt that next year several thorough-going democrats will be returned.[213] In the event probably as many as eight radicals were elected in 1853, including one, the innkeeper Robert Shackleton, who opposed the official Liberal in West Ward.[214]

It soon became clear, though, that the Radicals were not to behave as the active ginger group which both their friends and enemies might have anticipated. Certainly, on two issues they *did* act in concert in opposition to the Liberal establishment. The first occasion was in a dispute which became known as the 'spice-cake corner affair' when Radicals and Tories joined forces to oppose Liberal plans to purchase and clear a piece of land in the town centre.[215] The ostensible reason for the clearance was to provide a site for a statue of Robert Peel, but opponents claimed that the real intention was to increase the value of adjoining property owned by various Liberal aldermen, including Titus Salt. The second instance of independent action by the Radicals was when they pressed the council to proceed with a second application to parliament for powers to take-over the water company in 1853, despite William Walker's attempt to make council members personally liable for the first application.[216] The Radicals were successful on both occasions, thanks partly to the force of public opinion. Such displays of independence were infrequent, though, and neither at local elections nor in the council chamber does the behaviour of Bradford Radicals justify their being regarded as a separate party.

1854–60

In 1856, the editor of the *Bradford Observer* contemplated the 'almighty stillness' of the political scene and contrasted it with the storms of 17 years earlier. In an editorial he applauded the shift to the political centre: High Toryism and Chartism were moribund and Palmerstonian Liberalism held the centre of the stage. Centrist politics reached their zenith in Bradford in 1857 when only two candidates were nominated for the general election and so the constituency was uncontested for the first time.[217] H.W. Wickham had stood as a Tory in 1852 when he had won a narrow victory over the Radical-Liberal Colonel Thompson. His election in 1852 had enraged many local Liberals but by 1857 he was sufficiently acceptable to stand with Thompson as a Liberal, unopposed. The *Observer* reassured sceptics: 'Mr Wickham started in life as a Conservative . . . but time works wonders. Mr Wickham is now as good a Liberal as most who call themselves by that name'.[218] True, some Radicals made an unsuccessful attempt to persuade Titus Salt to oppose Wickham, and a correspondent of the *Bradford Observer* ridiculed one result of the current consensus politics, that the prominent local Tory, John Rand, had seconded the nomination of the supposed Liberal, Wickham. 'Can you at the top of your voice and with your arms flying about like a windmill . . . say this is right or consistent'.[219] An almighty stillness had descended also upon municipal politics. In 1855, only two wards were contested at the November elections, in 1857 only one.[220] In the latter year the Liberals did not even trouble to oppose Edwin Bentley who had been a leading Tory opponent of the councils take-over of the water company. In 1858 the *Observer* reported, 'The apathy in reference to the coming elections was never so manifest as it is at the present moment. There is very little manifestation that any deep interest is felt in the results of the election'.[221] In the event not a single ward was contested, a far cry from the days of the church rates dispute, and the hard fought battles over incorporation and the Improvement Act. Even though the following year, 1859, seemed to witness a return to conflict in the local elections, with five wards contested, the *Observer* remarked 'that there was very little of the excitement we have observed in former years'.[222]

The truth was that municipal government as an issue in Bradford politics had been settled by 1859. The year before, Leeds Town Hall, that splendid monument to Victorian civic pride, had been opened by the Queen.[223] The acceptance of municipal government amongst the local community which such an event display-ed, may in the late 1850s have been accompanied by a measure of apathy. However, there existed also an acceptance of local government amongst towns-people of all political persuasions which had not been known a decade earlier. Perhaps it took a Joseph Chamberlain to give full expression to such feelings, as at the laying of the foundation stone of Birmingham Town Hall in 1874: 'For my part, I have an abiding . . . sense of the value and importance of local self-government, and I desire therefore to surround them by everything which can mark their importance. Therefore, just as in past times we have provided for our monarchs . . . palaces in which to live . . . so now it behoves us to find a fitting habitation for our local Parliament to show the value we put upon our privileges and our free institutions'.[224] Perhaps such sentiments might have seemed somewhat extravagant 20 years earlier, but it was in 1854 that a little known Bradford councillor had maintained bluntly that the people were delighted with self-government.[225] Delight was certainly felt by some, but more significantly there was acceptance by all. The last stage in the establishment of municipal government in Bradford was the agreement of the whole population that the corporation was a necessary and central part of the life of the community.

BIBLIOGRAPHY

Primary sources

Bradford Metropolitan District Council Libraries Documents Collection

Early political and local authority papers, MSS:
Miscellaneous letters, handbills and leaflets
Bradford Reform Society Minutes, 1835
Bradford Operative Conservative Society Minutes, 1837–
Bradford United Reform Club Minutes, 1841–
Bradford Improvement Commissioners Order Books, 1803–47
Bradford Board of Surveyors Minutes
Bradford Board of Guardians Minutes, 1837–50
Ratebooks of petition in favour of incorporation (1845)
Petition against incorporation (1845)

Bradford Corporation papers MSS:
Town Council Minutes, 1847–60
Council Finance Committee Minutes, 1847–60
Council Sanitary Committee Minutes, 1847–60
Council Watch Committee, 1847–60
Council Building and Improvement Committee, 1850–60
Council Street and Drainage Committee, 1850–60
Corporation Out-letters, 1847–60

Bradford Corporation papers, printed:
Reports of the Committees of Bradford Council
Bradford Corporation Yearbooks, 1853–66.
Bradford Burgess Rolls

Bradford Cathedral Archives

Bradford Vestry Minutes, 1830–50
Ratebook, Bradford Township East Division, 1841

Public Record Office

General Board of Health Correspondence, M.H.13, vol. 27, 1850–60
Home Office Correspondence, H.O.41/19; H.O.45/2410/AC
Home Office Police Returns, H.O. 63

Parliamentary Papers

1834–5 Select Committee on the Handloom Weavers Petitions, 1834 (X). 1835 (XIII)

1835 Report of the Royal Commission on the Municipal Corporations of England and Wales, 1835 (XIII, CCIV, XXV, XXVI)
1840 Reports of the Assistant Commissioners on the Handloom Weavers, 1840 (XXIII) Part II
1840 Report of the Select Committee on the Health of Towns, 1840 (XI)
1842 Report on the Sanitary Condition of the Labouring Population, (E. Chadwick) 1842 (H.L.) (XXVI, XXVII)
1844–5 Report of the Royal Commission on the State of Large Towns and Populous Districts, 1844 (XVII), 1845 (XVIII) Parts I and II
1852–3 Report of the Select Committee on the expediency of adopting a more uniform system of police in England and Wales and Scotland, 1852–3 (XXXVI)
1854 Report of the General Board of Health on the administration of the Public Health Act and the nuisances Removal and Diseases Prevention Acts, (1848–54) 1854 (XXXV)
1857–8 Reports of the Inspectors of Constabulary, 1857–8 (XLVII)

Parliamentary debates

Hansard, 1847–56

Census

Census Enumerators' Returns, Bradford 1851
Comparative Account of the Population of Great Britain in 1801, 1811, 1821, 1831 P.P. 1831 (XVIII).
Census of Great Britain, 1851, Part IX.

Newspapers

Bradford Courier and West Riding Advertiser
Bradford Observer
Leeds Intelligencer
Leeds Mercury
Leeds Times
The Times

Directories

1837 Whites *History and Gazeteer of the West Riding,* volume I
1845 Ibbetson's *Directory of Bradford*
1850 Ibbetson's *Directory of Bradford*
1856 Lund's *Directory of Bradford*
1861 Whites *Directory of Bradford*

Poll-books (parliamentary)

1806 *Yorkshire Election*
1807 *Yorkshire Election*
1835 *Bradford Election*
1841 *Bradford Election*
1847 *Bradford Election*
1848 *West Riding Election*
1852 *Bradford Election*
1859 Bradford Election

Secondary sources

West Yorkshire history

Books

E. Baines, *Account of the Woollen Manufacture of England* (1970 edn)
R. Balgarnie, *Sir Titus Salt baronet: His Life and Its Lessons* (1970 edn)
F. Barrett, *A History of Queensbury* (1963)
J. Behrens, *Sir Jacob Behrens 1806–1889* (n.d. 1925?)
J. Bischoff, *A Comparative History of the Woollen and Worsted Manufacture* (1968 edn)
R. Brook, *The Story of Huddersfield* (1968)
J. Burnley, *The History of Wool and Woolcombing* (1889)
J. Burnley, *Looking for the Dawn* (1874) [fiction]
J. Burnley, *Phases of Bradford Life* (1871)
F. G. Byles, *William Byles* (1832)
J.A. Cooper, *The Corporation Question* (1845)
W. Cudworth, *The Condition of the Industrial Classes of Bradford and District* (1887)
W. Cudworth, *Historical Notes on the Bradford Corporation* (1881)
W. Cudworth, *Histories of Bolton and Bowling, Historically and Topographically Treated* (1891)
W. Cudworth, *Manningham, Heaton and Allerton* (1896)
W. Cudworth, *Methodism in Bradford* (1878)
W. Cudworth, *Rambles Round Horton* (1886)
W. Cudworth, *Round About Bradford* (1876)
W. Cudworth, *Worstedopolis* (1888)
J. Farrar, *The Autobiography of Joseph Farrar, J.P.* (1889)
T.W. Hanson, *The Story of Old Halifax* (1920)
H. Heaton, *The Victorian Woollen and Worsted Industries from the Earliest Times to the Industrial Revolution* (1965 edn)
H. Hird, *Bradford in History* (1968)
H. Hird, *How a City Grows* (1960)
A. Holroyd, *Collectanea Bradfordiana* (1973)
J. James, *History of the Worsted Manufacture in England* (1968 edn)
J. James, *The History of Bradford and its parish with Additions and Continuations to the Present Time* (1866)
H.F. Killick, *Notes on the Early History of the Leeds and Liverpool Canal* (1900)
M.C. Law, *The Story of Bradford* (1972 edn)
E. Lipson, *The History of the Woollen and Worsted Industry* (1921)
W. Paul, *A History of the Origins and Progress of Operative Conservative Societies* (1838)
A.J. Peacock, *Bradford Chartism, 1830–40* (York, 1969)
B. Popplewell and G. Pollard, *A Brief Statement of the Bradford Church Rates Case* (1849)
T.W. Reid, *The Life of the Rt. Hon. W.E. Forster* (1888)
W. Scruton, *Bradford Fifty Years Ago* (1897)
W. Scruton, *Pen and Pencil Pictures of Old Bradford* (1889)
E.M. Sigsworth, *Black Dyke Mills: a History* (1958)
W. Stamp, *Historical Notices of Wesleyan Methodism in Bradford and its Vicinity* (1841)
F. Trollope, *The Life and Adventures of Michael Armstrong. The Factory Boy* (1840) (fiction)
R.G. Wilson, *Gentlemen Merchants. The Merchant Community in Leeds 1700–1830* (1871)

Articles

W. Cudworth, 'Courts Baron and Leet', *Bradford Antiquary,* II (1895)

W. Cudworth, 'Horton Lane Chapel and congregation', *Horton Lane Congregational Mag.* (1893–4)

C. Dodsworth, 'Low Moor Ironworks', *Industrial Archaeology*, VIII (1971)

J.H. Farrington, 'The Leeds and Liverpool canal: a study in route selection', *Transport History*, III (1970)

D. Fraser, 'The fruits of reform. Leeds politics in the eighteen thirties', *Northern History*, VII (1972)

D. Fraser, 'Improvement in early Victorian Leeds', *Publications of the Thoresby Soc.*, LIII, part I (1970)

D. Fraser, 'Leeds churchwardens, 1828–50,' *Publications of the Thoresby Soc.*, LIII, Part I (1970)

D. Fraser, 'The politics of Leeds Water', *Publications of the Thoresby Soc.*, LIII, Part I (1970)

D. Fraser, 'Poor Law politics in Leeds', *Publications of the Thoresby Soc.*, LIII, Part I (1970)

M. Hirst, 'Liberal versus Liberal: the general election of 1874 in Bradford and Sheffield', *Historical J.*, xv, 4 (1972) (see also D.J. Wright)

H. Long, 'Bowling Iron Works', *Industrial Archaeology*, v (1968)

M.J. Mortimore, 'Landownership and urban growth in Bradford and its environs, 1850–1950', *Trans. Inst. British Geographers*, IVL (1969)

C. Richardson, 'The Irish in Victorian Bradford', *Bradford Antiquary*, n.s. (part XLV, 1971)

C. Richardson, 'Irish settlement in mid-nineteenth century Bradford', *Yorkshire Bull. Economic and Social Research*, xx, no. 2 (1968)

T.R. Roberts, 'Bradford waterways' rise and fall', *J. Bradford Textile Soc.* (1962–3)

A.H. Robinson, 'Horton Lane Chapel – Bradford's cathedral of Non-conformity' *Trans. Congregational Historical Soc.*, Bradford Branch (no. 5) typescript

P. Ross, 'The old roads of Bradford', *Bradford Antiquary*, v (1907–11), 297–311

E.M. Sigsworth, 'Bradford and the Great Exhibition 1851', *J. Bradford Textile Soc.* (1950–1)

E.A. Smith, 'The Yorkshire elections, 1806–7', *Northern History*, II (1967)

F.M. Thompson, 'Whigs and Liberals in the West Riding, 1830–60', *The English Historical Rev.*, LXXIV (1959)

J.T. Ward, 'Squire Auty, 1812–70', *Bradford Antiquary*, n.s., XLII (1964)

D.J. Wright, 'Liberal versus Liberal, 1874: some comments', *Historical J.*, XVI 3 (1973)

D.J. Wright, 'A radical borough – parliamentary politics in Bradford 1832–41', *Northern History*, IV (1969)

Other local history

Books

G. Amey, *The Collapse of Dale Dyke Dam, 1864* (1974)

W.A. Armstrong, *Stability and Change in an English County Town, 1801–51* (1974)

T.C. Barker and J.R. Harris, *A Merseyside Town in the Industrial Revolution, St Helens, 1750–1900* (1954)

S. Bell (ed.) *Victorian Lancashire* (1974)

R. Church, *Economic and Social Change in a Midland Town – Victorian Nottingham, 1815–1900* (1966)

C. Gill, *History of Birmingham*, I (1952)

G.W. Jones, *Borough Politics: a Study of the Wolverhampton Town Council, 1884–1964* (1969)

W. Lillie, *The History of Middlesbrough* (1968)

S. Middlebrook, *Newcastle upon Tyne. Its Growth and Achievement* (1968 edn)

E. Midwinter, *Old Liverpool* (1971)

R. Newton, *Victorian Exeter* (1968)

A. Temple Patterson, *A History of Southampton 1700–1914* (vol. I, 1966; vol. II, 1971)

A. Temple Patterson, *Radical Leicester. A History of Leicester, 1780–1950* (1954)
A. Redford, *The History of Local Government in Manchester*, II (1940)
M.I. Thomis, *Politics and Society in Nottingham 1785–1835* (1969)
F. Vigier, *Change and Apathy: Liverpool and Manchester during the Industrial Revolution* (Cambridge, Mass., 1970)

Other secondary works

H.J. Dyos and M. Wolff (eds.) *The Victorian City: Images and Realities,* 2 vols (1973)
J. Foster, *Class Struggle and the Industrial Revolution* (1974).
E.P. Hennock, *Fit and Proper Persons – Ideal and Reality in Nineteenth Century Urban Government* (1973)
W.C. Hubenow, *The Politics of Government Growth: Early Victorian Attitudes towards State Intervention* (1971)
A.D. Stewart and E. Jenkins, *The Medical and Legal Aspects of Sanitary Reform* (1969 edn)
J. Toulmin-Smith, *Local Self-Government and Centralization* (1851).

NOTES

1 The population of Bradford rose from 13,264 in 1801, to 103,778 in 1951. General Census of Great Britain, 1861, Appendix, 103. For a detailed account of the economic growth of Bradford see, G. Firth, 'The genesis of the industrial revolution in Bradford, 1760–1830' (Ph.D. thesis, University of Bradford, 1974); E.M. Sigsworth, *Black Dyke Mills – a History* (1958).
2 Second Report of the Commissioners for Enquiring into the State of Large Towns and Populous Districts (1845), XVIII, 166.
3 Appendix to the First Report of the Commissioners Inquiring into the State of Large Towns and Populous Districts (1844), XVII, 2.
4 A. Briggs, *Victorian Cities* (1968), 149.
5 J. James, *The History and Topography of Bradford* (1841), 181–3.
6 For a detailed account of Bradford politics in these years see, D.G. Wright, 'Politics and opinion in nineteenth century Bradford, 1832–80' (Ph.D. thesis, University of Leeds, 1966).
7 Bradford Operative Conservative Soc. Minutes, 8 May 1838 (Bradford Central Library, hereafter cited as BCL)
8 See report in *Bradford Observer* (hereafter cited as *BO*), 2 April 1840.
9 *BO*, 7 Oct. 1841.
10 See N. Gash, *Reaction and Reconstruction in English Politics, 1832–52* (1965); and W.R. Ward, *Religion and Society in England, 1790–1850* (1972).
11 *BO*, 21 Nov. 1839.
12 *BO*, 28 Nov. 1839.
13 Bradford Vestry Minutes, March 1842 (Bradford Cathedral Archives).
14 *BO*, 13 June 1839.
15 Bradford Vestry Minutes, 24 March 1843.
16 Bradford Improvement Commission Minutes, 4 Nov. 1843 (BCL).
17 *BO*, 7 Dec. 1843.
18 For a Liberal account of the struggle see J.A. Cooper, *The Corporation Question* (1845).
19 For Manchester, see A. Redford, *The History of Local Government in Manchester*, II (1940), 13–16.
20 Ratebooks of petition in favour of incorporation and petition against incorporation in BCL.

21 *BO,* 14 Aug. 1845.
22 A 'cross voter' was one who cast his two votes for one Liberal and one Conservative candidate.
23 *BO,* 24 Oct. 1850.
24 Bradford Board of Surveyors Minutes, 19 April 1850 (BCL).
25 *BO,* 9 May 1850.
26 *Ibid.*
27 Briggs, *op. cit.,* 43.
28 *BO,* 29 Aug. 1850.
29 Public Record Office (hereafter cited as PRO) M.H. 13 vol. 28, in letters Bradford to General Board of Health (hereafter cited as GBH), 24 June 1850.
30 *Ibid.,* 27 June 1850.
31 *BO,* 16 March 1854.
32 Report on the Sanitary Condition of the Labouring Population of Great Britain (1842). House of Lords, XXVII, 74.
33 For disputes over water in these towns see E. Midwinter, *Old Liverpool* (1971); R. Newton, *Victorian Exeter* (1968); and M. Walton, *Sheffield: Its Story and Achievements* (1968).
34 For the early history of Bradford's water supply see 'Bradford Corporation waterworks: a review', *J. Assoc. British Waterworks,* xxxviii (1956), 302–16.
35 W. Cudworth, *Historical Notes on the Bradford Corporation* (1881), 72.
36 *BO,* 5 May 1853.
37 *Ibid.*
38 Bradford Town Council Minutes, 20 Sept. 1852.
39 *BO,* 23 Sept. 1852.
40 *BO,* 17 March 1853.
41 The bill was opposed by the Keighley Improvement Commissioners, the Earl of Burlington, W.B. Ferrand, the Lancashire & Yorkshire Railway Company, and numerous land and factory owners.
42 *BO,* 12 May 1853.
43 *BO,* 14 July 1853.
44 Cudworth, *op. cit.,* 132.
45 *BO,* 14 July 1853.
46 Cudworth, *op. cit.,* 131
47 *BO,* 15 Sept. 1853.
48 *Ibid.*
49 *Ibid.*
50 *Ibid.*
51 *Ibid.*
52 *Northern Star,* 9 Nov. 1851.
53 Bradford Town Council Minutes, 28 Sept. 1856.
54 *BO,* 20 Oct. 1853.
55 At various times in this period economist parties emerged in Birmingham, Swansea, and Hull: see E.P. Hennock, 'Finance and politics in urban local government in England, 1835–1900', *Historical J.,* vi (1963:2), 217. In Leeds also 'increased costs produced periodic cries for economy and retrenchment'. D. Fraser, 'Areas of urban politics, Leeds, 1830–80', in *The Victorian City: Images and Realities,* ed. H.J. Dyos and M. Wolff (1973), 778.
56 *BO,* 3 Nov. 1853. The newspaper, embarassed by the Liberal divisions in the ward, played down the affair and remarked merely that 'the contest excited little interest'.
57 *BO,* 16 March 1854.
58 Cudworth, *op. cit.,* 140.
59 *BO,* 25 Sept. 1856.
60 *Ibid.*

61 *BO*, 1 June 1854.
62 In his manifesto in the Little Horton election of 1853 Wilkinson wrote, 'I pledge myself to the . . . right of Bradford . . . to have, water at the lowest cost at which it can be obtained'. (*BO*, 20 October 1853).
63 See H. Hird, *How a City Grows* (1966).
64 See below, 150.
65 *The Times*, 15 Oct. 1859.
66 PRO M.H. 13, vol. 27, in letters Bradford to GBH, vol. 28, 16 Jan. 1851.
67 *Ibid.*, GBH to Bradford, 3 Feb. 1851.
68 Borough of Bradford, *Reports of Committees of the Council* (1853), 6–7.
69 *BO*, 1 June 1854. An unsuccessful attempt had been made in the council to include a ban on back to back houses in the new by-laws. See also comments by Hennock on the effect of building by-laws in the nineteenth century: 'stringent bye-laws tended to produce a shortage of cheap houses and the subsequent overcrowding of existing accomodation'. E.P. Hennock. *Fit and Proper Persons Ideal and Reality in Nineteenth Century Urban Government* (1973), 115.
70 *BO*, 21 Feb. 1850.
71 The textile interest on the council was largely opposed to enforcement.
72 *BO*, 21 Feb. 1850.
73 *BO*, 1 June 1854.
74 Bradford Corporation Out Letters, Town Clerk to Privy Council (undated), 391.
75 *Ibid.*, 31 Oct. 1856.
76 *BO*, 17 March 1859.
77 *Ibid.*
78 *BO*, 13 Oct. 1859.
79 *Ibid.*
80 Karl Marx, *Capital* (orig. publ. 1887, repr. 1974), I, 620.
81 PRO H.O. 63, vols. 2, 4, 6, 8, and 10.
82 *Ibid.*
83 A.P. and E. Jenkins, *The Medical and Legal Aspects of Sanitary Reform* (orig. publ. 1867; repr. 1969), 50.
84 *BO*, 14 Dec. 1843.
85 Bradford Watch Committee Minutes, 15 November 1847.
86 *Ibid.*
87 J. James, *History of the Worsted Manufacture in England* (orig. publ. 1857; repr. 1968), 478.
88 Bradford Watch Committee Minutes, 20 Dec. 1847.
89 *Ibid.*
90 *Ibid.*
91 For accounts of chartism in Bradford see A.J. Peacock, *Bradford Chartism 1838–40* (1969); D. Thompson, *The Early Chartists* (1971), 280–6.
92 PRO H.O. 45/2410/AC. Bradford magistrates to the Home Secretary, 19 May 1848.
93 At least one Bradford policeman, John Ward, of Southgate, Horton, lived next door to a handloom weaver, an occupation well-represented in the chartist ranks. For a discussion of working-class resentment of the police, see R.D. Sturch, 'The plague of blue locusts: police reform and popular resistance in northern England, 1840–57', *International Rev. Social Hist.*, xx (1975), 61–99.
94 PRO H.O. 45/2410/A.C. Magistrates to the Home Secretary, 29 May 1848. See also *BO*, 1 June 1848.
95 *The Times,* 31 May 1848.
96 *BO*, 31 May 1848.
97 *BO*, 8 June 1848.
98 Bradford Watch Committee Minutes, 21 June 1848.
99 *Ibid.*, 15 July 1848.

100 J.T. Tobias, *Crime and Industrial Society in the Nineteenth Century* (1967), 237.
101 Bradford Watch Committee Minutes, 5 July 1856.
102 *Ibid.,* 1 September 1860.
103 Between 1847 and 1854, over 60 officers were disciplined for drunkenness, including five who were found drunk in brothels, and one who was reported to be drunk and fighting!
104 Bradford Watch Committee Minutes, 13 August 1859.
105 Reports of H.M. Inspectors of Constabulary, 1857–8, XLVII, 69. Woodford found the price to be 'complete in number and in a very satisfactory state of efficiency'.
106 *Ibid.,* 71–5. Woodford felt obliged to return to Leeds for a second inspection 'because of the general want of system'.
107 For discussion of such antipathy, see R.M. Gutchen, 'Local improvements and centralization in nineteenth century England', *Historical J.,* IV (1961), esp. 85.
108 *Ibid.*
109 R.A. Lewis, *Edwin Chadwick and the Public Health Movement, 1832–54* (1952), 304.
110 J. Toulmin-Smith, *Local Self-Government and Centralization* (1851), 338–9.
111 W.L. Burn, *The Age of Equipoise* (1964), 222.
112 *BO,* 9 March 1848.
113 *Ibid.*
114 S.E. Finer, *The Life and Times of Sir Edwin Chadwick* (1952), 437.
115 Lewis, *op. cit.,* 306.
116 PRO M.H. 13, vol. 28, Bradford to GBH, 10 Oct. 1850.
117 *Ibid.,* 31 Oct. 1850.
118 *Ibid.*
119 *Ibid.*
120 PRO M.H. 13, vol. 28, GBH to Bradford, 2 Nov. 1850.
121 E. Midwinter, 'Central and local government in mid-nineteenth century Lancashire', *Northern Hist.,* III (1969), 157.
122 PRO M.H. 13, vol. 28, Bradford to GBH, 26 Jan. 1852.
123 See chapter three.
124 PRO M.H. 13, vol. 28. Report by Robert Rawlinson, 3 February 1851.
125 *Ibid.*
126 *Ibid.*
127 PRO M.H. 13, vol. 28. Bradford to GBH, 8 May 1851.
128 Marx, *op. cit.,* I, 620.
129 PRO M.H. 13, vol. 28, 23 March 1852.
130 Finer, *op. cit.,* 467.
131 R. Lambert, *Sir John Simon, 1816–1904, and English Social Administration* (1963), 238–41.
132 PRO M.H. 13, 30 Mar. 1855.
133 *Ibid.*
134 Bradford Corporation Out Letters, Hudson to GBH, 10 Nov. 1856 (BCL).
135 *Ibid.*
136 *Ibid.*
137 R. Lambert, 'Central and local relations in mid-Victorian England: the local government Act Office, 1858–71', *Victorian Studies,* VI (1962), 133.
138 See J. Hart, 'The County and Borough Police Act, 1856', *Public Administration,* XXXIV (1956).
139 *Ibid.,* 406.
140 *BO,* 22 June 1854.
141 *Ibid.*
142 *Ibid.*
143 Toulmin-Smith, *op. cit.,* 204.
144 *BO,* 22 June 1854.

145 *BO*, 14 Feb. 1856.
146 *BO*, 21 Feb. 1856.
147 *Hansard*, CXL, 13 Feb. 1856.
148 *BO*, 28 Feb. 1856.
149 *Hansard*, CXL, 10 Mar. 1856.
150 H. Parris, 'The Home Office and the provincial police, 1856–70', *Public Law* (1961), 241.
151 Bradford Watch Committee Minutes, 22 Dec. 1857.
152 *BO*, 8 Apr. 1847.
153 *BO*, 19 Aug. 1847.
154 See T. Dixon's map of Bradford (10 ins:1 mile) of 1844; ward boundaries were added later.
155 See below, 139.
156 See B. Keith-Lucas, *The English Local Government Franchise* (1952), 228–9.
157 Party affiliation of candidates was ascertained from Bradford parliamentary poll-books of period (1841–68). Wherever possible votes in more than one election were checked.
158 *Bradford Corporation Yearbook 1866*, 188.
159 See, F. Vigier, *Change and Apathy: Liverpool and Manchester in the Industrial Revolution* (Cambridge, Mass., 1970), 210 (footnote).

Percentage of votes amongst all adult males 1851

	parliamentary	municipal
Birmingham	13.5	9.3
Leeds	14.1	18.8
Liverpool	22.1	10.5
Manchester	15.6	13.3
Sheffield	12.1	16.8

160 *Bradford Parliamentary Poll-books* 1835–68 and *Bradford Corporation Yearbook 1866*, 188.
161 Analysis of the poll-books and the burgess roll suggests that between 5 per cent and 8 per cent of entries were multiple i.e. names appearing more than once as a result of ownership of different properties within the same ward. The voter was only allowed one vote per vacancy however. *BO*, 4 Nov. 1852.
162 *BO*, 7 Nov. 1850.
163 *Ibid.*
164 *Northern Star*, 6 Nov. 1852.
165 *To the Burgesses of Little Horton Ward* (handbill) (BCL).
166 *BO*, 7 Nov. 1850.
167 *BO*, 4 Nov. 1847.
168 As in 1848 when the *Intelligencer* referred to 'the lavish expenditure and party feeling exhibited . . . by the so-called Liberals'. *Leeds Intelligencer*, 4 Nov. 1848.
169 *Northern Star*, 6 Nov. 1852.
170 *BO*, 9 Nov. 1848.
171 *BO*, 3 Nov. 1853.
172 T. Lloyds, 'Uncontested seats in British general elections, 1852–1910', *Historical J.*, VIII (1965), 260–5.
173 D. Fraser, *Urban Politics in Victorian England* (1976), 146.
174 Between 1854 and 1860 the *Bradford Observer* rarely troubled to record the votes cast for losing candidates.
175 The average turn-out in Bradford municipal elections in 1970 was 35.6 per cent. The highest turn-out was in Idle with 45.5 per cent and the lowest Wisbey with 29.8 per cent. 'Bradford municipal election results 1945–72' (BCL).

176 Calculated from vote in Bradford parliamentary elections 1847–59. Aldermen who had been councillors are not included in total of councillors although the mayors are included in totals for aldermen.
177 *BO*, 14 Nov. 1850.
178 Hennock, *Fit and Proper Persons*, 181.
179 See letter from a local Liberal, James Ellis to Robert Milligan (BCL, Box 17 Case 32): 'I fear great evil may arise from our first Chief Magistrate (who is known to be both Rich and Munificent) giving an entertainment on a scale which it may be very inconvenient for some of his successors to emulate.'
180 W. Cudworth, *Historical Notes on Bradford Corporation* (1881), 145.
181 *Ibid.*, 148.
182 A.H. Robinson, 'Horton Lane Chapel – Bradford's Cathedral of Nonconformity', *Trans. Congregational Historical Soc.*, v.
183 *BO*, 14 Nov. 1850.
184 Milligan was M.P. from 1852 to 1857 whilst Salt served from 1859 to 1861, when he resigned on becoming a Companion of Honour.
185 See Ruskin's lecture at the Wool Exchange, Bradford, 21 April 1864: 'Your railway stations, your warehouses, your exchange – all these are built to your Great Goddess of Getting on'. E. Cook and A. Wedderburn (eds.). *The Works of John Ruskin* (1905), 448.
186 J. Farrar, *Joseph Farrar, J.P.* (1889), 61.
187 Alderman William Murgatroyd was said to have given up the trade of manufacturer for the less exacting one of merchant. Cudworth, *op. cit.*, 139.
188 And a group who might 'act as a check to any imaginative approach to the problems of urban life'. Hennock, *Fit and Proper Persons*, 217.
189 Lund, *Directory of Bradford* (1856), 9.
190 Indeed an analysis of the votes of 50 Bradford innkeepers in the 1847 parliamentary election indicated that 29 voted Tory and 21 Liberal. A. Elliott, 'The establishment of municipal government in Bradford, 1837–57' (Ph.D. thesis, University of Bradford, 1976) 310–12.
191 Figures for Birmingham and Leeds taken from Hennock, *op. cit.*, 37.
192 *Ibid.*, 185.
193 D. Fraser, 'Politics in Leeds, 1830–52' (Ph.D. thesis, University of Leeds, 1966), 515.
194 Briggs, *op. cit.*, 108–9.
195 *BO*, 28 Oct. 1858.
196 G.M. Young, *Victorian England – Portrait of an Age* (orig. publ. 1936; 1960 edn), 87.
197 *Leeds Intelligencer*, 14 Aug. 1847.
198 These figures are obtained by taking the votes of the leading Tory and Liberal in the general election and of the leading Tory and Liberal in *each ward* in the municipal elections. (This system only works when, as in 1847, all wards were contested in the local elections). Technique devised by D. Fraser. See his 'Fruits of reform – Leeds politics', *Northern History*, VII (1972), 110–11.
199 See Elliott, *op. cit.*, 285.
200 *BO*, 4 Nov. 1847.
201 Bradford Town Council Minutes, 31 Dec. 1847.
202 J.R. Vincent, *The Formation of the British Liberal Party*, 1857–68 (1972), 161.
203 *BO*, 11 Nov. 1847.
204 *BO*, 10 Aug. 1848.
205 E. Baines, *Account of the Woollen Manufacture of England* (orig. publ. 1870; 1970 edn), 132.
206 See E.M. Sigsworth, 'Bradford and the Great Exhibition 1851', *J. Bradford Textile Soc.* (1950–1).
207 *Ibid.*, 44.
208 E.J. Hobsbawm, *Industry and Empire* (1969), 124.

209 In 1848 J. Binns had written to the Home Office of Milligan during Chartist demonstrations, 'where was our Chartist mayor?' PRO H.O. 41/19. J. Binns to Home Secretary, 25 May 1848.
210 *BO*, 4 May 1848.
211 *Leeds Intelligencer*, 4 Nov. 1848.
212 *BO*, 7 Nov. 1850.
213 *Star of Freedom*, 6 Nov. 1852.
214 Other Radicals included a basket-maker, a watchmaker, a butcher and a stationer.
215 See *BO*, 20 April 1852 and *Leeds Intelligencer,* 24 Apr. 1852.
216 *BO*, 15 Sept. 1853.
217 *BO*, 25 Sept. 1856.
218 *BO*, 2 Apr. 1857.
219 *BO*. The same correspondent later mocked Rand's leap from the 'yellow hustings at Bradford to the deeply, darkly beautiful blue at Wakefield'. *BO*, 9 Apr. 1857.
220 *BO*, 5 Nov. 1857.
221 *BO*, 28 Oct. 1858.
222 *BO*, 3 Nov. 1859.
223 See Briggs, *op. cit.*, 157–83.
224 C.W. Boyd (ed.) *Mr. Chamberlain's Speeches* (1914) 41–2 quoted in B.I. Coleman (ed.) *The Idea of the City in Nineteenth Century Britain* (1973), 159.
225 *BO*, 16 Mar. 1854.

INDEX